The Convergence of Distance and Conventional Education

This volume of essays from leading British, North American and Australasian contributors engages with the issues of the convergence of Distance and Conventional education. The term 'convergence' refers to the breaking down of barriers between open and distance learning and conventional education, and sees the creation of more and more institutions working across a range of modes. Such convergence has been driven by a number of factors, including the new technologies for teaching and learning, the impact of lifelong learning policies and the entry of larger than ever numbers of adult part-time students into tertiary education, and the demands of both employers and individuals for professional and work-related education throughout working lives.

The fourteen chapters engage critically with a range of aspects of convergence, including:

- how well is open and distance learning carried out in conventional institutions for which it may continue for a lengthy period to be seen as of secondary importance?
- to what extent will open and distance learning be more effectively carried out by conventional institutions able to offer a variety of modes to a wide range of learners?
- how well will the variety of learners be served by systems that are converging?
- what are the managerial issues at institutio̱   ᵇᵉʳᵉ ᶜonverging systems are being developed?

Alan Tait and **Roger Mills** are based in the Oper published widely in the field of open and distan

D1331788

Routledge studies in distance education
General Editors: Desmond Keegan and Alan Tait

The Convergence of Distance and Conventional Education

Patterns of flexibility for the individual learner

Edited by Alan Tait and Roger Mills

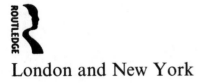

London and New York

First published 1999
by Routledge

Simultaneously published in the USA and Canada
by Routledge
29 West 35th Street, New York, NY 10001

Typeset in Times by
BC Typesetting, Bristol
Printed and bound in Great Britain by
Creative Print and Design (Wales), Ebbw Vale

British Library Cataloguing in Publication Data
A catalogue record for this book is available from the British Library

Library of Congress Cataloging in Publication Data
The convergence of distance and conventional education: patterns of
    flexibility for the individual learner/[edited by] Alan Tait and
    Roger Mills.
        p.   cm. – (Routledge studies in distance education)
    Includes bibliographical references and index.
    1. Distance education.   2. Open learning.   3. Continuing
education.   4. Educational technology.   I. Tait, Alan.   II. Mills,
    Roger, 1954–   .   III. Series.
LC5800.C67   1999
371.3'5–dc21   98-39659
                                                                      CIP

ISBN 0–415–19427–X (hbk)
ISBN 0–415–19428–8 (pbk)

Contents

Contributors

Mark Chambers is Director, Centre for Continuing Education at Victoria University of Wellington in New Zealand. Mr Chambers received a BA Philosophy at Berkeley and a JD (law degree) at Pepperdine University. In 1980 he and his wife emigrated to New Zealand, where he managed multidisciplinary research projects for a range of public and corporate clients. Before joining Victoria University in 1996, Mr Chambers was Head of School of Communication, Mathematics and Languages at the Open Polytechnic of New Zealand. He was recently awarded a Masters of Communication (with distinction) and was the winner of the New Zealand Minister of Information Technology Prize in 1996. He has been awarded a 1998 Winston Churchill Memorial Fellowship to investigate the implications of emerging new technologies for the future of the institution of the university.

Gail Crawford is an associate professor and instructional psychologist in Athabasca University's Centre for Distance Education and a faculty member in the Master of Distance Education (MDE) programme using distance-education methods to teach distance education to students throughout Canada and the rest of the world. Dr Crawford also consults nationally and internationally and conducts research in areas such as: student support and tutoring; instructional systems planning, design and development; the use of interactive technologies in course delivery; and formative evaluation.

Vicki Goodwin began teaching with the Headstart programme in the USA and then moved through junior and secondary schools and sixth form colleges in the UK to become Head of Department of Liberal Studies at Totton Community College. After teaching History of Education briefly at Warwick University, she began to work full-time for the Open University (UK) in 1987, having been a part-time tutor since 1979. Her interest in student support has remained constant since her involvement as president of a students' union in the 1960s, and her interest in seeking to make higher education more accessible through the development of study skills, and language and dyslexia support, has not flagged.

Lee Herman is Mentor/Co-ordinator at the Auburn, New York location of the State University of New York/Empire State College, and co-founder of the ESC Mentoring Institute. He has worked with adult students for the past twenty years. For many years, he has collaborated with Alan Mandell on understanding, practising and writing about mentoring.

Viktor Jakupec is Senior Lecturer in Education, Faculty of Education, University of Technology, Sydney, where he has developed graduate programmes in open, distance and flexible learning. Prior to joining UTS he was Director of Open and Distance Education Programs, Faculty of Education, Deakin University. He has extensive experience in developing infrastructures for flexible learning delivery and teaching of open and distance education courses. He holds a D.Phil. from FernUniversität Hagen (Germany). His research interests are in politics of distance, flexible and open education, and research methodology. He is the author of *Das Fernstudium in Australien* (Deakin University Press, Geelong), co-author (with R. McTaggart) of *Commercialisation and Flexible Delivery: Access in Vocational Education and Training* (Deakin Centre for Education and Change, Deakin University, Geelong) and co-editor (with T. Evans and D. Thompson) of *Research in Distance Education 4* (Deakin University Press, Geelong). He has published widely on the politics and policies of Australian distance education and higher education.

Sue Johnston is a professor in Higher Education and Director of the Teaching and Learning Centre at the University of New England, Australia. The Teaching and Learning Centre provides academic development, instructional design, multimedia development, academic skills support and the dispatch of distance-education materials for all faculties of the university. Sue's background is as a school teacher, an educational consultant and then a teacher educator. Her research interests revolve around her role over the past years in supporting academics and include a focus on academic work, professional development to enhance university teaching and learning, educational change and postgraduate supervision.

Denise Kirkpatrick is Senior Lecturer in the Centre for Learning and Teaching at the University of Technology, Sydney, where she works in the area of academic staff development with particular emphasis on flexible learning, managing change in universities with specific reference to implementing and managing flexible learning and the effect of such initiatives on academics' roles and practices.

Sharon McGuire (B.Ed, MA, PhD) is a faculty member of the Centre for Information and Communication Studies at Athabasca University. While at AU, Dr McGuire has served on various programme development councils including the Bachelor of Administration, Bachelor of Commerce, Master of Business Administration and Master of Distance Education degree programmes and has written and co-ordinated courses in

Organizational Communication and Organizational Behaviour. She has also served as a consultant to many organizations in both the public and private sectors. Current interests include organizational theory and design and academic work in distance education.

Alan Mandell is Director of the Mentoring Institute of the State University of New York/Empire State College, and Professor at ESC in New York City. He has been a mentor and administrator for more than twenty years, and has published reviews and essays on adult learning, including *Portfolio Development and Adult Learning* with Elana Michelson (Council on Adult and Experiential Learning, 1990). Ongoing collaboration with Lee Herman includes 'From teachers to mentors', a chapter in Roger Mills and Alan Tait's *Supporting the Learner in Open and Distance Learning* (London: Pitman, 1996).

Di Marks-Maran is Deputy Director of the Wolfson Institute of Health Sciences at Thames Valley University and Head of the Wolfson Institute's Centre for Teaching and Learning. She has recently completed a phenomenological study of adult learning methods in nurse education and is involved in a number of developments in problem-based learning. Her main fields of interest are open and distance learning and learning theory. This is as an academic co-ordinator for nursing and health programmes at the Open Learning Foundation where she is involved in the development of a framework for diplomas, degrees and masters programmes in health care by distance learning.

Roger Mills has been employed by the Open University (UK) in six different roles over twenty-six years, including that of pro-vice-chancellor for student support and teaching. He is currently Director of the Open University in East Anglia with responsibility for over 15,000 students, 700 part-time tutorial and counselling staff and 90 full-time academic, administrative and support staff. In addition he is the Vice-Chancellor's Delegate for Quality Assurance and has responsibility for the Open University's 1998 Quality Audit. He has undertaken consultancies, notably in India, Bangladesh, South Africa and Slovenia, and has written around twenty-five papers and articles on the broad subject of distance education. In 1996 he was co-editor with Alan Tait of *Supporting the Learner in Open and Distance Learning* (London: Pitman).

Jennifer O'Rourke is a consultant and researcher in adult and distance education and lives on Gabriola Island, BC, Canada. Her work in evaluation, programme planning, research and organization development is supported by a particular interest in the human aspect of open and distance learning. She was the principal researcher and author of *New Learning Technologies: Promises and Prospects for Women* (Toronto: Canadian Congress for Learning Opportunities for Women, 1997), sponsored by the Canadian Congress for Learning Opportunities for Women and funded by the Office of Learning Technologies, Government of Canada.

Rick Powell (BA, MA) has worked in the field of distance education for eighteen years, first as a researcher for the Open University (UK) and then as the director of research and evaluation for the Lesotho Distance Teaching Centre in southern Africa, an institution involved in using distance teaching for rural and secondary-school education. For the past thirteen years he has been Head of Institutional Studies at Athabasca University. He also teaches in AU's Master of Distance Education programme. Mr Powell's current research interests include activity-based costing, data warehousing and the structural changes distance-education institutions are undergoing in the fast-changing world of post-secondary education.

Pat Rickwood. After time spent in the army, the civil service and private industry, Pat Rickwood taught in a college of further education before moving to Wolverhampton Polytechnic. In the course of the 1970s and 1980s he witnessed successive changes in that institution's mission which inspired his interest in the quality of education for under-represented groups. Pat joined the Open University as a part-time student at both undergraduate and postgraduate levels, and one of the significant moments in his life was gaining his Open University degree in 1986.

Kate Stephens is currently Lecturer in Education at the University of Sheffield, where she teaches on a distance-learning masters course in English-language teaching, delivered to students working in the UK and overseas. She was previously employed as research assistant on a British-Library-funded project investigating the role of libraries in postgraduate distance learning. She has worked as a secondary-school teacher in the UK and overseas, and as a trainer and developer of second-language teachers in a variety of face-to-face teaching contexts.

Alan Tait is a staff tutor in the School of Education at the Open University (UK), based in Cambridge, managing tutors and student support systems, writing courses and doing research. He edited the journal *Open Learning* from 1989 to 1998, and has published widely in the field of open learning and post-secondary education. He has co-directed the Cambridge International Conference on Open and Distance Learning over many years, and has worked in a range of countries North and South.

Diane Thompson is a senior lecturer with the Deakin Centre for Academic Professional Development and Head of Academic Professional Development for the university. Her research interests are in the areas of academic discourse, most especially tertiary teaching, and the mediation of technologies on teaching and learning with a recent focus on the management of information technologies within the university sector. In 1997 she coauthored a federal government report on information technology and co-ordinated a desktop videoconferencing project. She is currently research-ing perceptions of the role of academics with a focus on the issue of change over the last decade. She is a member of the state and national executives of the Higher Education Research and Development Society of Austra-lasia (HERDSA) and is the convenor of the national Special Interest Group for Academic Development and co-convenor of the Research portfolio.

Ross Vermeer is an American by birth, but has lived and worked in Hong Kong for the past eight years. He is currently a course designer at the Open University of Hong Kong, and in the past taught English-language-skills courses at the Chinese University of Hong Kong. Mr Vermeer is interested in the ways in which using technology for teach-ing and learning influences our conceptions of self and agency, and in the ethical dimensions of on-line learning environments.

Gill Young is Reader in Educational Development and manages the Research Unit in the Centre for Teaching and Learning at the Wolfson Institute of Health Sciences, Thames Valley University. She is currently conducting evaluative research on a practice-based education project. Her main fields of interest are the assessment of theoretical and practice learning, and open and distance education. She is an academic co-ordinator for nursing and health programmes at the Open Learning Foundation where she is currently developing a framework for diplomas, degrees and masters programmes by distance learning in the field of health and social care.

1 The convergence of distance and conventional education

Patterns of flexibility for the individual learner

Alan Tait and Roger Mills

This book aims to offer a series of analyses of the current process of the convergence of distance and conventional education. Chapters from a range of countries offer viewpoints which can be characterized as driven by the perspective of the learner; of the teaching process; of institutional management; and of educational and social policy more broadly. They have predominantly been written by colleagues coming from the distance-education side, but with valuable contributions also from colleagues at what are increasingly erroneously termed 'conventional' universities.

It is clear from the chapters that a range of convergences is taking place with a rapidity that is bewildering from all perspectives. From the learner perspective we have seen on an international basis the arrival of more and more adult learners, many of them part-time, in institutions of post-secondary education. This has arisen both from demand by adult learners and from the late conversion of institutions to an interest in them as a cohort – an interest driven by the need to recruit larger numbers and fuelled by intermittent anxiety about the supply of school leavers.

Policy initiatives in the field of lifelong learning promoted governmentally in a number of countries, and by international agencies such as the European Commission, have also seen imperatives that learning opportunities for adults be offered on a flexible basis. Pressure on resources within institutions has seen an increasing emphasis on teaching and learning methods that demand less teacher contact and thus pave the way for more independent learning methods. The financial pressures have also been accompanied by progressive views about learning which see independence as a positive aspiration in its own right and part of a learner- rather than teacher-centred approach. While we share many of the values of progressive educators who support innovations in independent and resource-based learning methods, it would be naïve to think that their attractiveness at institutional and governmental levels is not also based on the need to expand within constrained financial climates. Indeed one of the problems in introducing new learning methodologies in conventional institutions is that of inadequate capital investment in learning materials and staff development. This can raise considerable suspicion and resentment on the part of teaching staff and students alike, and seriously impede the change process. The competitiveness of the institutional environments in many countries exacerbates these pressures, and a number of chapters in this book address the management issues which accordingly arise.

Fundamental to this change process are two elements. First of all, distance education has moved from the margins of educational policy and practice to being a respected and widespread mode of delivery alongside full-time and part-time study. A series of what we have learned from the Australian scene to call dual-mode institutions has emerged in the UK, as well as in the USA, Canada, Malaysia, many countries in Central and Eastern Europe, and no doubt others. Most influential now, however, at least at the visible level, are the new technologies for learning, which have accelerated the more widespread introduction of resource-based and flexible learning programmes in a wider range of educational institutions than ever before, and which are not necessarily termed distance programmes at all. CD-ROM, electronic communication methods including e-mail and electronic conferencing, web-based enquiry, application and guidance facilities, along with learning materials or topic-based investigative learning strategies, are making inroads into educational institutions irrespective of the primary educational descriptor of 'distance' or 'conventional'. We see in fact such sharp erosion of the distinction between distance education and innovative learning strategies based on the new information communications technologies (ICTs), that the continued existence of the distance-education tradition must now be in question.

There is a conflicting view which readers need to take into account. This is that adoption of distance-education strategies by conventional institutions is partial, weak in institutional policy terms, and weak on quality. This argument derives from observations that distance education is often only available for a few programmes in many conventional educational institutions, which are thus more accurately termed mixed-mode rather than dual-mode. This may be due to particular professional needs in one faculty or department which are not shared by others, or to the enthusiasms of a particular staff group or even an individual within an institution largely untouched by such thinking. The weaknesses in institutional policy arising from this mean that systems are not in place for anything other than an almost cottage-based distance-education operation, which suffers from disinterest or hostility from academic, administrative and operational areas alike. These factors in turn lead to lack of institutional commitment and investment, which impacts on the quality as well as the scale of what is done. It would be surprising if readers do not recognize some of these features in some institutions which they know. This line of argument leads to the view that only the dedicated open universities or colleges have the institutional strategy for significant distance-education programmes of high quality. The argument further draws on the continuing establishment of large-scale distance-teaching universities, the open universities, in particular in Asia (the most recent of which, for example, established in Bangladesh in 1992, already has some 50,000 students). While this argument acknowledges the increased use of distance education in conventional institutions, it sees the continued existence of distance education in the single-mode institutions as assured and as representing the most significant example of practice in the field.

While there are some persuasive elements in this argument, where we believe it looks increasingly vulnerable is in the face of the ICT revolution. This is at an early stage, relatively speaking, but will we suggest, following the International Council for Distance Education's assessment of what it termed the 'paradigm shift' (ICDE 1996), lead to a decisive break in the distinctions between distance and conventional education. It will also hasten the emergence of education and training in non-educational institutions, e.g. companies offering their own programmes in support of their businesses, as well as companies offering accredited educational opportunities in competition with educational institutions. It will also provide opportunities for business advantage on a global basis for what Daniel has termed the 'mega-universities', large universities behaving like businesses in the sense that they operate in entrepreneurial and competitive ways, advancing both by expanding markets and by moving into the markets of others (Daniel 1996). These mega-universities will in our view be as likely to come from 'conventional' institutions working with the new technologies as from distance-education institutions developing international business strategies. In other words the distinction in the future will lie between successful educational institutions using a range of teaching and learning strategies, substantially centred on ICTs, and less successful institutions which, as in the industrial and business environment, will be taken over or will go bankrupt. As with Otto Peters and his early and influential observations on the industrialized process of teaching which distance education brings, we do not propose or endorse these changes. However, we bring them to readers' attention as significant factors within the convergence process, which we see as more complex than simply the coming together of institutional traditions: more as a range of convergences of a socio-economic and technological nature.

From the learner's perspective the convergence of distance and conventional education will certainly bring the potential for increased access as a range of available modes of study becomes the norm, as is already the case in a number of major institutions in North America. A learner will thus be better able to ride the changes which family and work bring throughout life by switching between full-time and part-time, class-based and home-based study. It is also clear that the financial context within which these convergences are taking place may also see the idea of education as a social good being replaced by a more market-related approach to the payment of its costs. This will reduce access for some, as will the normative status of the more independent learner, which will exclude some students who start from a position of needing more support or having poor conditions at home in which to study.

There is a range of attitudes to this change process. The work of Daniel on the mega-universities sees strong potential for both increased opportunity and high quality. At the other end of the continuum there has been a spate of work recently which sees higher education in particular, when subject to some of the convergences identified here, as transmogrifying into a diminished and commoditized servicing of corporate agendas (Readings 1997; Shumar 1997). What is certain is that these convergences are taking place, and that reflection on them is the only effective preparation for managing them.

We should conclude by acknowledging the source of the thinking of this volume, and indeed of some of the chapters in origin, which was the Seventh Cambridge International Conference on Open and Distance Learning, which took place in late 1997. It is a pleasure to thank the colleagues who contributed to that meeting, including the keynote speakers Professors Raj Dhanarajan of the Commonwealth of Learning, Diana Laurillard of the Open University (UK) and Lesley Wagner of Leeds Metropolitan University.

References

Daniel, J. S. (1996) *Mega Universities and Knowledge Media*, London: Kogan Page.

ICDE (1996) *The Educational Paradigm Shift: Implications for ICDE and the Distance Learning Community*, Oslo: International Council for Distance Education.

Readings, B. (1997) *The University in Ruins*, Cambridge, Mass.: Harvard University Press.

Shumar, W. (1997) *College for Sale: A Critique of the Commodification of Higher Education*, London: Falmer Press.

2 The efficacy and ethics of using digital multimedia for educational purposes

Mark Chambers

Introduction

An important element in the widely reported growing convergence of distance and conventional modes of education has been the increasing use of digital multimedia in programmes of higher learning (see Mason and Kaye (eds) 1989). Digital-learning media are most often encountered in the form either of self-contained courses of instruction on CD-ROM discs or of interactive learning programmes on the World Wide Web. In the future, other digital technologies including digital video discs (DVDs), digital satellite transmissions and fibre-optic cable are anticipated to supersede CD-ROMs and the Internet (as we currently know it) (see Negroponte 1995 and Gilder 1995). Although courses on a CD-ROM disc and Internet-based programmes engender fundamentally different learning experiences, both of these new modes of educational delivery have provided individual learners worldwide with new patterns of flexibility in the pursuit of their tertiary studies.

As with the widespread adoption of any new technology, the introduction of digital multimedia into higher learning raises ethical issues concerning how such innovations may impact upon the individuals who use them and the communities into which the technologies are disseminated. Accordingly, any assessment of the suitability of digital multimedia for educational applications, whether by CD-ROM or on the Internet, should include consideration of the following fundamental questions:

1 Does the new technology bestow an added benefit upon the learners who use it relative to the modes of learning which the new technology displaces?
2 Considering the impact of the new technology upon an individual learner and the society of which the learner is a part, is it ethical for an educational institution to promote such digital modes of learning?

The efficacy of digital multimedia for learning purposes

The first question, concerning the efficacy of digital multimedia in learning, raises a number of subsidiary issues, including:

1   By what criteria may we usefully assess the effectiveness of a digitally mediated learning experience?
2   What are the inherent strengths and weaknesses of digital media which either promote or hinder a learning experience?
3   Considering 1 and 2 above, by what strategy should we seek to optimize the effectiveness of digital multimedia in the learning process?

Although it is beyond the scope of this chapter definitively to resolve these questions, the efficacy of digital learning media is considered from each of the three perspectives they imply.

Criteria for assessing the effectiveness of a digital learning experience

When designing a learning experience, whether it is to be mediated by classroom activity, correspondence, television, CD-ROM, the Internet or any other means, one must first ask, 'What is it that we want our learners to learn?' The literature is replete with evidence that best educational practice most highly values those learning experiences which foster a capacity for critical thought (Clift and Chambers 1994). This trend reflects the growing influence of the constructivist school of cognitive psychology on educational design, which seeks to promote understanding rather than the retention of information. Research into the nature of learning and the role of technology in education has identified widely accepted principles which provide benchmarks for assessing the design of digitally mediated learning programmes:

1   The primary purpose of the educational process should be to assist learners to develop their own cognitive strategies for using, managing, discovering and deriving their own meaning from knowledge (Wittrock 1977), because: 'Information is not knowledge; knowledge is not understanding' (Taylor and Saarinen 1994), and 'Wisdom cannot be told' (Bridges and Hallinger 1995, invoking the words of Harvard educationalist C. Cragg).
2   Learning media should seek to foster in learners the skills and knowledge required for deriving solutions, evaluating their validity and judging the most appropriate solution for a given situation (Eisner 1993).

Inherent strengths and weaknesses of digital multimedia as learning media

Measured against the criteria that the efficacy of educational multimedia be judged according to how well they promote critical thinking, many digital learning applications can be seen to be deficient. Such shortcomings are particularly evident in many of the pre-packaged learning experiences offered on such mass storage media as CD-ROMs. Speake and Powell (1997), for example, castigate much of the currently available multimedia learning materials as 'multi-mediocre' or 'awfulware'. Although CD-ROMs are excellent for asynchronous presentation of vast amounts of data, many CD-ROM courses fail to engage learners in the process of critically assessing the merits or utility of such data. CD-ROMs and Internet-based courses appear to have been designed to present a set of 'correct' facts which the learner is expected to commit to memory by rote. This shortcoming is particularly apparent in those computerized assessment systems which grade a learner's ability to feed back such 'correct information' to a computer.

The literature suggests that computer-mediated communication (CMC) is mode of choice for task-oriented communication and problem-solving (Palmer 1995) and excellent as a medium for providing learners with drills for testing generic skills such as mathematics and languages. However, in a survey of studies, Palmer (ibid.) delineated a number of perceived deficiencies of CMC as a means of interpersonal communications which limit the transmission of interpersonal and social information, including the restriction of 'social presence', diminished social-context cues and restricted number of channels, particularly nonverbal vocal and kinesic modes of expression.

Educational multimedia may supplement a learning experience by presenting a powerful simulation of a particular facet of the external world. However, what digital multimedia commonly lack is the ability to interact dynamically and intelligently in a discourse with every learner about what such a simulation means. The provision of a dialogue is the role of the human mentor who facilitates and manages the learning experience of an individual acquiring the cognitive and domain skills of a discipline. Again what is sought is not the acquisition of specific content knowledge but rather the growing sophistication of a learner in addressing problems typical of a discipline by using theories and concepts as tools of analysis. This process of development in a person's cognitive reasoning capacities is best facilitated by a dialogue with an accomplished mentor. Until machines are capable of fully simulating the cognitive and social repertoire of humans, the role of a mentor will continue to be an irreducible element of an optimal higher-learning experience.

Paradoxically, the emergence of new information and telecommunications technologies may assist traditional distance-learning organizations increasingly to incorporate attributes of quality conventional university programmes into their distance-delivery activities. Formerly, the cost of telephone communications and the slowness of study by correspondence often produced a stark contrast between asynchronous modes of distance learning and synchronous experience of a contact university. Now, synchronous interactions with one's cohort via Web 'Chat' and Internet-based bulletin boards as well as nearly synchronous e-mail interaction between tutors and their learners raise the prospect that distance-learning materials and procedures will increasingly resemble their contact-course analogues.

Possible strategies to optimize the use of digital multimedia in learning

Considering the advantages and limitations of digital multimedia for use in educational applications, this section offers three design strategies to optimize the efficacy of learning media:

1   The learning strategy known as problem-based learning (PBL).
2   Recognition of the importance of synchronous interactions between a learner and his or her mentor for optimal learning experiences.
3   Bohm's worldview of 'wholeness and implicate order'.

Incorporation of problem-based learning into digital learning media

Problem-based learning is founded on the premise that learning involves both knowing and doing. Advocates of PBL regard the ability to use knowledge as equally important as acquiring it (Bridges and Hallinger 1995). What is valued in the PBL approach is the opportunity for learners to gain practical skills by learning how to solve difficult, novel and ambiguous problems by applying theoretical concepts as analytical tools to prior knowledge in a context relevant to their own present circumstances. Learners come to 'understand' a vocational discipline, or a domain, by deriving meaning from new information in the context of their prior knowledge (Burns, Clift and Duncan 1990).

Clift and Chambers (1994) recommend that problem-based learning techniques be used for learners to attain understanding of a 'body of knowledge' by seeking solutions to a series of tasks of increasing complexity. Students are challenged to discover what information and theory as 'tools of analysis' they will need to discover possible solutions to such tasks. A final task may inspire the student to 'reflect' on the process and their solution(s). Problems should be designed without a single correct solution path and learners should be encouraged to draw from all aspects of the materials available on the CD-ROM (or Internet) in an integrative fashion to synthesize a solution. Problem-based learning focuses on the process, not the product. This approach challenges learners to derive solutions to a series of tasks of increasing complexity. Learners are stimulated to seek useful information and focus on the process of thinking about problems rather than learning subject matter by rote (Gibbs 1991).

PBL may be incorporated into digital learning media by providing a learner with a set of problems which he or she may reframe to be relevant to his or her life circumstances and interests. In solving a given problem, a learner will first be encouraged to formulate subjectively the criteria by which an optimal solution may be judged. The learner will then be encouraged to utilize the digital technology (CD-ROM or Internet) only as a starting point in the search for the required solution. In this manner, the self-confidence and initiative of the learner will be fostered, as will the recognition that all knowledge is conditioned by the assumptions one makes.

Synchronous interactions between a learner and his or her mentor

A theoretical rationale for the indispensability of interpersonal interaction between a mentor and a learner, in an optimal learning experience, can be found in the work of the social constructionists who contend that all perceptions of reality, including learning, are constructed from discourse and negotiation (see Schutz 1967). Social constructionists contend that the language used in a culture shapes the reality in which that culture exists. Gergen (1985) summarizes the constructionist logic as follows: As the world is known through human experience mediated principally by language, and categories of language used to classify things are situational and derived from social interaction, therefore reality is socially constructed by the continuing communicative interactions of members of a social group or culture.

Biocca has theorized about the social construction of a learning experience embedded within the design of the course materials (Biocca and Levy (eds) 1995). As suggested above (p. 7), this chapter advocates that the use of digital multimedia in higher learning be viewed as a potentially useful supplement to, but not displacement of, the learner's interactions with a mentor. Each educational technology entails the communication of a discourse that influences how learners think about reality. The pre-programmed, self-contained course materials frequently encountered on CD-ROM and many Internet-based courses are not able to simulate a dialogue that will meet the learning needs of any individual learner. This requires personal interaction with an intelligent and perceptive mentor. Accordingly, an optimal learning strategy recognizes the essential role of human interaction to facilitate a supportive dialogue as the learner constructs meaning from the educational experience.

The new Internet-based communications technologies afford university course lecturers and distance-learning tutors alike new opportunities to develop their mentoring skills in order to tailor and target support directly for individual learners. One need merely reflect on the relative ease of composing and transmitting e-mail in contrast to corresponding by letter, to recognize the versatility and cost-effectiveness of e-mail. This device facilitates both intimacy and remote interaction and thus new flexibility to accommodate the diverse learning requirements of contemporary university students.

Bohm's worldview of 'wholeness and implicate order'

A third strategy for effectively utilizing digital multimedia in the learning experience embraces the worldview of the late physicist and philosopher David Bohm, who argued that study of social phenomena, as well as of quantum mechanics, should be undertaken from the perspective of a 'wholeness and implicate order' of an entire system rather than by mastery of individual parts considered in isolation (Bohm 1980).

An application of Bohm's methodology to the design of educational multimedia rejects structured non-linear instructional modules, as well as the production of mere linear digital textbooks, in favour of media which present problems without any predetermined solution paths. Such non-structured learning experiences will require the participation of a mentor who can provide cues and Socratic support to the learner as he or she constructs meaning relevant to a specific context or vocation.

Bohm's vision resonates with the constructivist problem-based learning strategy advocated above. It is highly desirable that learners are empowered to draw creatively upon the totality of the resources available to them in the search for solutions to their problems. Presenting problems in which it is clear that no preferred solution path has been determined compels a learner to utilize his or her own judgement in formulating a solution rather than seeking to replicate the solution intended by course designers. An application of Bohm's methodology to the design of multimedia rejects predetermined non-linear structures for learning materials on CD-ROM or the World Wide Web, as well as linear programming, in favour of media which present problems without any predetermined solution paths.

Adoption of the Bohmian approach to making sense of the world by grasping whole systems, rather than minute analysis of their perceived parts, reinforces the central role of the mentor in the learning process. Without an interactive guide, an 'unstructured wholeness' approach to the presentation of problem-based learning modules could leave a learner submerged in his or her options in a labyrinth of information.

Design principles for digital presentation of learning media

The widespread adoption of digital learning media requires academic staff to completely rethink the nature and practice of higher learning (Brittain, Chambers and Marriott 1997). The advent of digital learning media profoundly alters the relationship of the learner to his or her university, tutor and course material. The control of when, where and how one learns shifts from the 'course instructors' to become the primary responsibility of the individual learner (ibid.).

An extensive literature search was undertaken in order to delineate contemporary views of educationalists of the best practice for the design and delivery of digitally presented learning media. The main thrust of the design approach advocated in this chapter is to shift the teaching process from 'subject-based' instruction to 'problem-based' learning. The problem-based learning format is intended to challenge learners to:

1   Discover what they already know about a subject and attempt to apply that knowledge to find methods of solving similar problems which are likely to arise in their professional and private lives (Clift and Chambers 1994).
2   Attempt increasingly difficult tasks supported by hints, model approaches and methodological suggestions (but not 'correct' answers). Such problems should be supported by Socratic instruction (whereby student questions are answered by questions which encourage the students increasingly to rely on their own powers of analysis).

There may be a temptation for some academic administrators to regard digital delivery as a potential cost-saving device whereby classroom lectures may be recorded and then mass-produced for presentation internationally. Such possibilities will not escape large multinational corporates who may wish to offer pre-packaged educational experiences as a new product line. Developments of this kind may promote a commodification of higher learning and a general decline in academic standards unless the course materials reflect the 'student-focused' philosophy articulated in this chapter.

If one accepts the basic premise that the fundamental purpose of higher learning is not the transmission of information but the acquisition by the learner of critical thinking skills, then it follows that the new digital learning media should be used in a manner which best facilitates a discourse between the learner and his or her mentor, rather than a one-way transmission of 'facts'.

The literature reflects growing interest in the use of e-mail as a particularly efficient and inexpensive mode of interpersonal communication which can be used to facilitate highly individualized tutoring of learners. Perhaps, for example, through the medium of e-mail, the 'Oxford Method' of weekly one-on-one tutorials may become more commonplace as a feature of the programmes offered by prestigious universities worldwide.

The ethics of incorporating digital multimedia into conventional programmes of higher learning

We live in a time when the electronic semblance of things is displacing the objects it represents. A predictable consequence of the widespread integration of digital multimedia into programmes of higher learning will be a rise of 'virtual classrooms' and 'virtual universities'. There is a growing body of comment in the educational literature concerning how digital technology may ultimately displace the bricks and mortar of schools and tertiary institutions (Tiffin and Rajasingham 1995). Those who seek to usher in a new age predicated upon technology have a social responsibility to examine how such technology will affect those who use it and the communities within which it is disseminated.

Before entering a virtual classroom it may be instructive to ponder who is in charge of the educational process. Although one may attend a virtual university in the comfort of one's home, the institution may be operating from anywhere in the world. Once education is no longer situated in a local community or even within a national boundary and can be remotely delivered, the possibility opens that large transnationals such as Time-Warner, Microsoft, IBM and Disney Corporation may set up their own universities and enrol students across the globe. As the educational process has a powerful influence upon an individual's sense of self-identity and loyalties, the potential for adverse social consequences of the widespread adoption of digital technologies in higher learning cannot be lightly dismissed.

The introduction of information technologies into higher learning in general and the advent of the virtual classroom in particular present a range of ethical issues, including:

1   Cost and equity of access.
2   Diminution of the role of the university as a 'critic and conscience of society'.
3   Erosion of civil society and true (proximal) communities.

Again it is beyond the scope of this paper to do more than raise these issues and provide brief comment.

Cost and equitable access to higher learning

The proponents of virtual universities often cite the enormous potential for government-spending reductions as the bricks and mortar of traditional universities are displaced by the computer hardware and software investments of learners logging into virtual universities from their homes.

Although IT innovations promise to reduce central government expenditures, the aggregate expenditure on higher learning may increase as individual learners are required to invest in the products which enable them to participate on-line. Some students will, of course, find the cost of technology prohibitive and others may regard such expenditures as wasteful, particularly as personal computers are notorious for their rapid decline in value into obsolescence. The financial burden of providing an educational infrastructure will merely have been shifted in great measure from the state and on to the students.

There is evidence in New Zealand that the adoption of IT for educational purposes is increasing rather than diminishing the cost of higher learning. For example, the deputy vice-chancellor of Auckland University (Hotere 1997) has reported that electronic delivery has been responsible for the escalating operational costs of the university and has contributed to the rise in student fees. In his view, the savings expected to be achieved by replacing the traditional campus services with electronically mediated learning are an illusion.

The role of the university as a 'critic and conscience of society'

Advocates of the virtual classroom typically focus on the purported benefits of remote participation. It cannot be doubted that there are indeed many students whose life circumstances are such that distance education is the best mode of learning. For these learners, the virtual classroom promises truly enhanced learning opportunities with their cohort and mentors. However, the dispersal of the campus into a virtual community will potentially adversely impact other functions of the university such as its role as a centre of research. A conventional university campus is a place where unpopular and unconventional thinking can first challenge dogma and ignorance. In this capacity, a university is able to serve as a 'critic and conscience of society'.

The very idea of a virtual university is at odds with the role of the critic and conscience of society. By their nature virtual universities are located in cyberspace and are dependent upon software and telecommunications corporations for their existence. The law of the free marketplace and economy-of-scale economics dictate that ultimately international virtual universities will compete for global markets. But how will a virtual mega-university based in Seattle, Tokyo or Cambridge serve as a critic and conscience for such places as New Zealand, Kenya or Costa Rica?

The cost of the loss of a local university as a concerned social critic would be very great because there are few alternatives in contemporary society to the contribution of independent scholars to philosophy, ethics, psychology, sociology and a host of other disciplines. An IT-driven 'lean and mean' university may produce effective workers and managers serving what Lyotard has defined as the 'performativity' agenda of the corporate sector to organize all activities according to market-sector efficiencies (Lyotard 1984), but would such institutions produce creative *and critical* thinkers whose integrity is not compromised by the need not to displease one's employer or sponsor?

The potential erosion of civil society and true (proximal) communities

Many commentators, such as Lanham (1990), interpret the impact of information technologies in a largely optimistic light. Lanham believes that the primary influence of the computer on modern thinking is humanistic, with the digitization of the arts serving radically to democratize them. He argues that as digitization makes all art forms radically interchangeable and accessible, we have entered a new age of interactivity which shifts the locus of creation from the author to the consumer.

What seems lacking in the analysis of the benefits of the new communications technologies is consideration of the implications of the technology for the constitution of the subjective self of an individual adapting to the electronically mediated realities of the emerging information age. The historian Mark Poster (1990) argues that a person's sense of self is constituted in acts and structures of communication. In the digital age, Poster observes, people derive much of the information about the world through electronically mediated communications such as television. These modes of communication filter and frame the messages we receive to the extent that they begin to constitute our collective sense of reality.

We must examine the extent to which the increasing use of Internet and other emerging information technology will transform the context and quality of our collective intercultural experience. Technology is never neutral, but has enormous potential for configuring the ways in which we inter-relate and influencing with whom we communicate, as well as transmitting the content of our communication.

Marike Finlay (1987) has provided a framework for evaluation of the social impact of emerging communications technologies. Finlay argues that any assessment of the social impact of communications technologies must take into consideration three fundamental tenets of contemporary media theory:

1   Communication is not a mirror reflection of brute unmediated reality.
2   Communication relations both mediate and constitute society.
3   Communication is more than content; it is also a set of rules for how social interaction may occur.

Finlay contends that all communication activities (and the technologies which facilitate them) should be understood as modes of discourse which contain presuppositions about the nature of society and what we know about the world. When we change the technology we use to communicate we fundamentally change those presuppositions and ultimately how society organizes its affairs.

What we choose to do with our time precludes other activities. The Berkeley educationalist Theodore Roszak (1986) considers that through our electronic preoccupations we may be losing our sense of shared cultural experience. He questions whether the imaged 'virtual communities' forming on the Internet will prove a true substitute for proximal interaction of people. Many commentators believe that in the future, traditional contact universities will evolve into distance-learning organizations serving a global catchment area. Yet Roszak's gloomy vision need not come to pass in the realm of higher learning if we make appropriate applications of emerging technologies to preserve and even enhance what we value most in the traditional university. Indeed, the digital convergence of the traditional contact and the distance universities may mean that the very Fordist concept of the university 'classroom' itself may be abandoned as an obsolete mass-production device in favour of that classic educational ideal since the time of Plato's Academy: one-on-one tuition. Perhaps in the future, instead of enduring Economics 101 in a crowded lecture hall on a dreary Monday morning, our learners will interact with fellow learners in synchronous electronic seminars and with their mentors in an e-mail version of the hallowed 'Oxford Method'. With the widespread reticulation of fibre-optic technologies the prospect that we shall increasingly interact through telepresence looms before us. Whether or not we make wise use of such technologies is ultimately our choice.

References

Biocca, Frank and Levy, Mark R. (eds) (1995) *Communication in the Age of Virtual Reality*, Hillsdale, NJ: Lawrence Erlbaum Associates.

Bohm, David (1980) *Wholeness and the Implicate Order*, London and Boston: Routledge & Kegan Paul.

Bridges, Edwin M. and Hallinger, Philip (1995) *Implementing Problem Based Learning in Leadership Development*, Eugene, Ore.: University of Oregon Press, ERIC Clearinghouse on Educational Management.

Brittain, Michael, Chambers, Mark and Marriott, Philip (1997) 'Design considerations in the development and delivery of digital learning media', paper presented at ED-Media Conference, Freiburg, Germany.

Burns, Janet, Clift, John and Duncan, J. (1990) 'Understanding of understanding: implications for learning and teaching', *British Journal of Educational Psychology* 61: 276–89.

Clift, John and Chambers, Mark (1994) 'Educational considerations in the development of a generic degree program', report to the New Zealand Qualifications Authority, Dec. 1994.

Eisner, E. (1993) 'Reshaping assessment in education: criteria in search of practice', *Journal of Curriculum Studies* 25(3): 219–33.

Finlay, Marike (1987) *Powermatics: A Discursive Critique of New Technology*, London: Routledge & Kegan Paul.

Gergen, Kenneth J. (1985) 'The social constructionist movement in modern psychology', *American Psychologist* 40: 266–75.

Gibbs, G. (1991) 'The CNAA improving student learning project', in A. Viscovic (ed.), *Research and Development in Higher Education: Volume 14*, Wellington: Higher Education Research and Development Society (HERDSA), pp. 8–19.

Gilder, George (1995) *Telecosm*, New York: Simon & Schuster.

Hotere, Andrea (1997) 'Technology pushes up the cost of education', *New Zealand Education Review*, Wellington, 14 May.

Lanham, Richard (1990) 'The extraordinary convergence: democracy, technology, theory and the university curriculum', *South Atlantic Quarterly* 89(1).

Lyotard, J. F. (1984) *The Postmodern Condition*, Minneapolis: University of Minnesota Press.

Mason, Robin and Kaye, Anthony (eds) (1989) *Mindweave: Communication, Computers and Distance Education*, Oxford: Pergamon Press. Retrieved from World Wide Web at < http://www-icdl.open.ac.uk/mindweave/chap1.html >.

Negroponte, Nicholas (1995) *Being Digital*, Rydalmere, NSW: Hodder & Stoughton.

Palmer, Mark T. (1995) 'Interpersonal communication and virtual reality: mediating interpersonal relationships', in Frank Biocca and Mark R. Levy (eds), *Communication in the Age of Virtual Reality*, Hillsdale, NJ: Lawrence Erlbaum Associates.

Poster, Mark (1990) *The Mode of Information: Poststructuralism and Social Context*, Cambridge: Polity Press.

Roszak, Theodore (1986) *The Cult of Information: A Neo-Luddite Treatise on High Tech, Artificial Intelligence, and the True Art of Thinking*, Berkeley: University of California Press.

Schutz, Alfred (1967) *The Phenomenology of the Social World*, trans. George Walsh and Frederick Lehnert, Minneapolis St Paul, Minn.: Northwestern University Press.

Speake, Terry and Powell, James (1997) 'The missing link in multimedia', *The Times Higher Education Supplement*, 14 Nov., p. xii, Multimedia.

Taylor, Mark and Saarinen, Esa (1994) *Imagologies: Media Philosophy*, London and New York: Routledge.

Tiffin, John and Rajasingham, Lalita (1995) *In Search of the Virtual Class: Education in an Information Society*, London and New York: Routledge.

Wittrock, M. (1977) 'The generative processes of memory', in M. C. Wittrock (ed.), *The Human Brain*, Englewood Cliffs, NJ: Prentice-Hall.

3 On access

Towards opening the lifeworld within adult higher education systems

Lee Herman and Alan Mandell

> The spirit and meaning of education cannot be enhanced by addition, by the easy method of giving the same dose to more individuals. If learning is to be revivified, quickened so as to become once more an adventure, we shall have need of new concepts, new motives, new methods; we shall need to experiment with the qualitative aspects of education.
>
> (Lindeman 1926, p. 4)

Introduction

It is just and good that more people and more people of different kinds have access to higher education. It is just, because through access to higher education people are more likely to acquire power and prosperity. It is good, because achieving such success is so commonly understood as a necessary condition of happiness. Higher education is thus an all but necessary instrument for fulfilment in today's world. In turn, access to higher education becomes an important political demand because, despite the hugely growing numbers of people attending college, the majority remain excluded, possibly for lack of ability, but assuredly for lack of means and for who they are. The struggle for access to the academy is a powerful reminder that our social and educational ideals have not yet been achieved.

At its simplest, access means opening opportunities for people to attend college who were once excluded. But increasing access has more than numerical consequences. It has led to the presence of populations of students and faculty which are increasingly diverse in age, ethnicity, gender, class and other ascriptions that were once seen as disqualifying. With these new persons, new voices are heard and new experiences become available to the entire academic community. As a result, many basic assumptions of academic institutions have been opened to question. These include assumptions about curriculum and canon, the organization and process of learning, the constitution of knowledge, the grounds of intellectual authority, and the purposes of education. Thus, the predominantly pragmatic aspects of access open on to normative perspectives, to questions about our fundamental values.

What began as a matter of making more room for more people has become a persisting battle over the very architecture of the academy (Herman 1992). Some thirty years ago, new institutions of 'distance', 'open', 'individualized' and otherwise 'non-traditional' education were created. These colleges were intended to provide both access and experimentation – to become laboratories where new modes and philosophies of learning with 'new' students could be explored. But even while change and invention thrived, various factors moved those alternative programmes towards more traditional practices and purposes. These factors include the struggle for legitimacy within the world of higher education; the normal processes of institutional routinization; the persistence of historical faculty roles, values and rewards; and especially the exigencies of the market, which mould student demands and university responses. At the same time, traditional, even elite colleges have made themselves more accessible to 'non-traditional' students. They now offer professional degrees and certificates, evening and weekend classes, satellite locations, and distance-learning opportunities that make it possible to reproduce the classroom any place at any time. Such innovations have allowed these conventional institutions to capture new markets necessary for their financial viability.

Thus, non-traditional and traditional colleges are converging (Tait 1997). Their pedagogies, goals and student bodies are increasingly similar. It might therefore be asked whether the call for access has stimulated normative transformations within the academy and in society beyond it. While there is no doubt that it is easier to be an adult college student than ever before, the practical advantages of convergence could also mean that the interrelated problems of social justice and basic educational values are pushed aside.

From a historical perspective, the access debate has never been simple. It has never been about practical issues alone. Whether it was a matter of women being allowed to go to college, or African-Americans, or older students (such as GIs returning from war), every 'new' population was suspect. Were they intellectually and temperamentally eligible for authentic participation in higher learning? Would they disrupt the stabilities presumed necessary for serious scholarship? (Nasaw 1979, pp. 170ff.). Even today, when it might be commonly assumed that such questions have been put to rest, 'unusual' students by their very presence are thought to dilute the quality of educational activity. For example, some undergraduate and graduate programmes continue to deny admission to part-time students on the grounds that only a full-time commitment to scholarship would enable one to partake in the most advanced exercises of the life of the mind. This normative claim thus has the practical consequence of excluding most adult students. The example also illustrates the more general point, that seemingly practical decisions are embedded in normative claims about what is true, what is just and what is fitting. And our responses to such normative questions always have practical consequences. The issue of access continues to have the authority that it does because it turns on just this conjunction of the practical and the normative. The issue is not and never will be only about room and resources in the academy for those admitted. It is also inextricably about who belongs, and the true and proper nature of the learning to be done there.

In this chapter we shall explore the intimate connections between the practical and normative aspects of access. We shall first discuss contemporary criticisms of a largely pragmatic approach to access; then we shall critically examine those criticisms; finally, we shall offer an alternative approach. It is our contention that fully appreciating the normative implications of the access question is necessarily both political and pedagogical. In other words, from this critically informed normative perspective, addressing questions of who learns, and how, what and why they learn, also means confronting decisions about fairness, authority and democracy. Opening up the problem of educational access in this way thus demands that we deal with how students and faculty struggle with the tension between succeeding in a harsh world and thriving in a cherishable one.

Throughout this chapter, we shall draw on the work of Jürgen Habermas, especially his analyses of the tensions between 'system' and 'lifeworld'. We shall understand 'system' to mean the realm of rationally related, calculable pragmatic functions, dominated by the values of efficiency, money and power. In contrast, the 'lifeworld' refers to the realm of normative values – truth, justice, beauty – which enduringly attract both human affections and rational enquiry (Habermas 1989). Our understanding is also informed by our own experiences of and reflections on the practices of adult education, on opening institutions and the faculty role to accommodate student experiences, interests and hopes (Mandell and Herman 1996). This exploration, at its heart, confirms two things: no adjustment of the educational system and the larger social system it reproduces, no matter how critically sophisticated, can avoid responding to the normative claims of the lifeworld; and no concern for the basic values of everyday life, no matter how caring or politically committed it may be, can ignore the implacable demands of impersonal systems. We shall hopefully offer an approach to accessible education which we believe works simultaneously in the domains of both system and life world.

Here is our argument: making educational opportunities more accessible to those it has excluded does not ultimately make the system fair. But bringing out the curricular and learning-process implications of truly listening to and sharing authority with non-traditional learners does challenge systemic assumptions about legitimate learning and knowledge. Acting on these new practices with students creates within the academy a set of democratic learning relationships, a kind of 'in vitro' community. Forming this democratic community 'in vitro' has, we contend, direct consequences for the 'in vivo' conjunctions between system and lifeworld in the public sphere beyond the academy. Thus, the occasions of academic learning are 'miniature public spaces' (Rose 1995, p. 5) which can be preparatory schools for thought and action in the larger public spaces beyond. At the beginning of the twentieth century John Dewey introduced the idea that schools should be transformed into places of 'embryonic community life': 'When the school introduces and trains each child of society into membership within such a little community, saturating him [*sic*] with the spirit of service, and providing him [*sic*] with the instruments of effective self-directions, we shall have the deepest and best guarantee of a larger society which is worthy, lovely, and harmonious' (Dewey 1959, p. 49). The conclusion of our argument is that such a vision of education is no less relevant for the adult students in today's world than it was for the children in Dewey's time.

We prepare for and complete this line of thought in three 'moments'. In the first, we explicate the limits of a purely pragmatic understanding of increasing access to higher education. We look at the ultimately self-contradictory qualities of education sought and provided mainly as an instrument of upward social mobility and increased prosperity. In the second, we follow the 'critical theorists'' analysis of the processes of adult learning as a 'commodification' of learning itself in the service of systemic imperatives. We track the consequent diminishment of the opportunity for both students and faculty to engage the normative issues of human life, the very substance of the lifeworld, which have traditionally been the hallmark of 'higher' education. And in the third moment we part company with the critical theorists. Applying maxims of what Habermas calls 'discourse ethics' (1990), we demonstrate the claim that with careful attention to the normative implications of genuinely collaborative enquiry between faculty and students, lifeworlds are created within the academy and can reverberate beyond it. We believe 'co-governance' (Shor 1996, p. 200) of students and faculty over both curriculum and learning process offers significant possibilities for reforming both the academic and the socio-economic system.

Such an effort requires not only commitment from students and faculty, but also a hospitable institutional environment. The public college in which we work, Empire State College, can be such a place. Like all colleges, ours is susceptible to the domination of systemic imperatives, including market forces; however, our institution does offer chances to create and sustain lifeworlds of enquiry with students. These surviving manifestations of the idealism in our college's original mission enable us to engage in genuinely 'student-centred' education: to work with students individually and in small, improvised groups; to develop 'learning contracts' and 'degree programmes' with students which reflect their individual experiences, curiosities, abilities and educational goals; and to set the schedule and place of learning to suit student needs. Because this hospitable institution actually exists, we can offer examples, case studies, of our work with students to demonstrate our abstract analytical and normative claims. Perhaps even more important, we believe that through the very process of reflecting on our work with students, we have been better able to understand, develop and keep faith with the idea of creating a lifeworld-in-enquiry.

Moment 1

The call for access to higher education began as part of a broad movement that demanded spreading opportunity to participate in the prosperity and power of contemporary society. It was supposed to become a matter of common sense and simple fairness that all citizens should be able to acquire the learning they needed to succeed. However, rather than simply an expression of social justice, public policies that eventually responded to collective voices for these demands (for example, in the 1960s) could equally well be understood as the outcome of a series of pragmatic calculations intended to preserve social order and established interests. Keeping people out of decent jobs and out of the growing culture of consumption was just too costly in both money and stability. Opening up the universities to people of colour, to more women – indeed, creating 'alternative' programmes and institutions for 'non-traditional' students – was, in fact, a victory for moral idealism (Kett 1994, pp. 447–8). But it also became and still remains an extremely lucrative and effective means of certifying and portioning social mobility. That is, although more people of different kinds can now gain access to higher education, college degrees are now more necessary for people to get ahead at all (Lehmann and Maehl 1995).

In this perspective, for both the policy makers and managers of the higher education system, as well as for its potential 'clients', access to educational services increasingly becomes a solely practical goal. But, as critics have so persuasively argued, even an educational system governed by such practicality is inherently self-contradictory. That is, while the system opens itself to new participants, it simultaneously imposes two practical restrictions. First, for those people who *do* get in, the requirements for social success and security multiply in terms of continuing (and often expensive) education, certificates and degrees. (Just as more and more people of different kinds are now getting into college, many jobs which had never required degrees at all now do, and those that did now require more advanced degrees and even 'lifelong' credentialling.) Second, for those people who are *excluded*, the social, economic and personal consequences are more drastic than ever. (At the same time that women and 'minorities' are more represented in workplaces proportionate to their numbers, permanent job security is increasingly obsolete and productivity requirements have dramatically escalated [cf., among others, Reich 1990].) In the name of our so-called 'knowledge society', learning itself becomes a harsh and uncivil tool in the competition for money, power and national prestige.

But there is a third restriction as well. This is a normative one, which, whether explicit or taken for granted, accompanies and serves to legitimate the dysfunctions of a wholly pragmatic approach to access. The very claim to openness justifies marginalizing those who are altogether excluded and those who never get very far. Deflecting attention from systemic dysfunctions (which are also social inequities), it is supposed that those who do not

prosper, do not *deserve* to prosper. They fail, it is supposed, for lack of sufficient individual initiative to take advantage of the opportunities available to
them. In fact, for the social economic order to function as it currently exists,
it must not only preserve its prosperity through the declining real incomes of
most working people and the dismantling of reliable and sufficient securities
for the poor, it must also distribute its unequal rewards according to ever
finer stratifications of credentialled achievement.

Access thus shows two faces: invitation and exclusion. While offered as a
new path to freedom and expression of democratic opportunity, access to
higher education also introduces a sequence of markers for legitimating
inequality. These ideas are echoed in the experiences of our students as
they encounter the Janus-like nature of higher education. They are grateful
for the welcome into institutions which had formerly been inaccessible to
them. However, they are also preoccupied with the oppressiveness of the
academic requirements now added to their already complex and demanding
lives.

Jim is one of our students whose experiences exemplify this tension.
In middle age, during a successful career as a facilities manager at a
manufacturing plant, he was told at first that in order to be promoted
or even maintain his current status, he would have to complete a two-
year college degree. Jim had never before been to college; however,
through technical schools, on-the-job training and his own inquisitive-
ness, he was used to learning the newest information and skills pertinent to his work. Were it not for the opportunity funded and the
threat implied by his company, it's unlikely that Jim would have
been able or would have chosen to go to college. Though acutely conscious of the status of becoming a 'college-educated' person, he also
worried about fitting academic work into his already busy schedule
and about being 'smart enough' to do it successfully at all. Further,
while not strongly resentful, Jim noticed the unfairness of having to
'get an education', and under difficult circumstances, so as to be
allowed to keep the job he already so capably performs. Upon completing his two-year degree, Jim's company then informed him that in order
for him to be upgraded within his *current* job title, a four-year degree
would be necessary and that if he wished to be promoted, a master's
degree would be preferred. (Moroever, while the company would fund
the four-year degree, it would not fund the master's.) Jim is completing
a baccalaureate degree; he is considering a master's. For Jim, access to
college is a gift he gratefully receives and a blow he has to absorb.

* * *

Leslie, another of our students, is more acutely aware of the precarious-
ness of her own situation, of the power of certified learning both to offer
a way out of and to maintain it. As a former prison inmate, she is interested in establishing a career and in understanding the racial and social
ascriptions which have marked her life. She is eager to learn and to use
that learning both to earn the rewards she needs and respects, and to
critically evaluate the world she deeply resents. For Leslie, becoming
a student is an invitation to a form of intellectual exploration she's
always desired and been denied. She also knows that going to college
would almost be impossible were it not for publicly funded financial
aid, an accommodating admissions policy, and the support of her
superiors at the social service agency where she works. It is her goal
to acquire their learning and authority. Going to school offers her
that opportunity. But her situation constantly echoes for her a basic
unfairness: the insight and intelligence she's developed through her
life are not in themselves sufficient for her to penetrate institutional
judgements and barriers; she is expected to add the stamp of an academic degree to her record of skilled work and wise judgement. For
Leslie, access to college means entering a world of learning and
status she genuinely desires, but also going through the performances
imposed by a social system she has found little reason to trust.
Making it through college, she knows, is her best or only means of
escaping the lower margins of society where she has dwelled. Yet, in
an embittering irony, during the very time she is skilfully working to
improve that society in a human services agency, she is learning,
through her college studies, something more about the injustices in
that society. She is learning that the degree her employers require of
her, her access to individual success, also symbolizes the power and
authority of the institutions which enforce the oppressive social stratifications from which she and so many of her fellow citizens have
suffered.

These instances bear out the claim that increased access to higher education
really does increase the prosperity of adult students (Kett 1994, pp. 403ff.).
However, the experiences of these particular students also suggest the
powerful inequity of a system that uses educational credentials as a series
of excluding and stratifying gates. Educational access that does not offer
opportunities to reform the institutional and social systems it serves creates
its own inequities: it provides an increased chance of success for some, while
exacting a severe socio-economic punishment for those altogether excluded;
and it imposes arbitrary criteria of merit on everyone. We should therefore

ask: How is it that institutions, students and faculty, through efforts to achieve their own individual success, lend themselves to conditions which ultimately corrode their highest values?

Moment 2

Educational institutions marketing increased access for adult students have developed a variety of techniques, services and processes which make the delivery of learning more responsive to the practical learning needs and life exigencies of their new clientele. In addition, changing attitudes, sometimes prompted by fierce enrolment competition, have by and large removed the second-class status of older students. The convergence of traditional and non-traditional colleges thus offers adults a variety of efficient and well-endowed learning opportunities.

At the same time as these programmes of adult education have become firmly established and systematized, there has also grown a routine theoretical critique of those developments. 'Critical theorists' (Connelly 1996) have argued that adult education has succumbed to 'a business corporate ethos' and, in becoming so pragmatic, has lost its identity as an agency of positive social change through 'emancipatory learning' (Collins 1995, pp. 88 and 80). Indeed, as our experience and examples show, most adult students *do* choose to continue their education for quite practical reasons: they want to acquire the learning and the certification necessary to succeed in a changing economy (Merriam and Caffarella 1991). And the programmes which have accommodated them, even those that retain a patina of a liberal arts education, have not only acceded to this market demand but also claim that workplace-relevant or 'instrumental' learning is the most important product the academy can contribute to society. In other words, these changes in the academy not only reflect an institutional responsiveness to the perceived and expressed needs of new students; also, with even greater social consequence, adult education programmes build their legitimacy (and thereby seek to secure their financial viability) by presenting themselves as valuable instruments for sustaining economic growth. Claiming to serve a 'nation of lifelong learners', they offer themselves as allies of a social system which claims economic imperatives to be its most fundamental value.

Critical theorists have also maintained that educational institutions within this system are creating a caste of new faculty professionals. The faculty are trying to accommodate the demands of their students and a changing academic workplace. The faculty are also responding to their well-founded anxieties about tensions between the traditional value of scholarly work and a demanding new role as expert facilitators, academic entrepreneurs and managers of learning resources. In a market-driven, global and diversified post-industrial world, the professoriate is no longer valued as it once was. We cannot buffer ourselves from that world by maintaining our integrity as guardians and sustainers of a cherished cultural tradition. Ironically, this occurs in large part because we ourselves have deconstructed that once secure and admired ivory tower. As educators of adults (and of younger students preparing to enter the adult workforce), faculty have turned their efforts to serve these students and the market into a distinctive expertise. In so doing, the critics argue, the faculty have created a 'thoroughly professionalized practice' that legitimizes their standing by wholly serving the demands of the market system (Welton 1995, p. 132).

In such an 'educational service economy' (ibid., p. 133), methods and processes of learning, with an emphasis on efficient and comfortable access to information, become the centre of education. Attention to the abiding questions of human life falls by the wayside. Matters at the heart of the life-world (the normative dimension), such as efficacious social criticism and alternative visions, are lost. Thus, at the same time that faculty are framing a socially valuable identity niche for themselves in an academy whose traditionally contemplative enterprise is no longer sheltered from the market-place, they inevitably participate in transforming the learning of which they had been the creators and conservators into a commodity. That is, learning becomes largely understood in terms of its exchange value, as something to be accumulated and traded for something economically useful, such as a job-marketable skill. The knowledge most worth having no longer has as much to do with enlightened and liberating enquiry as it does with promoting success.

Ellen is a classic case of upward mobility. She had devoted herself almost entirely to work since graduating high school. Over a decade, she rose within a company from assembly-line worker to supervisor. Then, when she had completed her associate's degree (majoring in business), she became a middle-level manager, and, upon finishing her baccalaureate degree (majoring in operations management), she had charge of the production of an entire division and was on the verge of a vice-presidency. As she began to design her baccalaureate curriculum, Ellen was clear, certain and assertive about three goals: completing her undergraduate education as soon as possible, obtaining maximum college credit for the learning she'd acquired through her work experience, and studying only work-relevant subjects. The policies and procedures of our college accommodated these goals quite smoothly. Her agenda was well satisfied by our flexible enrolment options, curricular customization and variety of study modes suitable to her schedule and preferred learning style. Moreover, by most criteria of institutional performance, Ellen was definitely a success for our college: she helped us meet our enrolment target, her company paid her tuition because her degree was work-related, she contributed to our rates of retention and graduation, she made good use of the variety of our learning resources, and she spoke well of us to other potential students. Her pragmatic attitude to learning and her sound academic skills profited our system and cost it little.

Because of our college's one-to-one approach to advisement and teaching, Ellen and her faculty mentor formed a good working relationship. Even so, her intense and nearly exclusive concentration on practical learning was sometimes troubling. She rarely seemed to take advantage of making the contemplative, reflective possibilities of her work and personal life into deeper academic enquiries. In our college, those possibilities could have easily been turned into meaningful, individualized liberal arts tutorials. However, Ellen's priorities were elsewhere, and here too, the malleability of our academic requirements allowed her to meet them in her own way.

*   *   *

Just as Empire State College helped Ellen become a 'captain' of the industrial system, we helped Bob become a 'guardian' of that system. He came to our college because he needed to accumulate, as quickly as possible, enough credits towards a bachelor's degree to be eligible for a police lieutenancy. Achieving that rank, he would have, in addition to job security and good pay, the prospect of retiring prosperously at age 40 and enviable public status.

The degree programme Bob created imitated the criminal-justice curricula of other institutions whose requirements he had researched. He transferred the credits he had earned at a two-year college and added to them credits we awarded him for learning he had acquired at the police academy and through on-the-job experience. For his remaining credits, Bob chose a number of liberal arts studies. In conversations with his faculty mentor, he voiced an interest in American history, and the two of them decided to include work on research writing and a final study on the Bill of Rights. Through that, he might link his knowledge of criminal justice with learning about American politics and political philosophy. He was a most competent student, who carried out his assignments according to schedule in the face of a demanding and always shifting calendar. He was certainly interested in the content of his studies. Moreover, he understood, with a lingering cynicism, that his place of employment had added to its promotion criteria a set of academic requirements that he was sure were unfair and only tangentially related to job performance. Nonetheless, both

Bob and his mentor accepted the overriding fact that he would do what was required to accumulate the credits necessary to get ahead.

In Bob's case, the faculty role was to facilitate his progress towards a degree, to arrange that the learning and certification he required would be met smoothly and efficiently. As a part of a growing market of student clientele, upon which our college is increasingly dependent, it was important for the faculty to suit Bob's academic needs. But in doing so, it could be asked whether the faculty had become more adept providers of pre-packaged academic material generically relevant to *any* police officer in his circumstance, rather than thoughtful teachers helping this individual person to question, explore and reflect. Judged by the criteria of professional facilitation, Bob and the college were served well. Judged by the criteria of active learning, opportunities were missed to engage with Bob in deep academic enquiry.

Predominantly, as in Ellen's case, conventional academic standards were adhered to, the college produced a graduate, the student achieved what he wanted, and he has, no doubt, spoken well of his experience to other potential students. Bob and Ellen will acquire high and prosperous places in the social system. We were pleased to have helped them. But we were also troubled by lubricating the reciprocity between powerful academic, industrial and law-enforcement institutions. We made access to and progress through college easy for Bob and Ellen, and their satisfying experiences sustained our access to ready-made, somewhat 'captive' markets of potential students who need us to improve their prosperity and social power.

This troubling experience of success expresses a problem: satisfying everyone's pragmatic interests, but failing to find a place for the lifeworld. Robert Kegan, in *In Over Our Heads* (1994), nicely describes the dilemma:

> In some quarters adult education as a field of practice is paralyzed by what it perceives as a choice it does not want to make: Shall it support its traditional, noble mission – the liberation of the mind and the growth of the student – at the risk of losing a large portion of its adult clientele, who will feel that what it has to offer is irrelevant to and neglectful of their adult practical needs? Or shall it respond to what it perceives as its adult clients' demands for practical training, expedient credentialing, increased skills, and a greater fund of knowledge at the risk of demoralizing or losing its best teachers, who are dismayed to find their professional and career identities being refashioned according to those of vocational education? (p. 273).

One way to understand this problematic tension is that educational goals have been 'colonized' by the imperatives of a market-driven economic system (Habermas 1989, pp. 325–7). Students are pressed to see their academic learning mostly in terms of its exchange value. Educational institutions, and thus we who hold positions within them, are driven by the same exigencies. And, even though we might express discomfort at this instrumentalization of learning, more and more we find ourselves placing our skills in service to those goals. We come to practise a somewhat mechanical facilitation which does not call upon us to touch the lifeworld – to engage with our students in reflective, deep enquiry which faculty have cherished as the heart of their professional identities.

To be sure, faculty cannot claim a monopoly on attending to lifeworld issues. In fact, a persistent feature of academic culture is the presumption that the more formal education one has, the wiser one is about the fundamental meanings and highest aspirations of human life. This claim to wisdom is foolish, something which Socrates long ago showed at the expense of the Sophists. However, such an attitude still endures even in modern democratic societies, where sometimes understanding basic values and virtues is taken to be a matter of mastering difficult technical information, as if it were an 'expertise' rather than an enquiry or discourse.

A much more hopeful and admirable idea is that all human beings can carefully contemplate their lifeworlds and honourably work to integrate them with the practical necessities, such as food, shelter, safety and comfort. Leisure and learning certainly do help those intellectual and creative efforts. Thus, the academy has been *one* place where the great normative questions are addressed in relative freedom from domination by practical issues; the academy's responses responses have indeed contributed to the lifeworld of the larger society. Whether a society's conversations are academic or part of everyday talk, the lifeworld is literally constituted, according to Habermas, by discourse about what is true, what is just and what is authentic or beautiful (1984, pp. 70–1). It is through respectful discussion of these topics with each other, in taking 'communicative action' with each other, that we form and live in fully human communities. In so doing, we rationally express our identities as individual selves, family members, friends, teachers, associates, neighbours, and as responsible and free citizens of a democratic society (Habermas 1996).

For Habermas, when education becomes a commodity and teaching-learning becomes largely instrumental, our lifeworld shrinks. The more attenuated our conversations about the normative questions of our lives (about truth, justice and beauty), the weaker our lifeworld becomes. We also become less capable of speaking for human values in the face of pervading reduction of ourselves to merely functional and expendable parts of a system (Habermas 1989, pp. 284–5). There was little room for meaningful conversations of this kind in our work with Ellen and Bob. Moreover, in our own scholarly activities, and even in our communication with our colleagues, we have bound ourselves to 'cultures of expertise' (Fischer 1990). We are preoccupied with ever more finely framed and constrictingly self-referential specializations. In effect, our scholarly work feeds a tremendous and complex academic system (comprised of journals, conferences, grants, departments and tenure processes), as though it were an end in itself. We faculty thus offer less than we might to the sustenance of the lifeworld.

It would of course be presumptuous to assume that students and faculty are unconcerned about this lifeworld or normative dimension. At issue, however, is that there is so little space for attending to it within the very institutions, colleges and universities, which have historically offered themselves as the special place for doing so. The academy has become too much a function of a much larger lifeworld-diminishing system upon which all of us depend. Thus, respect for the laudable ease with which many adults gain access to college and for our facilitating their progress should be tempered. It should be tempered with the critical reservation that our students' workplaces, as well as the academic workplace we share with them, are domains in which systemic powers are exercised. At its most extreme, academic systems are places where 'unfettered partnership or communication cannot enter', places of 'dumb necessity . . . solitary and silent' (Keane 1984, p. 136). We should therefore ask: What are the opportunities for emancipation in such a misleadingly accessible environment?

Moment 3

From the perspective of the critical theorists, it would appear that answers to this question demand direct action, both within and outside the academy. Professors can lend their expertise to political work that provides criticism of and even revolutionary challenges to current arrangements in non-academic spheres, such as families, workplaces, governments and the legal structures of the marketplace. As Habermas might say, academics can act directly on the 'steering media' of society: money and power (1989, p. 183). Within the academy, we could teach, by more or less traditional means, 'an education for life' (Hart 1992, p. 214), overtly increasing the room for 'deliberative discourse' about society in relevant moral and theoretical matters (Plumb 1995, p. 188). Instead of curricula designed to prepare students for success in the current system, we could offer knowledge that is normative, lifeworld-enhancing: information, skills and abilities that are life-affirming and socially responsible, which are relationship-building, and which engender self-expresssion and sensuous enjoyment even in the work-place (Hart 1992, p. 21). In other words, through such a 'transformative' approach to teaching, we could directly teach students about a better way to live (Giroux 1988). However, this method of teaching can become condescending, and its efficacy doubtful. One might ask whether we professors actually possess the wisdom, the normative knowledge, upon which such teaching depends, and even how one could decide whether we do.

An alternative to this approach is to take a more relativistic point of view. We could teach by encouraging students to pursue their own interests and questions, to explore and learn from their own backgrounds and experiences, and to respect their own abilities. In such an education, since no single normative perspective or tradition could be judged superior to any other, diversity becomes inherently valuable. Moreover, if such an educational system is not to be chaotic, then respecting differences and teaching students to do so becomes essential. That is, in consequence of the postmodernist deconstruction of objectively legitimated normative claims, this relativistic approach ostensibly clears the way for accepting and appreciating 'all varieties of educational tradition' (Usher and Edwards 1994, p. 31). However, while this may be a sentimentally attractive idea, it is necessarily based on its own normative assumption that diversity is a fundamental good. If one accepts the deconstructivist premise that such a normative claim could not be objectively legitimated, the value of diversity is left to stand solely on the brutal mercies of money and power – on exactly the dehumanizing systemic imperatives celebrants of postmodernism intend to dethrone (cf. Herman and Mandell 1996, pp. 58–9).

These two approaches should be taken seriously. Indeed, we largely agree with their critique of inequity, domination and alienation in contemporary social and academic arrangements. We also share their desire for a more 'utopian perspective' to guide our educational practices (Hart 1992, p. 200). These practices would include making space for genuinely diverse disputation and opposition within the academy (hooks and West 1991, pp. 27–58). However, we believe it is essential that this very urge towards emancipatory learning should not result in undercutting access to higher education. Just as the critical and utopian perspectives of educational theorists should be respected, so should the instrumental goals which apparently motivate so many students. That is, to allow more people into the academy, only to alienate them once they are there by condescending to or disregarding the very hopes which motivated them to come, would be absurd.

Instead, we propose that through nurturing a practice of listening to and honouring students' instrumental goals, the potential for emancipation arises in communicative dialogue. This quality of listening is not about recording information from students, which faculty then evaluate and transform into expert recommendations about their needs. Rather, it is about faculty involving themselves in student interests and purposes – working with their concerns and questions, however instrumental, as the legitimate grounds of collaborative enquiries. In such communication, faculty deliberately take the stance of not presuming to know students' interests better than they do. In other words, what motivates faculty is to find ways to share authority with students. As our examples will illustrate, in this very collaboration is the shared construction of a little lifeworld, a Deweyan 'embryonic community life'. Such an experience will naturally generate moments – new starting points – in which normative and fundamental issues, themes and questions arise, for both students and faculty. Thus, what faculty might have initially taken as impediments to depth, reflection and critique, in fact become materials and occasions for just such learning. Instrumental learning about making one's way in systems becomes integrated into normative learning about living in the lifeworld. Moreover, by genuinely sharing authority with students in the enquiries faculty undertake with them, we also believe that democratic learning relationships are formed within the academic context which can have important consequences outside it. That is, by enchancing experiences of reciprocal, collaborative and open communication within formal higher education, faculty and students help to expand the lifeworlds within and around it.

For Habermas, an appropriate response to the shrinkage of a lifeworld colonized by systemic imperatives is to engage in 'communicative action'. This does not mean only introducing into discussion the contents of the lifeworld, the normative topics of truth, justice and authenticity. There is also an absolutely essential regulative or process-attentive dimension of communicative action – a 'discourse ethics' (Habermas 1990). This kind of communication, such as an everyday conversation, is properly regulated by a set of ethical maxims, which Habermas offers (ibid., pp. 86–90) and which could be summarized as follows. Everyone with an interest and competence to participate (i.e. the ability to communicate) may do so. Force or coercion may not be used to exclude communication or to establish a position. Every participant should assert only what s/he really believes. Participants should not contradict themselves or use the same expressions with different meanings. Every participant who makes a claim or disputes one should give reasons and/or evidence to support it. Any assertion may be questioned. From these maxims identified by Habermas, two more can be derived: no conclusion should be held binding on the participants unless all can sincerely assert that they believe it; and all conclusions are provisional until the participants can raise no more questions about them.

In effect, these maxims legislate the lifeworld. They also serve as guides to rational enquiry. Moreover, it is in the very practice of such a discourse ethics that human beings in societies like our own, where system imperatives dominate, can gain the experience of a democratic lifeworld.

What would it mean, what would it look like, to use these maxims in formal higher education? It is easy to imagine what genuinely communicative enquiry would be in a non-institutional setting. It would be something like the free-flowing and never quite completed Socratic dialogues taking place in the relatively open space of the agora (Herman and Mandell 1996). In such dialogues, the participants can be aristocrats or slaves; the conversations are spontaneous, improvisational, playful and deep; and although the participants learn, none leave or should leave the conversation with the belief that they have now finally acquired the truth. However, unavoidably, learning taking place and credited within a modern formal system, an academic institution, cannot be so open-ended. Indeed, it is in working with the tensions between the maxims of the lifeworld and the demands of life within systems that we actually generate freedom within academic discourse. The faculty role, student expectations, definitions of important knowledge and even our normative imaginings of genuine communicative action – all must float within this tension.

It is essential to appreciate the sources of such tension. One is the sheer coercive force of social reality as it happens to be. We should not give it normative authority; we should not give this social reality the right, as it were, to define education. Nonetheless, these exigencies must be taken into account if education is to exist at all. Our students, our faculty jobs, our academic institutions would simply not exist were it not for the systemic force or imperatives of social prosperity and power. We can criticize, we can try to learn to shape and regulate these forces according to normative, emancipatory imperatives. But they cannot be disregarded. The second source (and this is essential for understanding the dialogues we are about to describe) is the maxim that the sincere claims of every participant deserve full attention. This means that in genuinely collaborative enquiries with our students we must care for and respect the instrumental educational goals and interests which our students bring into their academic work. It is not only the pragmatic concern that we risk losing their engagement (or, for that matter, their enrolment) if we fail to attend properly to those claims. Also, our normative responsibility to the ethics of discourse means that we ought to give our students' instrumental interests the status they deserve. This propriety does not come from our friendly or condescending regard for students, but from the recognition that we must take seriously any reasoned conclusion, of which our students' instrumental judgements are surely an example. And, in giving these practical values their due – in engaging them not as impediments but as opportunities – we are saying that both faculty and students will be able to recover truly meaningful connections between system and lifeworld. If we embrace the inevitable tension between system and lifeworld in our formal academic work with students, the abstract imagining of the lifeworld becomes lived experience.

We shall return to two of our cases to illustrate how emancipating explorations of the lifeworld can emerge from respectful attention to our students' preoccupation with system demands. We take the first from Moment 1 in order to show that even when a student is caught by having to go to college as protection from unfair socio-economic demands, communicative collaboration between teacher and student opens up intellectual and political freedom. We take the second case from Moment 2 in order to show that even when student and teacher focus on practical learning that offers success in their respective systems, they can still create learning that draws them into the lifeworld.

For Jim, certainly, practical goals were his primary and only expressed concern when he began his studies at ESC. He had no formal college background, his training and work experience were technical, he was not a reader (save for technical literature), he was not politically active nor, seemingly, much interested in community affairs, and he urgently wished to complete his undergraduate degrees to secure and advance his position within the company for which he worked. On the other hand, Jim was naturally curious, both appreciative and concerned about the quality of life in his organization, and very committed to providing a 'good life' for his family. Early student–mentor conversations and studies focused on the questions which concerned him most. How much college credit might he obtain from the learning he'd acquired through his work experience? How quickly could he finish a degree? What workplace-related learning might he turn into topics and projects for his remaining studies? His mentor offered him encouraging but reasonably estimated responses, cautioning him only that since he was seeking a degree from a liberal arts college, he would be required to do a certain amount of perhaps unfamiliar, less vocationally oriented studies. After telling him that these traditionally included subjects like literature, philosophy, history, maths and social studies, the mentor also explained that perhaps there might emerge during our conversations about his work and other experiences themes and questions important to him and upon which we might focus these liberal studies.

He listened patiently, and at first non-committally. He gradually became more relaxed, more skilful with academic tasks and more confident that his practical primary concerns would be fairly addressed. Jim and his mentor got to know one another better, and in fact became more genuinely interested in one another's very different interests: the mentor was curious about Jim's complicated, high-pressure industrial workplace and visited it a couple of times; Jim was curious about his mentor's background in literature and philosophy. It became apparent that, as a manager, Jim was very attentive to the 'human' needs of his supervisees and often went out of his way to design responsibilities for them which suited their interests and abilities. He'd thus 'saved' several employees whom, he noted, other managers in the company had given up on and would have fired. (This virtue also manifested itself in the intense care Jim demonstrated for his disabled son and for several friends, also in late middle age, who were suffering from dangerous or fatal illnesses.) Jim said he wanted to learn something about philosophy, literature and history.

Rather than selecting survey courses on these subjects, Jim and his mentor gradually devised themes for their 'learning contracts', themes which seemed to him to express focal points of his increasing reflectiveness about his own experiences: honesty and compassion in the face of force, the obligations and abuse of authority, the collective power of weak and exploited persons. He supplied the 'data' (i.e. his workplace experiences) and purposes of the enquiry. The faculty role was to describe and suggest some pertinent authors, works and topics Jim could study. (He eventually read, among other things, Plato, Aristotle and Nietzsche; *The Heart of Darkness*, *King Lear* and selections from the Bible; and American social history, with a particular emphasis on the labour movement.) Just as important, the mentor's responsibility was to academically legitimate Jim's curiosity by helping him name his ideas and, especially, by simply taking them seriously. Jim was fascinated and in all respects a 'good' student; the mentor was fascinated and often enlightened by the richness of the work and other life experiences that Jim brought to the readings. Now that Jim is contemplating a master's degree, no doubt affected both by his non-technical studies and his increasingly sharp notices of how expendably his organization often does treat its employees, he is considering designing a graduate curriculum focusing on both politics and human-resources management. Jim and his mentor learned to trust, be interested in and admire one another. And from this little lifeworld they created, Jim has not only expanded his intellectual concerns but is also thinking about how the care he was accustomed to show his associates might be extended within organizations as a whole and the socio-political environments in which they function.

* * *

The same elements were present in the academic work Ellen and her mentor did together: priority was given to her instrumental educational goals; they learned to understand and appreciate more about one another's work and interests, discovering therein a mutual concern, though exercised in vastly different contexts, for 'normative meanings' (as her mentor would call them) and 'good values' (as she would). Together, they eventually designed learning explicitly addressing those common interests; and our college's curricular and procedural flexibility allowed them time and inventiveness with content to do so. As suggested above, Ellen's practical goals, her desire for success, remained paramount. Perhaps presumptuously, the mentor rarely believed that she deeply engaged – relaxed into, as it were – the normative, lifeworld possibilities inherent in the pragmatic density of her experiences.

But there came a moment, during an almost idle chat, when Ellen contemplatively described a large, very expensive machine she was about to purchase for her production department as 'beautiful'. The mentor asked her why she thought it so. The student was intrigued by her own observation. Their collaborating curiosity became an enquiry into aesthetic and then other kinds of normative judgements. This conversation, which lasted several months, was in a sense a 'pure' dialogue. It was given form through a written learning contract, which very briefly sketched the initiating topic of discussion, set some guidelines for continuing and concluding it, and identified general criteria for evaluating the outcomes. There were very few assigned readings; neither mentor nor student presupposed specific answers to their questions. They simply committed themselves to wondering and responding as reasonably, thoroughly and clearly as they could to the questions they continued to generate about the meaning of the observation that the machine was beautiful.

They looked at how machinery and other features of the workplace might be satisfying and even inspiring stimulants to productive and self-expressive work. They considered how managers, as workplace leaders, might have obligations, moral obligations, to care for the aesthetic sensibilities and ethical culture of individual and groups of employees. They speculated on how managers might weigh the truths of workplaces as communities (where inhabitants might live a third or more of their waking hours) and as places of production (without which there would be no workplaces). They talked about beauty, societies, morals, quantitative and qualitative judgements. Sometimes their language was abstract. However, because a common language grew as a result of their dialogue, even abstract statements were viscerally connected to simple observations and comments about life in a factory. When they agreed to stop, that is, when Ellen felt ready to summarize her insights and reflections, mentor and student concluded their formal learning contract.

The mentor was never sure how much these enquiries reverberated beyond their discussions. However, it is notable that shortly thereafter, Ellen disassociated herself from a male colleague who had consistently abused and suppressed her. She certainly strengthened her lifeworld. And the mentor too learned to believe that industrial machinery might be 'beautiful'.

Conclusion

We have tried to show that when access to higher education is considered as a laudable goal, it can no longer be understood as a solely practical matter. The issue of access can never only be about the efficiency with which the educational system serves greater numbers and varieties of people. To be sure, we must always continue to look for ways to keep our doors open to people who need to acquire learning and degrees to survive and thrive in this society. However, although this pragmatic dimension should never be lost, it is also never sufficient. Normative claims always do press for and ought to occupy more and more attention in shaping both the content and process of learning.

We have argued, first, that if universities treat access only as a matter of enrolling larger numbers of formerly excluded people, the systemic socio-economic inequities which impelled those people towards college will be perpetuated. Second, if our efforts are mostly directed towards smoothly servicing these 'new' students, then both faculty and students neglect the opportunity to struggle with the deeper issues of life, whether in terms of traditionally humanistic studies or, as the critical theorists advocate, in terms of a programme for the political, cultural and economic reform of society. Finally, we demonstrate that when faculty actually share authority with students in creating both the content of curriculum and the process of learning, little lifeworlds form within the academic system. In these lifeworlds, faculty and students experience something often denied in our everyday lives: we glimpse qualities of reciprocal communication and gain practice in listening, in respectfully taking the position of 'the other', in critically reflecting on our own assumptions, in questioning the definitions of valuable knowledge and in learning to manage the inherent tension between the pragmatic and the normative. In short, faculty and students learn the practices of democratic community. We acquire the satisfaction of nurturing and experiencing those practices within the academic system, and thus some well-founded hope and transferable skills for enlarging the lifeworld beyond.

The case studies we have offered illustrate these ideas. However, they also reveal how important a hospitable academic environment is to actualizing them. Just as the pragmatic purposes of students cannot and should not be ignored, sustenance – both economic and moral – from an institutional system is a necessary condition of creating rational lifeworlds. We urge faculty to use their acumen to find opportunities within their colleges to explore the normative meanings of 'access' by the practice of student-centred learning. And we urge faculty, students and administrators to use their collective power within academic institutions to legislate lifeworld-enhancing conditions of learning (Habermas 1996, pp. 28–32). We must reform policies, structures, standards, contents and processes of learning so as to increase the hospitality of the university to lifeworlds of collaborative enquiry.

Finally, our case studies, representing only several of hundreds of possible examples, also demonstrate the value of 'learning from experience' – an aspect of reflection which has a vital place in opening potential lifeworlds. Within conversations with students about their pragmatic concerns, we gradually uncover vital normative preoccupations. So too, by reflecting on these experiences, we have gained our own access to understanding that secreted within the brutal imperatives of systems, living seeds of the lifeworld can be germinated.

We expect, with Eduard Lindeman, that education is 'an adventure'. From deep within access comes a call to conscience. We are called to struggle to listen for normative resonances in pragmatic impulses. We believe the adventure of learning what is necessary to live successfully – this adventure, this enterprise – demands a quest for truth, justice and beauty, a quest which makes human life worth living.

Acknowledgements

We thank Mayra Bloom, Rob Koegel, Alan Tait and Lois Zachary for reading this chapter and helping us to improve it.

References

Collins, M. (1995) 'Critical commentaries on the role of the adult educator: from self-directed learning to postmodernist sensibilities', in M. R. Welton (ed.), *In Defense of the Lifeworld: Critical Perspectives on Adult Learning*, Albany, NY: State University of New York Press, pp. 71–98.

Connelly, B. (1996) 'Interpretations of Jürgen Habermas in adult education writings', *Studies in the Education of Adults* 28(2) (Oct.): 241–53.

Dewey, J. (1959) 'The school and society', in M. S. Dworkin (ed.), *Dewey on Education: Selections*, New York: Teachers College Press, Columbia University.

Fischer, F. (1990) *Technology and the Politics of Expertise*, Newbury Park, Calif.: Sage Publications.

Giroux, H. (1988) *Teachers as Intellectuals*, New York: Bergin & Garvey.

Habermas, J. (1984) *The Theory of Communicative Action, Volume 1, Reason and the Rationalization of Society*, trans. T. McCarthy, Boston: Beacon Press.

Habermas, J. (1989) *The Theory of Communicative Action, Volume 2, Lifeworld and System: A Critique of Functionalist Reason*, trans. T. McCarthy, Boston: Beacon Press.

Habermas, J. (1990) 'Discourse ethics: notes on a program of philosophical justification', in J. Habermas, *Moral Consciousness and Communicative Action*, trans. C. Lendhardt and S. W. Nicholsen, Cambridge, Mass.: The MIT Press, pp. 43–115.

Habermas, J. (1996) *Between Facts and Norms: Contributions to a Discourse Theory of Law and Democracy*, trans. W. Rehg, Cambridge, Mass.: The MIT Press.

Hart, M. V. (1992) *Working and Educating for Life: Feminist and International Perspectives on Adult Education*, London: Routledge.

Herman, L. (1992) 'Making room', *Golden Hill* 6: 1–4.

Herman, L. and Mandell, A. (1996) 'The authority of uncertainty', *Educational Foundations* 10(1) (Winter): 57–72.

hooks, b. and West, C. (1991) *Breaking Bread: Insurgent Black Intellectual Life*, Boston: South End Press.

Keane, D. (1984) *Public Life and Late Capitalism: Toward a Socialist Theory of Democracy*, Cambridge: Cambridge University Press.

Kegan, R. (1994) *In Over Our Heads: The Mental Demands of Modern Life*, Cambridge, Mass.: Harvard University Press.

Kett, J. F. (1994) *The Pursuit of Knowledge Under Difficulties: From Self-Improvement to Adult Education in America, 1750–1990*, Stanford, Calif.: Stanford University Press.

Lehmann, T. and Maehl, W. (1995) 'Putting lifelong learners first', a background paper prepared for discussion with the Commission for a Nation of Lifelong Learners.

Lindeman, E. (1926, repr. 1961) *The Meaning of Adult Education*, New York: New Republic Inc.

Mandell, A. and Herman, L. (1996) 'From teachers to mentors: acknowledging openings in the faculty role', in R. Mills and A. Tait (eds), *Supporting the Learner in Open and Distance Learning*, London: Pitman Publishing, pp. 3–18.

Merriam, S. and Caffarella, R. S. (1991) *Learning in Adulthood: A Comprehensive Guide*, San Francisco: Jossey-Bass.

Nasaw, D. (1979) *Schooled to Order: A Social History of Public Schooling in the United States*, New York: Oxford University Press.

Plumb, D. (1995) 'Declining opportunities: adult education, culture, and post-modernity', in M. R. Welton (ed.), *In Defense of the Lifeworld: Critical Perspectives on Adult Learning*, Albany, NY: State University of New York Press, pp. 157–94.

Reich, R. (1990) *The Work of Nations: Capitalism in the 21st Century*, New York: Alfred A. Knopf.

Rose, M. (1995) *Possible Lives: The Promise of Public Education in America*, Boston: Houghton Mifflin Company.

Shor, I. (1996) *When Students Have Power: Negotiating Authority in a Critical Pedagogy*, Chicago: University of Chicago Press.

Tait, A. (1997) 'The convergence of distance and conventional education: some implications for social policy', in A. Tait (ed.), *Proceedings of the Cambridge International Conference on Open and Distance Learning*, Cambridge: Open University, pp. 182–90.

Usher, R. and Edwards, R. (1994) *Postmodernism and Education*, London: Routledge.

Welton, M. R. (1995) 'In defense of the lifeworld: a Habermasian approach to adult learning', in M. R. Welton (ed.), *In Defense of the Lifeworld: Critical Perspectives on Adult Learning*, Albany, NY: State University of New York Press, pp. 127–56.

4 Introducing and supporting change towards more flexible teaching approaches

Sue Johnston

Introduction

In Australia, as in many countries throughout the world, there has been a blurring of the boundaries between distance education and on-campus teaching. Universities are now more commonly using terms such as 'flexible delivery', 'flexible learning' or 'flexible approaches' to label moves towards the provision for *all* students (on and off campus) of teaching and learning approaches which are less time- and place-dependent. Such moves have been stimulated by many diverse factors, including: equity and access issues; higher levels of mobility among students; the tendency for many full-time students to have significant levels of employment to support their studies; a recognition of the range of student learning styles and needs; reductions in funding and staffing levels of universities concurrent with increases in student enrolments; the potential offered by various technology and media developments; and a recognition of the need to develop students as lifelong learners.

Although some universities in Australia have long-established traditions of involvement in distance education and can therefore relatively easily transfer their resources, support and 'know-how' to bring about more flexible approaches across the board, other universities have no such established tradition: policies and practices have been based on the assumption that students attend classes and are taught in ways largely based on face-to-face interaction. In these universities, the changes required to implement flexible approaches must begin from a very low base of experience in this area, and such changes can be quite daunting for all concerned. This chapter will provide a case study of the process. Although it is based on a scenario of a university moving towards flexible delivery from a tradition of face-to-face teaching, many of the points made will be applicable to all universities introducing some form of change, whatever their position on the continuum between very flexible approaches and traditional face-to-face approaches.

For those universities that have resolved to increase the flexibility of their teaching approaches, the changes required are far-reaching. They impact not only on the teaching approaches of individual academics but also on

administrative procedures, curriculum and assessment practices, the provision of student support, general timetabling and organizational arrangements, library and computer support, technical and infrastructure
provision and support, procedures for allocating workload for academic
and non-academic staff, and reward structures for academic staff. Such
change is often a slow, difficult and complex process. This chapter will
draw on literature related to educational change in general and also on
studies specifically of change towards flexible approaches to suggest some
general steps that need to be considered when managing such changes.

What do we know about educational change?

Over the years, much has been written about educational change, including
change in university settings. One of the enduring observations about change
is that it is most often a complex, non-linear process. In large, multifaceted
organizations such as universities, the complexity and slowness of change
are particularly evident. A favourite axiom is that change is a process not
an event. Fullan (1993) has synthesized much of the literature and experience
about educational change into eight 'lessons' or points:

1   You can't mandate what matters – the more complex the change is, the
    less you can force it.
2   Change is a journey, not a blueprint. Change is non-linear, loaded with
    uncertainty and excitement and sometimes perverse.
3   Problems are inevitable and you can't learn without them.
4   Vision and strategic planning come later. Premature visions and plan-
    ning can blind.
5   Individualism and collectivism must have equal power. There are no
    one-sided solutions to isolation and group-think.
6   Neither centralization nor non-centralization works. Both top-down and
    bottom-up strategies are necessary.
7   Connections with the wider environment are critical for success. The best
    organizations learn externally as well as internally.
8   Every person is a change agent. Change is too important to leave to the
    experts.

For an institution wishing to embark on a process of change, these points are
somewhat confusing and even pessimistic. Although some general principles
and good common sense appear in the literature on change, these often do
not offer sufficient guidance about the process needed at an institutional
level to bring about a specific change such as that required to introduce
flexible approaches.

One of the important issues to consider when embarking on a conscious
and planned change process is that the starting point is different for different
individuals and groups within the university. Even in a university for which

there has been little support and need for flexible approaches in the past, there will be individuals and perhaps groups who have already moved some way along the track towards flexible approaches. Within any university which does not have an established distance-education tradition, there is likely to be a wide range of opinions, attitudes and levels of expertise in the area. There will also be disciplinary differences in the attitudes of academic staff to changes towards flexible approaches. Waggoner (1994) has suggested that attitudes towards using technology in teaching depend on such factors as experience as a teacher, ethos of the discipline, environmental context, assumptions about students and perceptions or beliefs about technology. Some staff will be experimenting with flexible approaches on their own initiative and may be already quite advanced, using cutting-edge approaches. Most, however, will be much more uncertain about the efficacy of such approaches and the means by which such approaches may be integrated into their own teaching. It is likely that attitudes will range from enthusiasm and interest to ignorance, apathy and resistance. Those individuals and groups with some experience of flexible approaches will be advocating their particular ideas and there may well be a tendency for different groups to be working in conflicting directions, possibly causing confusion and even antagonism.

At this early, somewhat disparate, stage of development, there is need for a managed change process even if, as the literature suggests, such a process will not be followed sequentially. A managed change process will provide some direction and confidence to those who seek more certainty and guidance. The managed change process does not need to be rigidly adhered to but rather should provide a framework for action which is itself open to scrutiny and re-evaluation.

The role of early adopters

With flexible delivery, particularly those forms involving the use of technology, it is important to consider the role of early adopters because they dominate much of the literature and they will be the ones who will be providing much of the impetus to the directions which changes will take. In any change process, there is a relatively small percentage of the population who embrace the change quickly. Geoghegan (1995) has argued that the early adopters of technology in teaching, as for any new approach, comprise about 10 per cent of academic staff. The idea of the differential uptake of innovation has been offered within the literature on educational change over many years. Rogers (1965) and Havelock (1970) suggested that any educational innovation will initially be taken up by a small proportion of the population. Some characterizations have termed those who are more reluctant to take up innovation as 'resistant' or as 'laggards', but Geoghegan (1995) uses the less value-laden term of 'mainstream majority' to describe those who are not the early adopters of innovation.

The early adopters are the people who feature in much of the literature about flexible approaches and who contribute the 'success stories' which are often used as a gauge of how the field is progressing. Some writers have drawn attention to the problems of using the experiences of these early adopters as indicators of any depth in acceptance of such approaches throughout the academy (Caladine 1993; Spotts and Bowman 1993). These writers have suggested that the 'success stories' of early adopters give a false impression of how widespread developments are.

Geoghegan (1995) characterizes early adopters of information technology in their teaching as:

- favouring revolutionary change;
- visionary;
- strong in their technology focus;
- risk-takers;
- experimenters;
- largely self-sufficient;
- 'horizontally networked' (used to working across disciplinary boundaries and across groups).

In contrast, the mainstream majority who are slower to take on such new teaching approaches are characterized as:

- favouring evolutionary change;
- pragmatic or conservative;
- strong in their problem and process focus;
- risk-averse;
- wanting proven applications of compelling value;
- needing support;
- 'vertically networked' (used to working within the boundaries of their discipline).

The major implication of Geoghegan's distinction is that the support needs of both groups are quite different and that 'a veritable chasm' has developed between the two groups. He argues that the systems that campuses have put into place have been designed 'by and for the early adopters themselves, under an unstated assumption that all potential adopters need the same kinds of encouragement, facilities and support, differing from one another by degree, perhaps, but not by kind' (p. 31). Instead, the needs of the two groups are quite different, with the mainstream majority approaching the change with caution and needing additional support. More particularly, the mainstream majority will not be swayed by the excitement of the technology, but rather by the practical benefits the changes will bring for their own teaching and for the learning of their students. Therefore, we need to be careful that planning for developments towards flexible approaches is not left to the early adopters who have little understanding of the needs of the mainstream majority. While recognizing the importance of capitalizing on the expertise and enthusiasm of the early adopters, we must not use these as the benchmark of what is possible for all staff and for defining what staff need in order to take up flexible approaches with ease.

CASE STUDY

The University of Canberra is one of Australia's smaller universities with approximately 9,000 students who undertake a variety of applied professional courses. The university moved from college of advanced education to university status in line with national policy developments in the early 1990s. Unlike several other universities in Australia, the University of Canberra has no established tradition of distance-education provision. Teaching in the university has largely been organized around face-to-face interaction. The library and administrative arrangements rely on students using the services personally. In recent years, the Centre for the Enhancement of Learning, Teaching and Scholarship (CELTS) as part of its support of teaching and learning in the university has been encouraging the use of technology to enhance teaching. In 1995, external funding was used to bring two developers-in-residence to the university to work with staff in a consultancy capacity to help them integrate technology into their teaching in educationally sound ways. The developers-in-residence conducted a series of workshops and also worked with staff individually to support projects of varying size, focus and stage of development. In 1996, university funding was used to release key people from several faculties to provide further support to colleagues to develop initiatives in this area. Grants were available for specific projects which linked technology with teaching. In 1997, a cross-faculty flexible-delivery project was funded. The funding was used to develop the means of offering two courses and a single subject in flexible mode using different approaches. This project was intended as a pilot to determine the range of changes and support needed in the university to teach more flexibly. Those involved in the project presented seminars about their experiences so that ideas were progressively reported to the rest of the university community.

In the latter part of 1997, the university took a major step to formalize intentions in the area of flexible delivery, announcing in its strategic plan an objective to increase the university's ability to offer courses that are less time- and place-dependent and to make all courses more flexible over a period of time. This broad objective stimulated discussion papers, forums and a specific strategy to implement flexible approaches. Within the discussion papers there was a recognition of the need to build on the developments already occurring in 'pockets' within the university and to mainstream these as a major thrust within the university's planning. The documents articulated the need to move the initiative of flexible approaches beyond the early adopters to the mainstream majority.

Elements of a change process

What follows is a discussion of some of the key elements of the change process at the University of Canberra and a commentary which relates these to more general issues about educational change. The general context for the discussion is one of moving from a situation in which early adopters have taken up the approaches with enthusiasm to a more co-ordinated strategy designed to broaden these pockets of enthusiasm into a coherent, institutionalized policy.

Building the base for change

Given the complexity and slowness of educational change, large-scale innovation will not occur easily from a starting point in which there is no expertise or commitment to the change within the university. The formal moves towards flexible approaches at the University of Canberra followed more than three years of support at the grass-roots level to build expertise and develop working examples of the practices eventually spelt out in the formal policies. Largely, this grass-roots support was directed at the early adopters but there was also a conscious strategy to increase the pool of early adopters and to share their experiences more widely. This was done by providing incentives through grants to those considering piloting flexible approaches, importing the required expertise from outside the university to support their initiatives and then providing exposure to the early developments through show-cases, resource materials, publicity and workshops. CELTS made the support of flexible approaches one of its priorities, thus signalling to the university's staff the importance of these developments and also ensuring that resources were available to support individuals or groups wanting to try new approaches. It was the responsibility of CELTS to keep flexible approaches on the university's agenda and to frame this agenda in terms of effective teaching and learning.

Associated with these early developments directed at the teaching staff of the university, the division responsible for information technology was also working towards building the infrastructure and technical support necessary for flexible approaches. A university working party which examined the use of technology in teaching suggested the need for upgrading hardware and software access for staff and students because difficulties with these forms of infrastructure were a major barrier to staff and students wanting to explore the use of technology in teaching and learning (Clark et al. 1995). The availability of technology infrastructure and support to staff and students was seen to be variable across the university and a barrier to innovation by many staff. There was a need to move towards a technologically comfortable teaching and learning environment in the university. There were suggestions for minimum standards of software and hardware as well as an increase in the resources available for training staff and then supporting their ongoing use of information technology.

The message from these early developments towards flexible approaches within the university was that knowledgeable, confident individuals and working models are an essential starting point for change. Before formal policies and university-wide strategies can be put in place, there is a need to work less formally with those groups and individuals in the university who are most interested and amenable to the change. The early adopters, because they are 'horizontally linked', will establish networks of support which are not easily available to the majority of academic staff and they will work to overcome barriers which most staff would find daunting. The experiences of the early adopters can be used to determine which of the organizational and support aspects of the university need to be changed to accommodate flexible approaches. Building this base can take some time but such efforts are a worthwhile investment. It is also interesting to note that even before the official policies and directions were set, those academics and support staff who had been trialling approaches and piloting projects were beginning to look for the university to formalize its intentions and legitimate the activities that they had begun. It was as though they realized the importance of a policy framework to give their individual initiatives some scope for further development.

Articulating a vision

In 1997 the important step was taken to set out the formal objective within the university's strategic plan of offering some courses which were less time- and place-dependent and of ensuring that all courses were offered more flexibly. This was followed by a university discussion paper which helped define what was meant by flexible approaches and which demonstrated the benefits of these approaches for students, for staff and for the university. It was at this stage that the task within the university moved from supporting the early adopters to considering ways of moving flexible approaches into the mainstream. Care had to be taken to acknowledge sufficiently the efforts of the early adopters, while also recognizing that the task was not a simple one of expecting them to tell everyone else how to do it. For flexible approaches to become a mainstream concern of the university, it was necessary for the developments to be supported by top-down strategies as well as grass-roots strategies.

One of the tasks at this stage was to articulate a sufficiently clear vision of what was to be achieved while not constraining the diversity of flexible approaches. Flexible delivery takes many forms and means different things to different people. The decision was made to place flexible delivery in the broader framework of flexible learning. This provided a sound educational framework for the developments because flexible learning was defined as student-centred learning, giving students more control over their learning and allowing them to choose when, what, where, how and at what pace they learn. Flexible delivery was defined as a form of flexible learning which was less time- and place-dependent than more traditional forms of teaching. It was necessary to explain that flexible delivery is not confined to approaches that involve technology. Even those which do involve technology differ in terms of their teaching approaches and technical requirements. Suggestions were made about the full range of possible flexible approaches and the forms of flexible delivery we wanted to support in this university. Rather than being presented with a huge array of options and possibilities, the more conservative staff members preferred demonstration of some examples which had already been shown to work with available resources.

The mainstream majority are persuaded by arguments that change will have practical benefits for the university, for staff and for students, so such benefits had to be carefully articulated and agreed upon. Moreover, efforts were made to show the developments as fitting with the overall mission of the university and its staff. Issues such as why flexibility was important for this university and for individual staff were addressed. Such a rationale, tied to the university's mission and strategic plans, is important for gaining staff support.

Leadership

Many writers (for example, Laurillard and Margetson 1997; Taylor, Lopez and Quadrelli 1996) stress the need for strong leadership when introducing flexible approaches. This applies to all innovations. Such leadership not only creates a context in which change is seen to be important, but also works towards creating an environment conducive to change, by developing policies and providing incentives, support and resources. Strong leadership does not necessarily imply a top-down approach. Rather, it suggests an environment in which bottom-up action is encouraged and supported in order to meet shared goals. This required the deputy vice-chancellor to take charge of developments for flexible approaches. Responsibility for developing strategies and planning for support was also given to the university's Education Committee, which had the chief responsibility for educational policy. This committee then co-ordinated the work of other groups and individuals who had an interest in flexible delivery. It was important to embed developments for flexible delivery within the key structures of the university so that all staff would feel that leadership was being provided and would see flexible approaches as a major initiative of the university.

Developments of this type cannot proceed simultaneously across all parts of a university. At Canberra, decisions were made at the faculty level as to whether there were particular faculties, departments, programmes, courses or units into which the university should direct its resources so that these could act as exemplars for further developments. Some resources were made available on a competitive basis so that faculties could bid for support for projects which would further the goal of flexibility. Here, care was needed so that all funds and support did not go to the early adopters and to developments confined only to a small group of staff who were at the cutting edge. It was considered likely that the early adopters would continue their developments with minimal support and resources while the more widespread institutionalization of flexible delivery across the majority of staff would require considerable support. The limited resources available needed to be targeted strategically to those groups and initiatives which could then be used as exemplars for others. Faculty strategic plans incorporated targets for flexible approaches so that all areas of the university could see that objectives had been set, even if those targets could only be achieved some years away.

At every opportunity, flexible approaches need to be mainstreamed and institutionalized so that they are perceived by staff as an important element of a university's overall strategy. Although plans will not necessarily achieve change by themselves, they send messages that such changes are important and expected. Collaboratively developed plans allow staff at all levels to interpret a university's mission in terms of their own particular discipline or area of responsibility and determine what flexible delivery might mean in the local context and how it might be implemented. Strategic plans also have in-built monitoring and accountability procedures, thus ensuring that developments towards flexible delivery are documented and reported upon.

Given the diversity of interest and expertise in a university, it is likely that some staff can offer expertise in flexible delivery even if this does not form part of their current responsibilities. It is important to build a sense of what expertise exists, to determine ways of using this expertise and to plan to fill gaps when expertise is not available locally. Gaps in expertise may be filled by recruiting new staff, by bringing in the experts from elsewhere on a temporary basis or by building the expertise of existing staff through staff development. Physical resources should also be documented and considered in a similar way. The sharing of physical resources with other institutions may be an option worth investigating.

Supporting staff

Staff development and support form a vital element of introducing flexible delivery, a point which has been stressed by a number of writers (Land and Rist n.d.; Taylor, Lopez and Quadrelli 1996). MacKnight (1995) has highlighted that the level of comfort staff must reach to integrate these new approaches into their teaching is not achieved through a single event, but rather 'through continuous exposure, encouragement and support from colleagues, students and academic support personnel. The process involves moving from one successful experience to another' (p. 35). Such comments contradict any tendency to equate staff development and support with simple, one-off courses or workshops. Although these might form one component of a comprehensive staff development programme, alone they are unlikely to bring about changes in teaching approaches. Johnston and McCormack (1996) have argued that supporting the needs of the mainstream majority involves such all-encompassing considerations as: developing an institutional culture which values and rewards innovation in teaching; assisting teaching staff to reflect critically on their teaching; raising awareness about the potential of different approaches to enhance teaching; providing instructional design assistance; supporting production and implementation of new approaches; and ensuring that the university is a technologically comfortable working environment. These suggestions form a much more comprehensive approach than simply expecting one-off courses to bring about changes in teaching practice. They also cater for the mainstream majority by placing the focus on enhancing teaching and learning rather than using new technologies for their own sake.

Given the strong discipline interests of the mainstream majority it may be necessary to work with disciplinary teams in the first instance and then to encourage the formation of networks across disciplines. More than many other innovations, flexible approaches require input from people with a range of expertise and the formation of cross-disciplinary teams often composed of academic as well as non-academic staff. For academic staff used to the autonomy of teaching students in the privacy of their classroom, this is a new way of working which not only opens up their teaching to wider scrutiny but also has the potential to make them feel de-skilled because they cannot manage these new developments entirely on their own.

Monitoring and evaluation

Although written as a final step, monitoring and evaluation cannot be left until the end. Rather, evaluative procedures must be built progressively into all new developments. It is important not only to evaluate outcomes but also to evaluate the processes used to achieve those outcomes. It is likely that moves towards flexible delivery will use considerable resources through investment of both time and money. Evaluative procedures must ensure such resources have been used effectively and that the process and outcomes are worthwhile. Such issues are not addressed through simple data-collection procedures and, for this reason, formal evaluation is often a neglected step in the change process.

Concluding comment

The strategies outlined above are not necessarily the only or even the best ones to use in situations of mainstreaming educational innovation. They are offered as examples of possible approaches. They deliberately attempt to combine grass-roots support with a more centrally developed policy framework on the assumption that educational change cannot be facilitated by either a top-down or bottom-up approach alone: a combination of the two is necessary. It is far too soon to gauge the success of these strategies at the University of Canberra. There is no doubt that flexible approaches at the university will take many twists and turns. New strategies will be developed for managing and supporting the change. The lessons learned from early experiences will be used to modify plans and set new directions. According to the literature on educational change, all of this is to be expected.

Although these elements might appear like a carefully orchestrated and rigid series of steps, this is not the intention and no strict chronological sequence is implied. It is unlikely that the stages of educational change will ever be sequential, with many or even all of these steps occurring concurrently and iteratively. Sometimes energies will be devoted to some of the steps at the expense of others. The overall process involves senior management because of the expectation that leadership should come from at least that level. However, genuine consultation and involvement of all staff at all levels should characterize the process. Furthermore, although key issues such as academic workload and rewards have not yet been tackled explicitly, they are certain to arise during discussions among academic staff. They will need to be resolved before commitment from academic staff will be forthcoming. Changes towards flexible teaching approaches, as with many educational changes, impact broadly on all aspects of life and work within a university.

There are strong indicators that the distinct boundaries between on-campus and distance teaching are being dismantled. Distance and open learning approaches which in the past have been confined to off-campus teaching are now seen to provide benefits to all students. Flexible approaches to teaching and learning have formed the bridge, with all students now seeking offerings which are less time- and place-dependent. For universities set up to cater for distance students, this transition is relatively easy.

However, there is now pressure for universities not previously involved in distance education to make the transition to more flexible approaches. For those universities whose infrastructure and organization are built around students attending classes on campus, changes to more flexible approaches can be costly. Similarly, for academics whose careers and experiences have been centred around face-to-face interactions with students, the idea of moving towards flexible approaches can be daunting. It is not a simple matter of imposing new approaches on existing practices and structures. The change process is often slow and convoluted. Facilitating such a change process requires a recognition of the need for strategies which build on grass-roots support while also putting into place appropriate centralized policies and support.

References

Caladine, R. (1993) *Overseas Experience in Non-Traditional Modes of Delivery in Higher Education Using State-of-the-Art Technologies: A Literature Review*, Canberra: Australian Government Publishing Service.

Clark, E., Adams, D., Annice, C., Battye, G., Black, S., Bouvin, P., Brooks, R., Cheetham, A., Favre, J.-P., Johnston, S., Klein, D., McCormack, C., Thompson, B. and Mansbridge, L. (1995) *The Role of Information Technology in University Teaching: University of Canberra Working Party Report*, University of Canberra.

Fullan, M. (1993) *Change Forces: Probing the Depths of Educational Reform*, New York: Falmer Press.

Geoghegan, W. (1995) 'Stuck at the barricades: can information technology really enter the mainstream of teaching and learning?', *Change* 27(2): 22–30.

Havelock, R. (1970) *Guide to Innovation in Education*, Ann Arbor: University of Michigan Press.

Johnston, S. and McCormack, C. (1996) 'Integrating information technology into university teaching: identifying the needs and providing the support', *International Journal of Educational Management* 10(5): 36–42.

Land, R. and Rist, R. (n.d.) *The Staff Developer and Learning Technology: SEDA/UCoSDA Staff Development Paper No. 4.*

Laurillard, D. and Margetson, D. (1997) *Introducing a Flexible Learning Methodology: Discussion Paper*, Brisbane: Griffith University GIHE.

MacKnight, C. (1995) 'Managing technological change in academe', *Cause/Effect* 18(2) (Spring): 29–39.

Rogers, E. (1965) 'What are innovators like?', in R. Carlson (ed.), *Change Processes in Public Schools*, Eugene: University of Oregon Press.

Spotts, T. and Bowman, M. (1993) 'Faculty use of instructional technologies in higher education', *Educational Technology* 35(2) (Mar.–Apr.): 56–64.

Taylor, P.G., Lopez, L. and Quadrelli, C. (1996) *Flexibility, Technology and Academics' Practices: Tantalising Tales and Muddy Maps*, Canberra: Australian Government Publishing Service.

Waggoner, M. (1994) 'Disciplinary differences and the integration of technology into teaching', *Journal of Information Technology for Teacher Education* 3(2): 175–86.

5 Becoming flexible: what does it mean?

Denise Kirkpatrick and Viktor Jakupec

In Australia and elsewhere the introduction of flexible learning reflects a more general transformation of higher education influenced by technological change, public accountability, increased competition, restricted funding, and catering for the needs of a semi-mass rather than semi-elite system (Chubb 1993; Shapiro 1993). The growing trend for universities to focus attention and energies on the development of flexible learning and delivery has been given impetus by a range of factors including the rapid advances in electronic communications technology that introduce flexibility in production, distribution and interactivity in education and the consequent tendency towards globalization of education.

Commentators on information technologies argue that flexibility offers education providers an effective means of responding to the needs of the 'new' learner and hence is seen as a key to their survival. According to them, the needs of consumers will drive the direction and demand for knowledge, with legitimation of knowledge becoming largely a factor of its demand. To exist in such a climate educational institutions will have to structure information and 'knowledge' in flexible ways (for example, offering courses in different organizational and delivery modes, providing courses in a variety of locations including the workplace, modularizing existing courses, and providing continually updated information and just-in-time training). New technologies suggest different roles for universities. The growing range of information providers via the Internet, offering alternative sources of knowledge creation and credentialling, challenge conventional models of teaching and learning offered by traditional education providers. In this context universities will have to compete with multinational information providers for a market share of students. As a consequence of this globalization, the traditional notions of scholarship are replaced by continual just-in-time learning. Teaching is seen as less place-bound, replaced by networked learning using global connections.

Strategically, flexibility of operation and flexible learning are seen as both a defence and an offence for educational institutions in their competition for students. Higher education institutions in Australia, similarly to universities in other industrialized countries, are engaged in competition for market shares of Australian and off-shore markets, especially at postgraduate level. Flexible delivery and flexible learning can be exploited to give the competitive edge in a number of ways. Flexible learning gives universities the capacity to appeal to niche markets via approaches such as work-based learning programmes, and to open up new, remote markets using communications technologies or distance-learning modes. There is also a perception that institutions have to 'be seen to be doing flexible learning'; that it is the 'sexy' thing to do. By freeing up the space, place and time constraints of studying it can be used to attract students who previously may not have been able to attend classes due to various life commitments. By providing alternative ways of accessing university education, universities believe that they can attract more students.

This focus on alternative ways of delivering courses to students has also been encouraged by a recognition of the changing needs of students, business interests and industry. There are a range of reasons for thinking about providing education in different ways. The more flexible offering and delivery of higher education may achieve the desirable social goals of increasing access to education and democratizing teaching and the learning process by giving greater control to the learner. However, the relevant literature reflects a growing emphasis on the delivery aspect of education rather than thinking of ways of making student learning more flexible. This in turn may lead to the alienation of a significant number of students and members of the academic community, not only due to the requirement for cultural change, especially the culture of teaching and learning, but also due to the potential (perceived or real) loss of traditional academic values, quality and scholarly rigour. In addition, there are entrepreneurial considerations. The focus on delivery rather than learning will give rise to more intense competition for funding, resources and business among educational providers.

The terms flexible learning and flexible delivery imply an intention to increase learners' access to and control over particular teaching and learning environments. Flexibility is a characteristic that may satisfy many stakeholders in education. It can serve the interests of managers and politicians who focus on effectiveness, efficiency and budget solutions to the delivery of a service. Many business interest groups and politicians have argued that scarcity of resources provides a compelling argument to support the use of flexible learning. They argue that flexible learning is the answer to challenges which have emerged in international, national and regional higher-education and training sectors. For those marketing educational services flexible learning can mean the production of commodities which can be used competitively in a global market. For students and teachers it can suggest a student-centred approach to learning and democratization of processes of learning and teaching. For those students who either cannot or choose not to attend a physical site it can mean the opportunity to engage in education as it is delivered to the home or workplace in ways and times to suit the circumstances. For curriculum developers it may mean the availability of a range of service approaches to suit student diversity. Similarly it can imply the end of the suite of academics' offices as staff conduct their teaching from places other than the institution. In intent, as well as form, it can mean different things to different stakeholders and have markedly different consequences and implications.

The prevailing view in higher education has been (and is still held strongly in many quarters) that 'good' teaching can only be face-to-face, and that learning can only take place in specific environments and in the presence of the teacher. The onus is on flexible learning to demonstrate how it can meet traditional values and expectations. This creates potential tensions in any educational institution which is changing its culture from traditional face-to-face teaching–learning to a flexible learning and delivery culture.

What happened in one university

In this chapter we will describe the way in which flexible learning was established in a metropolitan Australian university. Since any educational initiative will affect the staff and students involved we will also consider the responses of academic staff and explore the staff-development implications of implementing flexible learning across a university.

The University of Technology, Sydney (UTS) is a multi-campus metropolitan university with a clearly identified student clientele, largely part-time and adult students. It has a strong reputation for professional and vocational education with good industry links and co-operative education programmes. The university had not previously been involved in the provision of distance education but had recently entered into off-shore delivery of educational programmes. In 1996 UTS identified flexible learning as one of its strategic initiatives, describing it as 'developing the university's capacity to offer learning independent of space and time' (UTS strategic plan 1996). The term was intentionally loosely defined, allowing individual faculties and academics within faculties to construct their own meanings in ways that were relevant to their current and future practices. A central committee was established to provide strategic guidance and support for flexible learning and to ensure a co-ordinated approach across the university. The university was keen to support early adopters of flexible learning in the first instance, and funding was provided to support the establishment of teaching projects and administrative practices that would result in flexible learning.

In the early stages of the introduction of flexible learning it was not surprising that many academic staff expressed concern about the exact nature of this 'new' approach and were eager to get some idea of what might be involved. To provide some guidance for staff a discussion document featuring flexible-learning case studies was developed. This document featured flexible-learning innovations that were information-technology based. Staff also drew conclusions about the forms of flexible learning that the university saw as valid and appropriate by looking at the type of projects that had been successful in the first round of funding. A large number of the successful project bids involved the use of technology, including the establishment of a website, the introduction of computer-mediated conferencing and the development of multimedia or web-based instruction. A second major thread was the development of distance-education-type materials and the conversion of traditional face-to-face teaching to remote learning. These projects were followed by the provision of competitive funding for strategic-initiatives projects from faculties. In an effort to increase the likelihood of lasting change resulting from these projects preference was given to projects that were team-based. Again, successful proposals focused mainly on the use of information technology.

While there was a level of discomfort among many staff at the perceived lack of guidance from 'the top' there was a high level of enthusiasm for the potential range of educational options created by the introduction of flexible learning. Every time funding to support flexible-learning initiatives was advertised a large number of applications were received and the total value of funding requested far exceeded the amount available. In response to expressed concerns, documents relating to flexible learning were issued by the office of the deputy vice-chancellor (academic) which offered a broad definition of flexible learning encompassing anything that increased student access to learning (for example, off-shore delivery, work-based learning, the use of peer learning and assessment, take-home labs, the use of web-based instruction, development of independent learning materials and the introduction of teaching periods that extended beyond the normal two semesters). An audit of existing flexible practices that had been carried out as part of funded projects was made available on the flexible-learning website to provide interested academic staff with data about the range of activity that was occurring and to facilitate communication with and among staff involved in various projects.

A range of activities were held throughout the university to support the idea of flexible learning and to provide information for interested staff. A flexible-learning symposium provided an opportunity for exploration of possible practices with an emphasis on existing practices. In part this was a response to criticisms that the approach that had been adopted appeared to value only 'new' practices and that many established teaching practices were already providing flexibility for students. Not only did this symposium provide a forum for discussion and the sharing of experiences, it publicly valued existing (and usually unfunded) flexible-learning practices. The central unit responsible for academic staff development offered university-wide workshops on specific aspects or forms of flexible learning such as the design of independent learning materials. Staff-development activities were also provided for specific projects or to support faculty-level groups who were interested in exploring the possibilities offered by flexible learning. Funding was provided to support the involvement of academic staff developers in funded strategic-initiative projects.

Emerging discourses in the institution

Four clear representations of flexible learning emerged: flexible learning as efficient practice; flexible learning as the means of gaining the competitive edge; flexible learning as achieving equity; and flexible delivery, particularly the use of information technologies.

Flexible learning as efficiency

Performativity is the principle of optimizing performance by technical innovation. This notion of performativity was clearly represented in the discourse of flexible learning as efficiency. The emphasis on the use of information technology in enabling flexible learning and the view that information technology will create a more efficient education system reflects Lyotard's claims about the impact of information processing on the transmission of acquired learning (1984): 'The result . . . will be the mercantilization of knowledge where knowledge will cease to be an end in itself.' Increasing attention is being given to the input–output equation in accountability in higher education and flexibility is represented as the means of achieving greater efficiencies.

There were no explicit statements that flexible learning was being introduced to save money although there was a groundswell of opinion among teaching academics that the primary reason for the university's attention to the development of flexible learning was economic. The drive to implement more flexible-learning strategies was interpreted by many teaching academics as an economic and political expedient. Implicit in this was a concern that the change is a short-term response, reactive rather than proactive, only secondarily determined by educational considerations. Teachers were also concerned that performance would be judged against externally determined criteria which neither learners nor teachers would necessarily endorse. Public documents made it clear that although some money would be spent establishing projects, ultimately course delivery should cost no more than it currently did. Many teaching academics expressed beliefs that flexible learning was all about doing more with less (and that they would be seen as responsible and lacking in some way if they were not able to do this effectively).

Flexible learning featured strongly in the university's and faculty's strategic goals and was reflected in planning documents. This managerial emphasis on flexible learning makes it increasingly difficult for individual academics to ignore the calls for increased flexibility. Linking funding for initiatives and development to the demonstration of increased flexibility added pressure for individuals and groups to be seen to be involved and communicated the seriousness with which the idea is regarded by the university. In order to win much-needed resources most departments agreed to 'take on' flexible learning, joining a desperate rush for funding. Not only did this require staff time and effort to develop proposals but it was frequently done with little or no consultation between managers and teaching academics, causing resistance from staff who had not been involved in the decision making but were expected to implement the changes. Consequently, a reasonable resistance to the introduction of different ways of teaching was heightened by feelings of anger at the imposition of innovation to which some staff had not agreed. The perception that flexible learning was being imposed on academic staff, accompanied by a belief that accountability was being shifted 'down', became more widespread.

Certain high-profile flexible-learning projects focused very clearly on developing mechanisms for dealing efficiently with large numbers of students. In at least one faculty there was a stated intention to use flexible learning to make faculty teaching operations more efficient and there were overt and covert actions that supported this. The notion that flexible learning could result in more efficient teaching was viewed by some as providing an opportunity to use flexible learning to handle administrative and organizational aspects of teaching more efficiently for staff and students, thus allowing more opportunity for teaching and learning. These views were most commonly voiced by academics who had been involved in the project for some time and had developed familiarity with technologies and were able to look beyond them. Like most users of new technologies it was not until they were comfortable with the routine use of the technology that they could envisage other ways of employing it.

Many teaching academics saw a decrease in the amount of face-to-face contact between teachers and students as a negative consequence of flexible-learning projects. While flexible learning may lower the cost of teaching a subject or course it removes an important source of teacher satisfaction and was the subject of some resistance. There was even greater resistance to the possibility that the ultimate efficiency may result from the development of flexible-learning approaches – the redundancy of teaching academics resulting from the use of stand-alone teaching packages, workplace mentors or web-based instruction.

Flexible learning as the competitive edge

While flexible learning was represented as the means of creating a more efficient university, there was a related discourse that portrayed flexible learning as providing the competitive edge. Flexibility was seen as the means by which the university could become more competitive in attracting students. This was portrayed in terms of the modes of delivery that were offered, creating courses for niche markets and offering them in ways that would be attractive to particular groups (for example, work-based learning qualifications). Much attention was directed at the marketability of various funded-project outcomes. Flexible learning was seen as the means of preserving the university's place in the current marketplace and of creating and consolidating niche markets.

The discourse of the competitive edge functioned at all levels within the university. In competition for scarce curriculum and development funding, one faculty's activity in the realm of flexible learning might give it the advantage over its rivals. The ability to develop courses that were more flexible and catered to the needs of particular potential student groups increased a faculty's capacity to attract more students and hence a greater share of funding.

The competitive edge also functioned among individuals. Flexible learning was frequently interpreted as something new or innovative. Individual teacher academics perceived pressure to be involved in the development of flexible learning and expressed concern that as the university was placing so much importance on it they would be judged as somehow lacking if they were not involved and successful. The inclusion of flexible learning in guidelines for promotion provided further reason for academics to think that involvement in projects would put them ahead of the competition. This reinforced the perception that flexible learning was something that staff needed to be seen to be doing. Just as the university was seen to be engaging in flexible learning because its competitors were, so too were individuals. Being involved in a flexible-learning project was seen to be something that would give an academic the competitive edge over his or her colleagues in attracting internal funding, getting promotion, having his or her contract renewed and so on. Others saw the inclusion of flexible learning in criteria for promotion as an appropriate reward, making extra effort worthwhile – a necessary way of encouraging staff to adopt new projects. In a context of economic restriction and threats of job cuts the performative function of flexible-learning initiatives became significant in regulating the behaviour of academic staff.

Flexible learning as equity and access

In order to promote the view of flexible learning as increased access, university documents presented alternative entry scenarios and policies were altered to support a third teaching 'semester'. Documents describing what flexible learning might be in the university made reference to increasing the access of students to education through the use of alternative modes of delivery. Recognition of prior learning and the freeing-up of entry and exit points can open higher education to students who would previously have been denied entry through traditional practices. This can suggest a student-centred approach to learning and democratization of processes of learning and teaching.

The practices of flexible learning can support views about teaching, learning and access which affirm liberal and humanistic views of education. Flexible learning and delivery can be represented as the method of enacting lifelong learning and student-centred learning. At UTS administrative procedures were reviewed to facilitate more flexible student entry and a board of studies was established to oversee the development of courses allowing non-traditional entry through work-based programmes. As equity and access, flexible learning implied an intention to increase learners' access to and control over particular teaching and learning environments. The more flexible offering and delivery of higher education may achieve the desirable social goals of increasing access to education and democratizing teaching and learning processes by giving greater control to the learner.

However, this was contradicted in many instances by the restricted access created by the use of technology. Not all students had personal access to the necessary technology and the level of university support through laboratories was limited. Distance education, the form of delivery which would increase the potential access of students by freeing up time, space and place, received some attention but little infrastructure support. A number of unfunded projects offered more freedom of access through the use of learning contracts, block teaching sessions, and the provision of independent study materials. For many, particularly those on the fringes of flexible learning, it was the funded projects which were more visible and hence seen as more privileged.

Flexible learning as information technologies

Despite policy documents reiterating the 'official' view that while flexible learning may mean teaching with technology this would not always be appropriate, there was a widespread sentiment that flexible learning did mean the use of technology. This is closely associated with the theme of flexible learning as the competitive edge. 'Early adopters' of information technology, specifically users of computer-mediated conferencing and (at least in the early stages) web-based instruction, received support for projects in which they had a special interest. This usually led to a raising of the faculty-level profile for people who were already seen as being associated with technological innovation. Many of these projects were not widely known or officially widely publicized, but as word spread about what various people were doing a sense of some individuals being 'in' while others were seen to be excluded from a select group began to develop. Those who were working with funded projects were seen as the 'anointed ones'; those who not only knew what flexible learning meant but were actively engaged in it and being rewarded by the institution – that is, gaining the competitive edge in the university.

The lack of a coherent method of circulating information about various projects and initiatives had several consequences; for example, it meant that there was duplication of effort (and in some cases resource provision) as staff introduced new approaches. There were several similar projects happening concurrently, but with little communication between teams simply because they were unaware of each other. Staff involved in overlapping projects responded with frustration when they heard that others were working in similar areas and that they had missed opportunities to share in each other's learning; those outside, meanwhile, showed cynicism. Some observers interpreted the failure of communication as evidence of the university wanting to make teaching staff responsible for the direction and the subsequent success of the venture; others viewed it as a deliberate ploy to keep information from staff. Measures to address this lack of communication such as information-sharing sessions and the establishment of a website and of support groups initiated the dissemination of information and opened up spaces for discussion and exploration of experiences and ideas.

Although, as we have noted above, policy documents stated support for a broad view of flexible learning, encompassing a diversity of ways of increasing access to learning, this was not the message perceived by staff. A large proportion of available funding was directed at technologically driven approaches and individuals interpreted this to mean that high-tech approaches were preferred. For many teaching academics flexible learning (and delivery) was the form of learning that was carried by the information technologies. Flexible-learning initiatives were accompanied by substantial highly visible infrastructure which emphasized the message that information technology was highly valued. This was particularly the case where most of the projects that were funded related to the use of computer conferencing and resulted in the formation of large teams, trialling and purchase of software and investment in infrastructure. Some consideration was given to the teaching and learning implications of this, but the focus was clearly on the means of delivery. The allocation of limited funding to the purchase of high-cost items that demanded time and attention indicated to staff the forms of flexible learning that the university saw as valid and valuable.

While some funding was allocated for the development of distance-education materials no provision was made for the central infrastructure to support this. Projects that involved the development or implementation of practices that placed the learner more centrally in the teaching–learning process were generally perceived as part of existing teaching practice and were not seen to require funding to support their development. This was also associated with the notion that flexible learning was about innovation and doing something different. Even in contexts where learning contracts, flexible assessment and so on were not part of existing practice they had a lower profile because such initiatives do not require large amounts of funding or a visible infrastructure. These were often unfunded, small-scale, individual projects and as such they did not appear on the advertised list of successful projects. In a culture that judges value partly by cost, these types of projects were seen as less valuable. This presents a dilemma for the university that is trying to encourage diverse practice – how to acknowledge the value of projects that do not have a high price-tag. This dilemma is deepened when the alternative route of rewarding involvement in such projects with promotion is viewed as either irrelevant, undesirable or coercive.

There were many unfunded projects and examples of teaching practice that could easily be understood as increasing flexibility of time and space. However, in the words of one academic, 'Well, I'm doing lots of things that you could call flexible learning but they're things like flexible scheduling, self-study groups and choice of learning modules. And that's not what the university is calling flexible learning is it? For the university it's using computers, putting it on the web. . . .' Staff who believed that their existing practices constituted 'real' flexible learning, albeit not what they thought the university saw as flexible learning, were perhaps complicit in marginalizing these other views. They acquiesced to what they saw as the official view, often eventually seeing themselves as not engaging in practices that represented flexible learning. In some faculties, where deans or managers publicly valued staff involvement in these other forms of flexible learning, there was a stronger association between the practices and the 'institutionalized' term, although staff still expressed the sentiment that they were currently engaged in and had 'been doing flexible learning for some time – it's just not what the university wants it to be'. This reinforced the technology-driven view of flexible learning within the university.

Consideration of the projects that were initiated suggests that, at this stage, attention was focused very squarely on flexible delivery. This is reflected in much of the literature relating to the development of flexible learning in Australia, which focuses on ways of delivering information or courses to students. If the technologies used overcome space–time constraints, then the focus on delivery may well improve student access to education, providing opportunities to attend to ways of making learning more flexible. However, in many cases, as in many other Australian universities, these projects featured a reconfiguration or repackaging of existing material which may well often lock students into more rigid ways of engaging in course content rather than offering greater flexibility. The emphasis on flexible-learning projects that used computer-mediated communications conflicted with discourses of access and equity. The use of computer-mediated communications as an integral part of a subject may create attitudinal as well as resource barriers to the access of particular groups of students or restrict access to particular times. This was the case where students did not have appropriate technology at home or work and were reliant on gaining access to limited university computer laboratories. Even when students have access to appropriate technology at work there may be real restrictions on the amount of access they have or the times at which they can make use of these resources for study purposes. As universities increasingly expect students to be able to utilize the technology resources of their employers, the possibility that employers will restrict access or charge employees for private use of resources becomes very real. It does not seem reasonable for universities, who themselves as employers are considering charging their staff for private use of the Internet, to expect that other employers will be more generous.

Regardless of the form of technology which was intended to support alternative modes of delivery this discourse was accompanied by concerns on the part of teaching academics about their lack of knowledge and skills in using the technology either in its own right, or more specifically, as part of the teaching–learning process. Individuals were concerned about their level of computer literacy as well as the most effective ways to use, for example, computer-mediated conferencing to encourage student learning. Technologies used in distance education also caused problems for academic staff who were not experienced in the design, preparation or production of independent learning materials. The extensive involvement in trial-and-error development was time-consuming, ultimately expensive and the source of frustration for many academic staff. For some this was perceived as further evidence that responsibility for the success of flexible learning was being placed squarely on the shoulders of teaching academics.

The university's use of the term 'flexible learning' became synonymous with technology-based flexible delivery and included any strategies that would increase students' access to learning, freeing learners from constraints of time, space and place. This suggested that almost any past and present practices could be adapted to fulfil this aim. The intention to increase flexibility implied that there would be particular demands on student administration in the area of enrolment procedures and entry and exit requirements. In the first instance this impacted most on administrative systems, but staff began to identify issues relating to the procedures for course approval as faculties and schools attempted to free up the way in which they offered their courses. This placed additional pressure for change on administrative procedures.

Implications for academic practice

Discussion of the representations of flexible learning has already highlighted some of the effects on academics. Not suprisingly there was considerable variation in the reactions of academic staff depending on the extent of their involvement in the innovations and the role that they had taken.

My job won't change   This response emanated from staff who believed that their current teaching practices already incorporated flexibility for learners, so there was no need for change. Staff who were strongly resistant to flexible learning also had no intention of changing what they were doing.

I can see it's going to change what I do and I'm not looking forward to it   Some staff were concerned or disturbed that flexible-learning practices would remove them from a primary source of academic pleasure or fulfilment: direct contact with their students. Other staff were intimidated by technologies or by the demands of learning to use these and were reluctant to expose themselves to uncertainty.

Professional identities are tied up with one's competence in performing one's job – teaching. The prospect of teaching in new ways raises the possibility that some may be less successful than in traditional, familiar teaching roles. Senior-level academics in managerial positions who had limited teaching responsibilities did not see that flexible learning would directly affect the nature of their jobs.

This is a great learning opportunity (for me and for my students)   Learning involved not just how to use the technologies (whether this meant computer-mediated conferencing, developing learning materials and packages or new assessment techniques) but more significantly finding out what worked, under what circumstances and for whom and how. As staff became more familiar with the technologies they were able to explore their potential to support teaching and learning in new ways. This presented them with the option of reconceptualizing their teaching in quite dramatically different ways.

A number of staff were also enthusiastic about the potential that flexible learning offered them for improving the quality of students' learning experiences and meeting the needs of their students in more appropriate ways. Generally individuals were not able to focus on student-learning aspects until they were comfortable with the strategies and techniques they were using, even where their initial interest had been motivated by the desire to improve learning.

Providing support

The introduction of flexible learning has important implications for the culture of the university. It requires a changed culture in order to accept and implement it, as well as developing a changed culture in response to it. In this section we will consider the support that the effective introduction of flexible learning requires. The introduction of more-flexible-learning approaches often requires sophisticated activities and technologies, technical backup and support structures.

Attitudes and beliefs of staff can also obstruct change (McNeil 1990; Stofflett 1994; Taylor, Lopez and Quadrelli 1996) and hence need to be supported. In this case staff attitudes and beliefs about the nature of 'valued' learning, the real reasons for the introduction of flexible learning, the contribution of flexible-learning techniques to achieving specific learning outcomes and their own roles in the learning process all operated as barriers to change. Staff also expressed concern that they lacked knowledge, skills and pedagogic practices necessary to use flexible-learning approaches effectively.

Providing a framework and clear direction

From our preceding discussion it is clear that the extent to which a central body, such as the executive of a university, defines the parameters of flexible learning is problematic. Rigid definitions and frameworks can limit creativity and restrict the breadth of possible initiatives, reducing flexible learning to little more than a recipe book or a rigidly defined set of practices. However, too little definition can have a negative effect on staff motivation as they expend time and energy attempting to define what is meant. Too little guidance can also discourage staff who may be reluctant to take respons- ibility for constructing a workable meaning of the concept. Taylor (1996) argues that a definition of the scope of flexible education for meeting the extended mission of a university is a key feature of policy that will provide guidance about what is permitted and possible. There needs to be a clearly understood and shared meaning (rather than a prescriptive definition) of the term. At UTS, while flexible learning was clearly associated with the uni- versity's strategic initiatives, there was no clear indication of the ways in which it would contribute to achieving the broader goals of the university. The provision of case studies and examples that illustrate the breadth of meaning of flexible learning can provide additional direction for staff without being too prescriptive.

Development in knowledge and skills

There are powerful barriers to taking seriously the problematic concerns embedded in flexible learning and delivery. If academics are to embrace this shift in emphasis they need to develop a knowledge base which allows them to understand the pedagogical practices which underpin approaches to teaching and learning that allow for independent self-directed learners and lifelong learning. The use of the term 'flexible learning' suggests the focus should be on student learning rather than the technologies. However, when proficiency in the use of the technologies (whatever they may be) is the primary concern of the individual who must use them in order to fulfil their teaching role (and maintain a public and private image of competence in teaching) it becomes difficult to direct attention to a focus on learning.

UTS made an intentional decision to leave the term 'flexible learning' as undefined as possible to allow for generations of locally relevant meanings. However, when staff were asked to adopt ambiguously defined innovations there was an understandable feeling of disquiet. Well-intentioned staff who wish to improve learning for the students want to know just what it is they should be doing. In the initial stages of introduction there is a need for the provision of opportunities for staff to explore possible ways in which flexible learning may be interpreted and what each interpretation would mean for teaching and learning.

Once staff have developed some idea of the options from which they may select, there is a need for training in and development of the skills involved. Such development may be offered in a range of ways: generic skills in instructional design may be appropriate, although these may result in limited transfer of learning. Alternatively, a range of introductory workshops presenting an overview and basic skills in facilitating flexible learning can provide staff with the confidence to begin work on a development. Follow-up workshops for project teams, specifically focused on the development of a project, allow staff to be supported in the course of learning about the 'best' way to use various flexible learning and delivery strategies. In flexible-learning approaches that involve the use of technologies there is a need for basic training in the use of the technologies, especially when staff are unfamiliar with them. Where software is involved staff also need to become familiar with ways in which the software works and its capabilities.

Until staff are comfortable using technologies such as computer-mediated conferencing, video- or teleconferencing they will not be able to consider the pedagogical demands of the new approach or the most effective ways to use it to enhance student learning. Attending to the pedagogical dimensions of new approaches is of particular importance. Where flexible-learning projects included the use of established approaches such as distance-education materials, peer teaching, learning and assessment, videoconferencing, take-home labs and interactive multimedia one could draw on an established body of literature dealing with teaching and learning principles and issues. This provided a base from which staff development could begin. In addition, such literature provided a source of evidence to support the decisions staff had made about selecting that approach as the most appropriate for their context. However, newer strategies such as the use of workplace-based learning, web-based instruction or computer-mediated conferencing have little empirical evidence suggesting 'best practice' or supporting their use to facilitate learning. This adds yet another 'layer' of learning to the staff's already heavy learning load – not only do they have to learn how to use the technologies in a technical sense, they have to learn how to use them effectively in an educational sense. This 'learning load' provides further support for the recommendation that a range of opportunities are made available for staff to share their experiences.

Once staff have developed familiarity with basic skills and technologies, attention needs to be given to exploring the pedagogical implications of using a specific approach. This may be done in generic workshops or carried out with project teams or faculty or sub-faculty groups. Ongoing work with teams on a specific project allows staff to reflect on their experiences under the guidance of a team leader or academic staff developer who can also draw on the experiences of other groups. Mentor schemes teaming more and less experienced users of specific flexible-learning approaches have great potential for enhancing the learning processes of academic staff adopting flexible approaches. The involvement of academic staff developers in ongoing project and developmental work can fulfil an important information-dissemination function in addition to their more obvious educational development role.

Time

Overwhelmingly the staff involved in developing flexible-learning projects reported that not only was the development time-consuming, it was consistently more time-consuming than they had expected. Even after strategies or programmes had been developed there were glitches and problems along the way. These not only took time to correct but often required the development of fallback positions so that teachers were not left without teaching materials when, for example, the server crashed or they lost vision from their videoconferencing. Provision of adequate preparation time is a critical factor in supporting staff. Where staff were involved in the development of flexible-learning approaches without some reduction in teaching or administrative load, flexible-learning development made heavy claims on their time and on them personally. Most teaching staff are prepared to go 'beyond the call of duty' but this can only be sustained up to a point. The current educational environment where staff are facing heavier teaching loads, larger classes and increased pressure to attract external funding and to publish challenges the commitment of most professionals. Of greatest significance to staff involved in flexible-learning initiatives at UTS was the need for realistic acknowledgment of the time required to establish flexible learning.

Provision of forums for discussion and dissemination of information

At all stages of the introduction of flexible learning the provision of opportunities for staff to engage in discussion and exploration of ideas and possibilities, share experiences and critique their practice is essential. In the early stages it is important to provide adequate opportunities for staff to explore the implications for their teaching, general academic practice and students. Later, as staff become involved in projects, they need opportunities to share their experiences with others providing a forum for displaying what they have done, articulating the processes they have gone through and the decisions they have made. This also allows others (especially those who may be reluctant to become involved) to find out what is going on. Sharing experiences allows individuals to learn from each other's experiences and to realize that others may be facing similar challenges.

At UTS a variety of forums for sharing experiences were held, ranging from informal team discussion to formal university-wide show-cases of projects. A number of symposia were held where staff involved in a range of flexible-learning projects presented their experiences and shared the lessons they had learned. An unintended outcome of some of these discussions was trouble-shooting as members of various teams worked together to solve an individual staff member's problem. These forums also facilitated exchange of ideas about teaching and learning between members of different faculties, providing valuable cross-fertilization and establishing useful collaborations and the sharing of expertise.

There is also a need to provide opportunities for staff to discuss the affective consequences of adopting flexible approaches. For many academic staff it is the face-to-face interactions with students that define their teaching selves (McInnis 1992); the use of forms of flexible learning which distance teacher from learner can unsettle these professional identities (McWilliam and Palmer 1995). Some staff viewed the removal of this contact as undesirable or threatening and expressed feelings of loss in relation to views of themselves constructed through interpersonal interaction with students. Staff need support to deal with these feelings and also to look forward and to explore the possibilities for developing different relationships between teacher and learners.

Similarly, adopting new teaching and learning approaches that often contain little in the way of established recommended practice can be both challenging and intimidating. 'Good' conventional teachers have well-developed skills in interacting with students in their classes. Studies of good teaching find it hard to go past personal interactive attributes when describing what it is that makes a good teacher. Staff need opportunities to explore and conceive of what will constitute a teacher in these more flexible learning environments. Individuals who were comfortable and competent in their previous teaching approaches will be trying out new and often untested techniques, opening up the possibility that teaching sessions may fail or at least be less successful than normal. In these circumstances the opportunity to hear of others' similar experiences (and their responses) and to receive collegial support provides encouragement and helps sustain activity and morale.

McInnis (1992) suggests that new university environments which include more flexible learning will be accompanied by a changing view of what constitutes academics' work. Flexible learning will not necessarily result in flexible teaching or flexibility for the academic. Changed patterns to the academic year resulting from block-mode teaching, summer schools, short courses, etc., will alter the autonomy of the individual to self-regulate their daily work practices. Flexible learning also challenges the direct and proportional relationship assumed between teaching contact time and productivity, and between teaching time and the allocation of financial resources. If more flexible learning involves greater liaison with industry there will be a need for academics to develop skills in negotiating curricula and learning contracts between student, university and organization, developing links with industry and increasing their knowledge of the world 'out there'.

Technologies have the potential to alter the nature of the traditional community controlled by teachers in university learning. Ideas of community, discourse and power within conventional teaching and learning situations are changed by the new relationships between production and delivery (Landow 1992). Technology alters the pattern of control and power that conventional education takes for granted in designing, delivering and evaluating teaching and learning. Conceptions of teaching and curriculum contain the idea of order, structure and sequence: information is part of an intentional route to learning. Technology allows access to a radically different situation in which information is unscreened and unordered. The possibilities of electronically mediated learning make redundant the idea of a self-contained classroom where teachers are the centre of most of the control and structuring of information and communication: instead there is provider control.

While it is important to look to developing new practices we must not lose sight of what was effective and valuable in our past practices. Suggesting that flexible learning demands 'new practices' devalues those activities which have comprised academics' previous roles. A consequence of an emphasis on flexible learning as innovation is the abandonment of past practices in the flurry to become part of the 'new wave'. It also creates a perception that flexible learning must be something which has not been done before.

Academics' sense of professional identity is also in part defined by the institution in which they work. Universities position themselves in the marketplace to develop a reputation for strengths in particular fields and in attracting particular types of students. Flexible learning has the potential to alter this. For a university such as UTS which has a clearly described local student client group and which has historically refused involvement in any form of open and distance learning, the introduction of flexible approaches opens up a whole new world of potential students. If universities (and individual academics) define themselves in part by the nature of their students, these changes in students and the nature of teaching and learning resulting from increased flexibility have significant implications for institutional and individual professional identities.

An effective and far-reaching method of communicating ideas among and between staff can provide support for staff who may feel isolated in their efforts and can capitalize on expertise that is developing and minimize duplication of effort. If staff have plenty of opportunities for finding out about various projects that are being developed, including projects similar to their own, the task of adopting a new approach is made easier. E-mail discussion groups, a website, occasional symposia, featuring flexible-learning projects in university newsletters can help to publicize initiatives and make information widely available. Building up a resource base, publicizing available information and support and providing adequate resources to support staff learning are essential.

Staff from central academic staff development or support units working across the university can provide a breadth of vision and different perspectives on what is occurring. They can act as a conduit linking members and projects across disciplines and can share learning and experiences between teams. The development of flexible-learning approaches does take time, and having a number of staff who are informed about what is happening in different projects can prevent replication of mistakes and duplication of efforts.

Acknowledging and rewarding efforts

There is always a dilemma that institutional efforts to reward staff achievements may be interpreted as techniques for ensuring compliance. At UTS, staff involved in developing flexible-learning approaches were spending large amounts of their own time and placing themselves in risky situations. The issue of acknowledgement of efforts was equally salient, however, for staff who had been working in ways that they regarded as flexible prior to the initiative and which they felt had not been acknowledged. Involvement in flexible learning was added to the criteria for promotion, offering a very real incentive and reward for those who were in a position to apply. However, there was no equivalent reward available for those for whom promotion was not a viable option. The linking of promotions to involvement in flexible learning presents the university with a dilemma: while it is important to reward involvement in strategic directives, care needs to be taken that what is rewarded *is* good teaching and that staff do not rush to embrace flexible learning for purely instrumental reasons. Linking promotion to involvement in flexible learning can also be read as punishing those who choose not to adopt flexible learning (for educationally sound reasons).

The university awarded a limited number of annual teaching excellence awards and these provided an avenue for staff who were actively seeking some incentive. However, it takes a certain amount of confidence or collegial support to put oneself forward as an 'excellent teacher', along with a significant time commitment preparing an application. As an alternative means of acknowledging staff efforts a week of special activities valuing teaching and learning in the university was held and staff involved in flexible learning were invited to participate in workshops, seminars, symposia, panel discussions and poster sessions that show-cased their work and provided public recognition.

Infrastructure support and technical assistance

The success of information-technology-based flexible approaches is dependent on the provision of sufficient infrastructure to support hardware and delivery. Staff and students at UTS reported frustration when technology failed them. If staff are to persevere with new developments they need to do so feeling secure that the technology is more rather than less likely to work.

Projects that involve student learning via web-based instruction or computer-mediated conferencing also need to be supported by adequate resources, for example access to computer laboratories. Lack of adequate computer access was a source of frustration for many students and limited the success of several projects. The use of information technology to deliver teaching implies around-the-clock access, which in turn demands readily available technical support.

A number of projects focused on the development of materials that could be offered as distance-education packages. There had been no provision for a centralized infrastructure to co-ordinate the production and distribution of this type of learning materials. This presented difficulties for teams involved in these projects and was not always resolved in a satisfactory manner. Academic managers and project teams need to be encouraged to give careful consideration to the implications and needs of projects before committing themselves to action.

Conclusion

Flexible learning has evolved in response to a range of social, cultural and economic factors. Examination of the introduction of flexible learning in one university identified the following dominant discourses: flexible learning as efficiency; flexible learning as technology; flexible learning as a means of improving student access; and flexible learning as innovation. These discourses both influence and represent what is valued in the university in terms of learning and teaching. Flexible learning has the potential to change significantly the way we teach and learn in universities, the role of the academic, the nature of our learners and what is learned. It offers potential challenge and excitement for academics as they adapt to these new ways of being and doing. However, unless the introduction of such a significant initiative is accompanied by appropriate support and staff development its effects are likely to be limited and disappointing. We have identified areas in which support and staff development are necessary and have suggested strategies that have proved effective in the case of UTS.

References

Chubb, I. (1993) Conference report in *The Transition from Elite to Mass Higher Education: Conference Proceedings of DEET and OECD*, Canberra: Australian Government Publishing Service.

Landow, G. (1992) *Hypertext: The Convergence of Contemporary Critical Theory and Technology*, Baltimore: Johns Hopkins University Press.

Lyotard, J.-F. (1984) *The Postmodern Condition: A Report on Knowledge* trans. G. Bennington and B. Massumi, Manchester: Manchester University Press.

McInnis, C. (1992) 'Changes in the nature of academic work', *Australian Universities Review* 35(2): 9–12.

McNeil, D. (1990) *Wiring the Ivory Tower: A Round Table on Technology*, Washington, DC: Academy for Educational Development, Inc. [ED 320 555].

McWilliam, E. and Palmer, P. (1995) 'Teaching tech(no)bodies: open learning and postgraduate pedagogy', *Australian Universities Review* 38(2): 32–4.

Shapiro, B. (1993) 'Mass higher education: problems and challenges', in *The Transition from Elite to Mass Higher Education: Conference Proceedings of DEET and OECD*, Canberra: Australian Government Publishing Service.

Stofflett, R. T. (1994) 'The accommodation of science pedagogical knowledge: the application of conceptual change constructs to teacher education', *Journal of Research in Science Teaching* 31: 787–810.

Taylor, P. G. (1996) 'Courses in university teaching: looking to practice-focused educational development', paper prepared for 'Preparing University Teachers in Australia and New Zealand', a symposium conducted by the Griffith Institute for Higher Education, Griffith University, Oct.

Taylor, P. G., Lopez, L. and Quadrelli, C. (1996) *Flexibility, Technology and Academics' Practices: Tantalising Tales and Muddy Maps*, Canberra: Australian Government Publishing Service.

6 Diversity, convergence and the evolution of student support in higher education in the UK

Roger Mills

Introduction

This chapter examines the way in which diverse approaches to student support have converged, improving services to students and leading to new and imaginative ways of teaching and learning across the whole sector.

Using an approach centred around the OUUK, we first consider the influence of other institutions on its development and in turn its influence on others. The convergence of ideas and methods of teaching and student support, driven in part by the development of new technologies and convergence in student demographics, forms the second part of the chapter, whilst the final section reflects on the influence of institutional teaching quality exercises in the UK in transmitting good practice across institutions, leading to convergence and evolution. It is argued that the ultimate driver for convergence is target audience, with students from a wide range of backgrounds, age groups and institutions all demanding greater flexibility, greater autonomy and easier access to learning resources of all kinds. In turn this leads to a student- rather than institution-centred system which encourages increasing levels of credit transfer between institutions. When the OUUK first opened its doors in 1971, one of the key issues of concern for the first vice-chancellor and the original students was the credibility of the OU degree. In her recent biography of Jennie Lee (the minister in the 1966 Wilson government with responsibility for the establishment of the OU), Hollis (1997) writes, 'they objected to any notion that the OU might be a remedial University, a "secondary modern" amid grammar school and public school players'. The acceptability of the outcome of study was a crucial requirement of the new university and although its approach to teaching and learning, its admissions policies and the close integration of academic, operational and administrative procedures were very different from the conventional institutions of the time, its basic governance and its mechanisms for quality assurance (a term which would not have been used then) in terms of external assessors and examiners were based on the systems which had proved so successful in establishing UK higher education as among the most highly respected in the world. The desire to be seen to be equal to traditional institutions manifested itself in the debate over academic dress for formal occasions such as degree ceremonies. Some of the OU staff were opposed to the notion of a modern university taking on the dated trappings of conventional institutions such as academic dress and honorary degrees, but it was soon made clear by the student body that they wanted academic dress in the same way as all other graduates.

Ecological and evolutionary analogies have been used by Mills and Tait (1997) to describe developments in open and distance learning (ODL) and in this chapter this approach is used again to analyse the convergence between different approaches to higher education. The diversity of higher education in the UK has been one of its strengths and has provided a rich source of variation which can be developed as the environment changes. Convergence between institutions, and especially between conventional and open and distance-teaching organizations, as a result of both the development of national standards supported by quality audit and assessment and the rapid impact of the new technologies on approaches to teaching and learning, might therefore be regarded with some concern. It is perhaps not helpful to create an environment where all institutions have similar aims and objectives. It is important for them to have clear missions which continue to demonstrate diversity of approach and which ensure that diversity remains within higher education such that the whole sector is ready for change, whether that be gradual or cataclysmic. At the same time benchmarking between institutions, leading to transmission of good practices and to greater clarity and commonality about standards, needs to be enhanced. It is acknowledged, however, that the Quality Assurance Agency in the UK has publicly stated that the retention of institutional diversity is an important goal for the future.

Early developments in UK open and distance learning

When serious and accredited open and distance learning was introduced at university level in the 1970s in the UK, the traditional university lecture was replaced with written course materials, television and radio programmes and home experiment kits. In this way students could read or listen to the 'teacher' in their own time and at their own convenience. Such freeing up of the time and place of interacting with the 'teacher' was a major driver for the development of both distance education and open learning; but it was not, of course, new: for many years correspondence education had done just that.

It can be argued that the development of distance education itself did little to improve teaching and learning, but simply introduced a new dimension to the process. However, when teams of academics began to work together to pool ideas and methods the quality of teaching and learning resources quickly improved. This 'opening up' of the conventional lecture theatre to the public and to other academics led to significant improvements in teaching. More input from instructional designers and educational tech-nologists helped the subject specialists to teach their subjects better, and of course students were able to study at their own convenience. At the same time students and teachers had started to question the value of the traditional university lecture both as an educational technique and as a method of trans-ferring information and knowledge from teacher to taught (see Bligh 1971). But if the basic approach to education improved, it did not change: the core was still the transmission of knowledge from teacher to taught through a variety of media. Where open and distance education diverged from corre-spondence education was in the use of multiple media and more particularly in the introduction of the notion of small-group and individual student support and teaching.

One of the longest-standing elite traditions in UK education at university level has been the small-group and individual tutorial work developed over many centuries at the universities of Oxford and Cambridge. The 'Oxbridge' system of lectures and practical work provided by the university combined with tutorial support or supervisions arranged by the individual colleges is a well-tried and tested approach which ensures that individual students are supported, their strengths and weaknesses noted and appropriate action taken. The basic approach is clear: that there is an opportunity each week for students to write an essay, to read and discuss what they have written and to engage in further reading with their supervisor and a very small number of other students. This experience is remembered by many Oxbridge students (the approach was tried by other universities, notably Durham, but was never developed more widely partly because of the costs involved in such individual support) as challenging and somewhat daunting; there is no place to hide in a system focused on providing individual support to the student. The lecture hall is ancillary, and although for science students laboratories also provided individual support in inescapable periods of skills development and learning, the main learning occurs through the individual act of reading and writing, together with the small-group activity of argument and discus-sion. This is active learning in its simplest manifestation.

Early systems of ODL, known as correspondence education before the advent of open universities, simply replaced the lecture theatre with cor-respondence materials. However, the advent of the UK and other open and distance-teaching universities in the 1970s and 1980s led to a con-vergence of the traditional Oxbridge approach with the best of distance education. Laboratories were replaced with home experiment kits for science students and many attended a week-long residential school to develop the skills and experience required of students studying practical subjects. But more significant and more universal was the emphasis placed by open and distance learning (ODL) systems on the interaction between the tutor and the individual student. As if to compensate for the absence of face-to-face lectures, ODL systems placed a firm emphasis on interaction by correspondence. Teaching by commenting constructively on students' scripts became a key skill in the distance tutor's repertoire. Much staff-development activity in ODL currently revolves around the skills and pedagogy of teaching by commenting in writing on a student's work and entering into a dialogue using this medium. The art and psychology of giving criticism in writing without visual and oral clues and cues is an area where much work has been done. Of course such a skill is also a vital part of the skills mix of a teacher in a conventional institution and now, especially with the growing numbers of students in higher education, it is increasingly important as opportunities for individual face-to-face sessions between tutor and student become fewer. In contrast, many ODL institutions have made much of providing some direct face-to-face support to students through the organization of a limited number of optional (or in some cases compulsory) evening tutorials, day schools and residential weekends or weeks.

It can be argued that the approach to teaching and learning in ODL has evolved from a correspondence course origin and converged with the pedagogic approach of the university lecture and the college tutorial developed and continuing today at the universities of Oxford and Cambridge. Having an essay commented on in detail by a fellow student and a tutor is a very different and more active type of learning than simply attending lectures, and although it is not quite the same as submitting an assignment for comment in writing, the common element is the treatment of the student as an individual. There are some signs of increasing recognition by staff in conventional universities that 'teaching by correspondence' or teaching by making detailed comments in a constructive but intellectually challenging way on students' assignments is one of the best ways at present to individualize teaching and learning. The basic principle is that teachers should make comments thoughtfully and in writing, as if they did not meet the student regularly. The advantage of this is that the student has a permanent record of the teacher's comments and that the teacher has to think more carefully in producing a written rather than an oral comment on a piece of work.

The above analysis demonstrates one of the major convergences between some ODL and conventional systems: the increasing realization that students need individual and small-group support. This will be achieved in part through the use of a range of resources, increasingly accessed by technological means, to support individual students.

The impact of other institutions on the OUUK

During the planning period of the OUUK the influence of other institutions was considerable, none less than the University of New England at Armidale in New South Wales where the OU's first vice-chancellor experienced the use of residential schools. This directly contributed to the decision to have residential summer schools for all the OUUK first-year courses. The argument was that in addition to providing library and laboratory experience unavailable to most students in their home environment, the residential experience provided a taste of what a 'real' university was like and gave opportunities for intensive interaction between students and staff. Since 1971 the situation has changed considerably: an increasing number of university students are non-residential: they attend their local universities on a part-time or full-time basis (and sometimes a mixture of the two) whilst continuing to live at home and undertaking paid employment.

There are other examples of how ODL institutions have learned from each other, but what is less easy to see is how conventional institutions have influenced distance-teaching institutions over recent years. Clearly they were a major influence when large distance-teaching institutions were set up and many of the quality-assurance procedures of the OUUK were developed from those well tried and tested in the conventional system. But what influence are conventional higher-education institutions having on ODL today? In one sense the influence is all the other way. However, because conventional institutions are structured in a significantly different way to ODL institutions, certainly in the UK, they have the opportunity to develop approaches to ODL on a small scale in a way that would not be economic in a large-scale institution such as the OU. Nevertheless as higher education (HE) institutions in the UK continue to be subject to common approaches to funding and quality assurance, the simple fact that there are over 100 'conventional' universities and just one open university means that the influence of these other institutions on national systems which equally affect the OUUK is very great. A recent example illustrates this. Institutions were asked to nominate staff to join national subject panels which are advisory in relation to the teaching quality exercises. The OUUK's input to this was to stress the need to have some panel members with experience of teaching part-time adult students, preferably at a distance.

Undoubtedly this convergence between ODL and conventional teaching, significantly speeded up by providing learning resources through new technology, is leading to increased competition which in turn is stimulating new developments. The ability to provide information about courses (and even offer them) on the World Wide Web, and to admit and accredit students on these courses means that all universities can open themselves up much more in the future.

Definitions of ODL are a continuing problem and vary to suit the individual institution. For example, one institution advertises a distance-taught programme which is defined by the tutor driving to a town away from the main university campus and providing face-to-face teaching! In the past this was regarded as extra-mural work. Now in many cases such an approach is misleadingly classified as distance education because ODL has become a powerful marketing slogan. Another example in the East Anglia region of England, a geographical area roughly the size of Israel, is where a conventional university has developed a distance structure by franchising its first- and second-year courses to local colleges. In this way the university moves away from the fixed location and brings university education to local colleges. Such approaches to extending the campus can be cheaper than ODL systems, especially when costs are marginal to the main teaching and learning system, but they may not provide the student with sufficient support and may not enable local progression to higher levels and more specialist subjects.

In countries such as Australia and Canada where dual-mode institutions (i.e., those which produce learning resources for use by both on-campus and off-campus students) are the norm rather than the exception, the notion of convergence is to some extent irrelevant. Many of these institutions simply regard ODL as another method of teaching; students move in and out of different modes of education and sometimes study in two different modes simultaneously. It is relatively easy to see how conventional institutions in the UK can add an ODL mode to their portfolio (although quality of materials is a real resource issue both in terms of cash and staff time) but much more difficult to envisage a major single-mode ODL institution such as the OUUK moving towards the conventional system by undertaking more face-to face work. The rapid development of technology may channel both types of institution into a single converging and eventually parallel path in the early part of the next millennium.

The impact of the OUUK on other institutions

Daniel (1997) in an internal OUUK paper reflects on this under the heading 'From monopoly of mission to convergence in competition'. His analysis is as follows:

> When Lord Crowther [the first chancellor of the OUUK] coined the statement, *open as to people, open as to places, open as to methods and open as to ideas*, he gave the OU a distinct mission. Although all universities claim to be open as to ideas, the OU had a near monopoly on openness to people, places and methods for much of the 1970s. During the 1980s the OU had increasingly to share the ideal of being *open as to people* with the developing polytechnics. In North America mass higher education was already a reality and open admission for adults had ceased to be radical. In the 1990s, partly goaded by the OU and greatly helped by the new technologies, most other universities realised that they too could be *open as to places* and launched distance teaching programmes.

It is clear therefore that some of the major ODL systems in the world such as the OUUK have had an enormous impact on conventional teaching, with their ideas and approaches flowing into the conventional systems, stimulating rapid development. This impact may be seen especially in three areas:

- the production of teaching materials
- staff development
- open admissions policies and student support.

Through teaching materials

The term 'resource-based learning' has become well established in many institutions and denotes increasing encouragement to students to use non-staff resources more actively in their study. Some institutions make available to students and staff resources produced by the OUUK in the form of written course books and of broadcast and recorded audio and video programmes. These resources replace or complement the long-established lecture approach which today usually seems to satisfy only the lecturer. We have come a long way since Donald Bligh (1971) wrote *What's the Use of Lectures?*, questioning the effectiveness of the traditional lecture both as a teaching and learning strategy and as a method of transferring facts. Over the past seven years many of the new universities have clubbed together to establish a resource base for collective materials production known as the Open Learning Foundation which enables co-operative development of resources across institutional boundaries. This is complementary to the provision of the OUUK and other agencies such as the UK National Extension College.

Through staff and staff development

Many OU associate lecturers are staff of other institutions. Through its consistent, well-resourced and acclaimed staff development programme for its part-time associate lecturers the OU has influenced the approach to teaching in many conventional universities, emphasizing the importance of the student as an individual and developing techniques for correspondence and small-group work. The use of OU materials for training tutors such as 'Supporting Open Learning' (1997) and the 'Open Teaching Toolkits' (1992 onwards) has had a significant impact on staff-development practices in other universities. One of the main recommendations of the Dearing Report (1997) on higher education is the establishment of an Institute for Teaching and Learning in Higher Education. This national institute will be charged with the training and accreditation of all university teachers and will not discriminate with regard to the mode of instruction. Its establishment will bring together staff-development practices from both the conventional and ODL sectors of UK higher education, leading to convergence of approach and in time to co-operation in practice.

Through open admissions policy and learner support

The encouragement of learner autonomy through student support is another area where the coming together of open and distance education with conventional systems is leading to further development. This is a convergence of a different kind. For many years the OU led the way in the notion that educational guidance and counselling was an essential element in the learning process. However, there has been a tremendous growth in the provision of counselling and guidance services outside the OU over the past twenty years and the developing understanding of the importance of these processes is noted by McNair (1997). He points out that higher education has addressed the development of independent learning in three distinct ways:

- through the processes of the mainstream curriculum: what is taught and how learning is supported, mainly by academic staff
- through academic tutoring: guiding individuals' learning, usually by academic staff
- through specialist services: careers, counselling, advice, etc., delivered mainly by specialist non-academic staff.

To this list one could add the growing acknowledgement of the importance of the development of key learning skills, as specified in the Dearing Report.

As McNair (ibid.) points out, 'the growing convergence between the above three issues has fundamental implications for who does what in higher education, and indeed for how we conceive of the process of higher education itself'.

Future convergence

The rest of this chapter looks to the future and argues that it is more appropriate to think of open and distance learning and conventional learning moving at the same pace and in the same direction. This direction is towards an increase in resource-based learning in both modes (the direct result of the development of the Internet and CD-ROMs) and an acknowledgement, through the use of computer-mediated communication to link student with student and with tutor, of the crucial importance of individual support.

A good example of the development of resource-based learning in a new but conventional university is that of the Effective Learning Programme (ELP) at the University of Lincolnshire and Humberside. Hunter (1997), the project manager, sets out the rationale (available on the World Wide Web http://Home.Ulh.Ac.Uk/Ldu/elpview.html). The aim of this programme, which is compulsory for all students, is

> to develop students' learning and study skills and to support the University's mission statement: to provide our students world wide with the best employment prospects and to equip them to become life long learners. . . .

The ELP is designed such that students will spend some time working alone and some time working with others. All the modules are written in an accessible, open learning format with plenty of opportunities for reflection, testing what has been done and for the application of tools and techniques, encouraging the students to learn in a variety of ways. There are no lectures in the 'standard' version of ELP – the aim is to develop independence in learning. . . .

When students are taking some modules, e.g. Information Technology modules, they are able to seek on-the-spot assistance from help desks.

Such an approach may not be new in an international context but in the UK the emphasis on the development of study competence through resource-based learning is breaking new ground and alongside the increasing use of computer simulations and CD-ROMs as resources for traditional students, demonstrates a real convergence with techniques pioneered by distance educators and their predecessors the programmed-learning specialists. The Dearing Report, with its emphasis on skills development and the importance of common standards relating to what graduates can do and what skills they possess, is certainly a driver for the convergence of teaching and learning approaches across the whole higher-education curriculum. Linked to this is the convergence stimulated by requirements for assessment systems to meet the growing need for a skills-based higher-education curriculum. These developments pose significant challenges for distance education and especially its assessment policies and practices.

Another example of a 'conventional university' using new technology in an innovative way is the University of Wolverhampton's Broadnet project which enables a wide range of learning materials to be accessed through the Internet. This system is used both within the university to link students studying on six campuses and also to deliver courses to industry and for out-reach work to places where higher-education provision has previously been the monopoly of the OUUK.

What is interesting is that the OUUK and other distance-teaching insti-tutions are now having to rethink their entire approach to teaching in the context of the power of computer-mediated communication, the World Wide Web and CD-ROMs. Whereas in a conventional institution sufficient access can be provided (at least in principle) for each student to have enough time on a PC for the work required, this is less easy in a distance-teaching institution which prides itself on ease of access both financially and in terms of admissions criteria. The developments in resource-based learning are a real challenge to the distance-teaching institutions and this is acknowledged in a recent thinkpiece by the vice-chancellor of the OUUK (Daniel 1997). The development of the concept of the university for industry in the UK is giving further impetus to the use of new technologies in deliver-ing smaller packets or 'chunks' of learning materials.

As institutions converge and begin to offer products (courses, programmes of study) of similar kinds taught in a variety of modes, competition will increase. To some this is a positive thing for the student, leading to more choice; but care must be taken that institutions do not spend too much of their creative energies on this activity. Burt (1997) in his internal paper 'Face to face with distance education' asks the question 'Is contemporary distance education inferior to contemporary classroom education?' He points out that the situation in conventional higher education is changing due to budgetary pressures and to increasing demands for access and the use of the new technology. He concludes that 'there is a convergence between conventional education and distance education'. With class sizes increasing the student in the classroom is becoming more 'distant'. At the same time the distance-education student is becoming less 'distant' due to the use of the new technologies. The use of e-mail and computer-conferencing systems such as First Class℠ has brought the distant student (or at least the one who can afford the equipment at home) much closer to other students, to tutors and counsellors and to the course writers, and this above all other developments is having a major impact on the development of distance education.

Wagner (1997) suggests that a large amount of convergence has already occurred. He reports a study conducted at Leeds Metropolitan University which suggests that 'students in conventional higher education spend significantly more of their time in distance education than in face to face activities. . . . And this is without any dramatic leap in the new technologies.' Of course such statements need some qualification, especially in relation to the definition of distance education, but the point is clear: even in a conventional 'face-to-face' system, students spend much of their time working on their own. It may always have been so, but the increase in resources for individual learning and especially those offered through the new technologies has provided students with far more powerful tools for independent learning.

The changing context

Many distance-teaching organizations were established to meet the needs of adults who had not had the opportunity to attend conventional universities, and in many ways – at least in the UK – the curriculum was different and distinct. A modular curriculum with an emphasis on personal development was and still is an important role for the Open University. In addition, from the start of the university there have been groups of professionals and individuals who have undertaken courses of study with direct career or professional outcomes in mind. However, as the average age of an OUUK student has dropped and the type of student has changed, so the demand from students and potential students for a modified curriculum has increased; hence the decision by the OUUK to introduce named degrees and to develop a more vocationally oriented curriculum in the post-Dearing era. (This parallels what is happening at Athabasca University in Canada; see Chapter 7 below.) At the same time there is a growing population of older students in 'conventional' universities as they broaden their admissions criteria and make learning opportunities available on a more flexible basis. Nearly half all UK higher-education students are now studying in a modular framework. Thus the ultimate convergence may not be one of mode but of student demographics. One of the big issues today is whether the distance-teaching approach of the OU should be considered as a very real alternative for 18-year-olds to the conventional system.

In most of the statistics on the take-up of university places in the UK, the OU is treated as a separate and additional institution. It is not included in the Universities and Colleges Admissions System (UCAS), nor does it advertise in its handbook. An increasing number of 18–24-year-olds qualified for conventional university entrance are deciding to start work at the same time as continuing their education; a decision undoubtedly reinforced by the sharp increase in the cost of HE to students themselves and to their families. They will increasingly look for flexibility and the opportunity to put together an employer-valued and relevant degree profile or statement of competence. With the increasing effectiveness of credit transfer, education will become more and more student- rather than institution-centred and students will be able to move in and out of face-to-face, distance, part-time and full-time modes with ease. As distance-education institutions move into the consumer territory traditionally monopolized by conventional institutions and vice versa we can expect increased competition, which if managed well may lead to increasing choice for the student and consequently a more effective higher-education system. There is no real need for institutions to be threatened by increased competition as there are large numbers of people who are still not involved in higher education and who would benefit from it. In the East Anglia region of the UK, which has a population of 5.2 million people, only 55,000 were studying part-time in higher education in 1994 and of these 16,000 studied through the OUUK. The fact that the OU's market share in this region has decreased by about 10 per cent over the past three years is a clear indication of increasing competition: more and more institutions are offering opportunities to study part-time.

However, if the distance-teaching organizations target the traditional consumers of HE at a time when those consumers are seriously considering whether it is worth their while to go to university full-time at 18, we can expect a much tougher competitive environment for older and part-time applicants to HE. This could lead to the withdrawal of study-centre and examination facilities currently provided to a large extent by the other HE and FE institutions which are potentially competitors. In addition, the OUUK depends to a large extent on the staff of other institutions for its associate lecturers. This joint use of staff has considerable benefits for students in both institutions. The ideas and approaches developed by the OUUK are used by its associate lecturers in their main jobs, and the teaching

Table 6.1 HEFCE Teaching Quality Assessment Process

Aspect of provision	Test to be applied	Scale points			
		1	2	3	4
1 Curriculum design, contents and organization	To what extent do the student learning experience and student achievement within this aspect of provision contribute to the meeting of objectives set by the subject provider?	The aims and/or objectives set by the subject provider are not met; there are major shortcomings which must be rectified.	This aspect makes an acceptable contribution to the attainment of the stated objectives but significant improvement could be made.	This aspect makes a substantial contribution to the attainment of stated objectives; however, there is scope for improvement.	This aspect makes a full contribution to the attainment of the stated objectives.
2 Teaching, learning and assessment					
3 Student progression and achievement					
4 Student support and guidance	Do the objectives set, and the level of attainment of those objectives, allow the aims set by the subject provider to be met?		The aims set by the subject provider are broadly met.	The aims set by the subject provider are met.	The aims set by the subject provider are met.
5 Learning resources					
6 Quality assurance and enhancement					

materials supplied by the OU to associate lecturers are also a resource for teaching in more conventional situations. On the other hand, OU students benefit from teaching resources which have been developed by associate lecturers in their primary occupation.

The impact of quality assessment

One of the values of external quality audit, whether subject-based or institution-based, is that it can potentially assist the exchange of good practice between institutions. A description of the current higher-education quality-assessment processes in the UK is given by O'Shea, Bearman and Downes (1996) and it is informative to look at the current criteria against which higher-education institutions are asked to assess themselves in the UK. The Higher Education Quality Assurance Agency asks each university the following questions:

- Can you tell us how you are sure that you are discharging effectively your responsibility for the standard of each award granted in your name and for the quality of the education provided by you to enable students to attain that standard?
- Can you convince us that the evidence that you are relying on for this purpose is sufficient, valid and reliable? (HEFCE 1997a).

These questions are tough but are couched in wide enough terms to allow for individual approaches. As the audit team's findings are summarized in a published report there are opportunities for all institutions to learn from each other.

Of interest here are the *Draft Guidelines on Quality Assurance of Distance Learning* at present being written for the Quality Assurance Agency (1998). The aim of these guidelines is to provide advice, mainly to conventional institutions, about what needs to be considered when assuring the quality and academic standards of programmes provided through distance learning. The draft document notes that 'the physical separation of programme design, delivery, learner support and assessment raises particular questions for institutions about the ways in which they "manage" teaching and learning to ensure quality of provision and security of standards'. It is interesting to observe the way in which distance learning is classified into three 'dimensions' in this document, none of which is the model used by the OUUK. The definition of distance learning in this document is revealing in its breadth, suggesting that it is 'a mode of provision of higher education that involves learning resources being transferred to the student's location, rather than the student moving to the location of the resources'.

The HEFCE *Teaching Quality Assessment Process* of individual subject areas (HEFCE 1997b) is more specific and correctly covers the broad spectrum of student learning. For each subject area there are tests to be applied to 6 different aspects of provision. These are set out in full in Table 6.1 and it is a measure of the convergence of open and distance education with 'conventional' approaches that the questions can be applied across the board to all higher-education institutions.

What is interesting in the context of this book is whether these processes are forcing institutional convergence of a negative kind, reducing variety and restricting future evolutionary development; or whether they are leading to an exchange of good practice – a mixing of 'gene pools', to use another evolutionary metaphor – resulting in greater potential within individual institutions.

It is clear that there is quite rapid convergence in the UK between the many different kinds of higher-education provision. On the one hand 'conventional' institutions are increasing access by moving towards modular degrees which can be taken in a variety of ways, part-time, full-time, resource-based, classroom-based and through distance learning. On the other hand the traditional approach to distance education, based on correspondence materials, broadcasts and video/audio tape supplemented by face-to-face and telephone teaching and counselling, is rapidly being augmented by access through communication technology to other students and staff from home. In addition, the Dearing Report, with its emphasis on skills development in higher education, is also leading to convergence of approaches because there is an increasing demand by employers to identify what it is that graduates 'can do' (the 'graduateness' debate). Even so, diversity has to be maintained for future development and in order to provide students with more options for realizing their potential.

One issue stands out above all others: in an increasingly complex environment with many choices of mode, pace, content and approach to study, there will be greater demand for educational advice and guidance and support. The waste of resources resulting from students choosing the wrong course or programme is significant and needs to be addressed urgently at a national level. Students now more frequently construct their degree profile by selecting modules from a range of institutions, and will in future include some accreditation of their own experience whether it be in the workplace, the home or elsewhere. The provision, by higher-education institutions or preferably by independent institution-sponsored bodies, of objective professional advice, firmly linked to vocation, concerning the best way of constructing a learning profile which can be added to throughout life, is likely to become one of the key measures of quality in the converging world of higher education.

References

Bligh, D. (1971) *What's the Use of Lectures?*, London: University Teaching Methods Unit, London University.

Burt, G. (1997) 'Face to face with distance education', internal OUUK Institute of Educational Technology paper.

Daniel, J. S. (1997) 'The Open University in a new era: reviewing the vision, renewing the mission, refreshing the image', Annex 1 OUUK Academic Board Paper AcB.84/10.

Dearing, R. (1997) *Report of the National Committee of Inquiry into Higher Education*, London: Department for Education and Employment.

HEFCE (1997a) *The Analytical Account: Guidance for Institutions*, Gloucester: HEFCE.

HEFCE (1997b) *Teaching Quality Assessment Process*, Gloucester: HEFCE.

Hollis, P. (1997) *Jennie Lee: A Life*, Oxford: Oxford University Press.

Hunter, R. (1997) 'The Effective Learning Programme', University of Lincolnshire and Humberside. www.http://Home.Ulh.Ac.UK/Ldu/elpview.html.

McNair, S. (1997) *Getting the Most Out of HE: Supporting Learner Autonomy*, London: Department for Education and Employment.

Mills, A. R. and Tait, A. W. (1997) 'The ecology of the Open University', paper presented to the 1997 ICDE Conference, Penn State University.

O'Shea, T., Bearman, S. C. and Downes, A. L. (1996) 'Quality assurance and assessment in distance learning', in R. Mills and A. Tait (eds), *Supporting the Learner in Open and Distance Learning*, London: Pitman Publishing.

Quality Assurance Agency for Higher Education (1998) *Draft Guidelines on Quality Assurance of Distance Learning*, Gloucester: Quality Assurance Agency for Higher Education.

Wagner, L. (1997) Keynote speech to 7th Cambridge International Conference on Student Support in Open and Distance Learning, Madingley Hall, Cambridge, Sept.

7   Convergence of student types

Issues for distance education

*Rick Powell, Sharon McGuire and
Gail Crawford*

Introduction

Educational programmers, in both the conventional and distance-education systems, generally have in their mind's eye a fairly clear notion of who they want to teach and what potential students' needs are. When distance-teaching universities such as Athabasca University (AU) were created in the late 1960s and in the 1970s, the target student population was clear: adults who had not been able to, or did not, take advantage of conventional higher education in their youth and could not use the conventional system in their later years. AU would be their second chance of achieving a university degree. This conception of educational need was in large part predicated on certain assumptions about what conventional, that is, face-to-face classroom teaching institutions were about. Specifically, conventional institutions were designed to serve 'front-end' learners, those entering the system directly from secondary education. The mind-sets that neatly separated the missions and mandates of conventional and distance-education universities and their respective roles in the higher-education system did approximate reality in their day. But this is no longer true.

Changes in student populations are occurring in many post-secondary jurisdictions. For example, at AU, the facts of rapid change are clear. Currently more than 40 per cent of new admissions are students who are concurrently enrolled at other educational institutions. Ten years ago only 17 per cent of new admissions were simultaneously enrolled in AU and in other institutions. In addition, the average age of the AU student population has dropped from approximately 35 years to 31 years over the same period. While, on average, AU's student population is still older than students in conventional universities, the difference has decreased. In conventional institutions, the average age of students is increasing, while in distance education the average age of students is decreasing. Indeed, age appears to be becoming an increasingly irrelevant characteristic in distinguishing between students in conventional and distance education.

This convergence of characteristics between distance and conventional students is not restricted simply to age. Student motivations and behaviour are also converging. Students in conventional universities are increasingly faced with balancing work, family and financial demands with their educational pursuits. As a result they are taking longer to complete their programmes of study and are making use of a variety of institutions to meet their specific programmatic needs. These changes in the behaviour of conventional university students have not arisen out of fickleness. Economic necessity and the need to marry programmes of study more closely to career-development imperatives are driving them. Students may well want to complete a four-year degree programme in four years and to take all their required courses at a single institution, but in today's social and economic climate even the traditional 'front-end' student is simply not able to do that. As a result, the profiles of conventional university and distance-education students are looking increasingly similar.

The convergence between the needs and behaviour of conventional and distance-education students has not necessarily resulted in a convergence of responses by the conventional and distance-education systems. The issue examined here is how distance-education systems, in particular, are positioned to meet emerging student needs and make use of the opportunities afforded. First, the phenomenon of convergence of student types will be examined in more detail. Second, a strategic analysis will be used to examine the position of distance education within the post-secondary education environment. Finally, we shall discuss some of the critical issues arising from these analyses.

Major trends in post-secondary education

Formal education has traditionally been seen as occupying the first twenty or so years of a person's life, after which people would enter the labour force and establish families. In the past, within this traditional framework, people who left school continued to learn and develop new skills. However, they did so largely outside the formal education system. Their days of formal schooling ended, usually, in their late teens or early twenties. This traditional role of formal education, for youth only, has changed markedly even over the last generation. This change is a result of several factors, including:

- the reduction in lifetime or even long-term jobs;
- the increase in two-income families and the need for one spouse to upgrade his/her skills;
- rapid advances in information and technologies;
- the necessity of developing and maintaining a highly trained and flexible labour force to enhance competitiveness in a 'global economy';
- the growth of 'credentialism', that is, the need for formal educational credentials as passports for entry into the job market;

- increasing expectations for students to pay a larger proportion of the costs of their education (for example, tuition fees in Canada rose by 86 per cent in real terms from 1983 to 1995 (Little 1997, p. 2)).

As a consequence of these developments, education is no longer exclusively or even primarily a 'front-end' activity. People need to return to formal education throughout their working lives and even beyond. Adults, once confined to the margins of the formal education sector, are now becoming important players.

Distance education: the third generation

Distance education, almost by definition, has been tied to technology – particularly communications technology. Two-way communication between students and teachers separated by distance only became practicable with the advent of railways and a relatively fast and efficient postal service. This was the first age of distance education. The near-universal access to telephones, radio and television on the part of prospective students in industrialized countries allowed for a variety of communications media, and the advent of the second age of distance education. Nonetheless, the direction of communications was still largely from teacher to student, not the other way around. Moreover, student–student interaction was limited, and in many systems all but impossible.

Garrison (1985) and Nipper (1989) point to a third technological age for distance education – one that comprises the capability for 'real-time' or 'same-time' teacher–student and student–student interaction through audioconferencing, videoconferencing and computerized versions of both. Each author extols the virtues of the technological possibilities inherent within the third age. Garrison seems to approve of such developments from the standpoint of improving teacher–student interaction. Nipper sees such communication possibilities as an enhancement of adult education, which historically has meant much group work.

Peters (1993) is much more concerned than Garrison or Nipper with the characteristics of the 'new-age' student and the consequences of 'post-industrial' society. He does not concentrate on the industrial/technological developments within distance education, but puts together a rather optimistic extrapolation of workplace developments in Germany and in some other European countries during the 1970s and 1980s. The 'third-generation' student, according to Peters, represents a reaction to the Weberian archetype of the Protestant ethic. The deferral of gratification is no more. Moreover, the workplace has been democratized, with a concomitant increase in empowerment.

In the recent literature on distance education, emphasis is placed on technological advances which have moved the production and delivery of course materials out of the mail and railway systems into a highly sophisticated system of interactive communications (Garrison 1985; Nipper 1989). However, Otto Peters looks beyond these technological advances to consider how in the light of such changes students will avail themselves of distance-education opportunities. He envisions a more democratized student who will have increased freedom of education/training choice.

Peters's humanistic optimism seems unfounded from the standpoint of most industrialized countries in Europe and America. Times are harder now – and so are student choices. The 'new student', we submit, is both an amalgam of our notions of front-end students and a throw-back to the traditionally held educational needs of adults.

Student archetypes

As mentioned in the introduction, the development of any educational system, whether conventional or distance, presupposes some conception of the type of students to be served and their educational needs. This conception might be referred to as a student archetype. The development of student archetypes inevitably involves simplifying the complexities of the real world. By putting forward and contrasting two student archetypes – the 'conventional student' and the 'non-conventional student' – we are not making claims for empirical exactness but only arguing that these abstractions have in the past informed, and continue currently to inform, education planning and decision-making across educational systems. The two archetypes to be described may have represented reasonable approximations of reality a generation ago in Canada, but they are increasingly becoming less accurate reflections of student characteristics and expectations as the century closes. Nonetheless, we submit that such archetypes continue to exert a strong influence on the ways both distance and conventional post-secondary institutions think of themselves, their students, their role in society and the ways they operate.

The conventional student

Archetypal conventional students proceed directly from secondary education to post-secondary education. As a result, being engaged in education is the primary, if not the exclusive, occupation of these students. Moreover, the state supports this archetypal student through the heavy public subsidy of post-secondary education. Archetypal conventional students progress through the system in a lockstep fashion. Furthermore, they take four years of highly structured full-time study to earn a four-year degree from a single educational provider. These are the 18–24-year-old students who might be described as 'front-end' learners.

The non-conventional student

Archetypal non-conventional students are adults who have completed their formal education, are participants in the labour force and may have started families and assumed community responsibilities. This archetype is roughly equivalent to other labels and descriptions such as the 'adult learner', the 'second-chance learner' and the 'lifelong learner'. In contrast to conventional students, non-conventional students do not have the luxury of devoting themselves solely to the pursuit of their education. Other work, family and community obligations necessarily intrude and have to be balanced with educational goals. The constraints of time, place and the pacing of studies effectively exclude non-conventional students from participating in most formal education even if formal credentials are desired. Finally, non-conventional students are often not able to rely on a single educational provider to pursue their studies, but have to 'patch together' their programmes through a variety of providers in both formal and non-formal settings. Consequently, they cannot rely on the generous public support afforded to conventional students. Non-conventional students have to be more reliant on the resources provided by themselves or by their employers to pay the costs of their education. Table 7.1 provides a summary of the contrasting archetypes of conventional students and non-conventional students.

Table 7.1 Student archetypes

Characteristic	Conventional	Non-conventional
Age	Under 24 years	25 years and older
Labour-force participation	Not in the labour force	In the labour force
Life roles	Student role is primary role	Student role is one of several competing life roles
Prior learning	Secondary-school education only	A variety of related formal and experiential learning
Need for credentials	Essential	May be important but not essential
Time and place of study	Able to study at institutionally set time and place	Constrained by locations, competing job, family and community obligations
Educational providers	Single institutions	Seek out multiple educational providers
Financial support	Largely public	Largely private

The convergence of archetypes: the emergence of the contemporary student

We have concentrated on contrasting the archetypes of conventional and non-conventional students at the risk of violating empirical accuracy. Conventional students at the end of the twentieth century do not look like or behave like their counterparts of a generation ago. This also holds true for non-conventional students. Nonetheless, traditional archetypes of students still drive the thinking of both distance and conventional educational providers, in defiance of the emerging realities of demands made on post-secondary education. But as these archetypes become increasingly less accurate reflections of student characteristics and educational needs, a new archetype emerges – an archetype that encompasses the elements of both of the older archetypes, but has its own characteristics. We will call this new archetype 'the contemporary student'.

The contemporary student, in part, represents a merging of characteristics of the conventional and non-conventional students (Wallace 1996). The demographics of the older archetypes are blurring. Age profile is becoming less of an issue as the previous age profiles converge. This convergence is a consequence of several factors. Because conventional students are having to bear a rapidly increasing proportion of the costs of their education many delay entry into formal post-secondary systems in order to earn money. Often, many continue to remain in the labour force in order to finance their education, thereby delaying the completion of their studies. In addition, conventional students bring with them other attributes of adult life such as family and community responsibilities. In other words, conventional students begin to look increasingly like non-conventional students and to have similar multifaceted needs. Like non-conventional students, contemporary students have to rely heavily on private (e.g., personal, family and employer) resources to meet the costs associated with their education while balancing competing life roles. Finally, conventional students are being forced to keep future career prospects more firmly in mind in choosing their educational paths.

Convergence of archetypes works both ways. Non-conventional students, while mostly relegated to the non-formal (i.e., non-accrediting) educational sector for upgrading and career development, have recently been driven by economic necessity to strive for programme credentials. Job tenure is becoming more tenuous. Moreover, even highly advanced knowledge and skill sets face becoming redundant – who needs the traditional skills of a typesetter, a stenographer, architectural draughtsman or a COBOL programmer now? Thus, job insecurity extends to career instability, necessitating the continual 'refining' of the labour force to meet arising economic demands. Finally, as the supply of labour outstrips demand both in Canada and in Europe, formal programme credentials have become a coin of increased value for workers changing jobs, if not their careers.

The 'contemporary student' is not just an amalgam of the conventional and the non-conventional student. Contemporary students bring some of the same needs of the older archetypes but they also bring different needs to the higher-education system. For example, contemporary students are apt to ask discomfiting programme-related questions of educational providers that neither conventional nor non-conventional students would pose, such as:

- How well does the subject matter of the course or programme offered fit with my personal programme, career or employer's needs?
- Why do I have to take this course when I already know the content from on-the-job training?
- Are courses available elsewhere that better fit my particular programmatic needs?
- Are courses that meet my needs available elsewhere at lower cost?

In other words, contemporary students are asking hard questions about the value added by educators to the achievement of their current educational and career goals. They are asking both about programmatic offerings and also about whether delivery methods fit in with their constraints on the time, place and pace of study. Contemporary students are forced to become more discriminating about their educational choices because they, or their employers, are footing most of the financial costs and all of the opportunity costs. Table 7.2 summarizes the characteristics of the archetype of the contemporary student.

Table 7.2 The contemporary student

Characteristic	Typical profile
Age	18 years and older
Labour-force participation	Part- to full-time participation
Life role	Must balance competing work, family, community and study obligations
Need for credentials	Very important
Time and place of study	Constrained by locations, job, family and community obligations
Financial support	A combination of public, private and employer support
Programmatic needs	Largely student- and employer-driven

Distance education and the contemporary student

So far in this chapter we have been dealing with trends that affect both conventional and distance education. These trends have resulted in a merging of the conventional and non-conventional student archetypes. These trends have also resulted in the emergence of a new type of student – the contemporary student – common to both conventional and distance education. As noted previously, the convergence of student archetypes does not necessarily mean the strategies used by either sector must also converge. Indeed, their strategies should be different, if each sector pays attention to what it can do best. As distance educators, we shall focus solely on the distance-education sector. To do this, we shall make use of a long-standing analytical tool for strategic planning, the SWOT analysis (Shermerhorn, Cattaneo and Templer 1994). The acronym SWOT stands for the identification of the Strengths and Weaknesses of an organization, as well as of the Opportunities afforded by and potential Threats arising from changes to an organization's economic and socio-political environment.

The social, political, economic and educational environments of distance-teaching institutions vary considerably from country to country. The following SWOT analysis is not comprehensive. Primarily it addresses the emergence of the contemporary student and the ability of distance education to respond. Although our SWOT analysis is rooted in a Canadian context, we submit that the phenomenon of the contemporary student crosses borders, even continents. Also, distance-education institutions share enough strengths and weaknesses to make a generalized SWOT analysis useful even though the particular opportunities and threats arising from place to place may differ.

A SWOT analysis of distance education

Strengths

Post-secondary distance-education institutions are well positioned to respond to the needs of the contemporary learner. Among their strengths are:

- The ability to remove barriers of time and place of study. For example, at Athabasca University there are no entry requirements for most programmes, students can be admitted to and register in courses year-round and study is unpaced. As stated previously, flexibility in study is often critical to the contemporary student who has to balance education with competing job and family demands.
- The fact that complex and multifaceted distance-education systems are no longer the 'new kids on the block'. Collectively such distance-education institutions share over thirty years of experience in designing self-contained educational materials using a variety of technological

modes along with tutorial support systems. These approaches to education have long passed the 'Beta stage' and are tried and true. There is a proven educational track record both in terms of successful teaching of students and the recognition of the value of credentials awarded.

- The ability to accommodate growth without substantial capital investments in classroom space, laboratories, dormitories and so on. Also, growth need not necessitate a concomitant increase in fixed recurrent costs such as academic salaries.
- The ability to utilize off-site academic expertise in materials development. Contributions to distance-education courses and programmes can be made from any place on the planet.
- The cost advantage of virtually eliminating relocation expenses and lost opportunity costs associated with campus-based education. As leaving the job market, even temporarily, becomes a more risky business this cost advantage will increase in importance. Moreover, the marginal costs of bringing in new students in a distance-education system are typically much lower than in the conventional system; for example, you don't need more classroom space to accommodate volume increases. Also, distance-education institutions have the ability to pass on the benefits of their educational economics to students by keeping tuition and ancillary fees down.

Weaknesses

Although offering many advantages to the contemporary student, distance education has weaknesses that may affect its ability to attract students. Some of these are:

- Distance-education organizations have typically been modelled in accordance with management principles first developed by Frederic K. Taylor (1911). Taylorism is well suited to meeting the needs of a mass, undifferentiated educational market. But Taylor's mechanistic approach to management brings with it an inherent inflexibility which makes organizational responses to change, such as the emergence of the contemporary student, difficult. This point will be elaborated later.
- Dependence on economy of scale to recover start-up costs. High start-up costs make small-market courses or courses in subject areas undergoing rapid transition (e.g., tax accounting) exceedingly expensive to offer.
- For economic reasons, there has been a reluctance to revise distance-education materials even when the materials are no longer current or pedagogically sound.
- Distance-education institutions are often unable to benefit from both informal and formal evaluative feedback mechanisms to enhance quality. The separation between the educational provider and the student militates against effective informal feedback. Formal feedback mechanisms

have to be expressly, and expensively, built in. Also, evaluative feedback is difficult to assimilate in a timely fashion.
- Distance education has a limited ability to offer socially significant opportunities for instructor-to-student and student-to-student inter-action given the exigencies of separation in time and place of study. Distance-teaching institutions have tried a variety of ways to re-create the experience of the classroom, the coffee shop or the campus pub, but only at great expense and with uncertain effectiveness.
- Getting locked into high-cost, high-risk technological ventures is a continuing weakness of distance education. This point will be explored later.

Opportunities

Many opportunities for the future will likely be centred on the incorporation of information technologies. Some opportunities are:

- Using such technologies as desk-top publishing to free the organization from the dependence on economics of scale. Large print-runs are not necessary and the time required for course development and revision can be considerably shortened. The potential for realizing technological efficiencies also applies to reducing the costs of adapting materials produced by external parties such as contracted subject-matter experts as well as materials produced by other distance-teaching organizations.
- Computerized course development and production techniques now make it possible to customize course materials to meet niche market needs.
- The introduction of wide-area computer networks (e.g., the Internet and the World Wide Web) allows low-cost synchronous as well as asynchronous student-to-student and student-to-institution interactions. The information resources available on these networks can also compensate for the lack of campus-based library resources. Additionally, commentaries on and contributions to course materials by experts around the world are possible.
- Distance education has always had the advantage of being able to reach students who are geographically dispersed. However, the scope has generally been regional or national. There is now the potential of offering high-quality, interactive distance-education programmes internationally.

Threats

Well positioned as they may be, distance-education institutions face threats that may affect their future viability. Such threats vary from institution to institution, but general concerns include:

- Increased competition from conventional institutions – now a serious factor. The conventional sector is becoming increasingly sensitive to enrolment levels and the tuition revenue they bring in. They are discovering any number of ways to draw students to their doors or to go out to students, and they bring considerable resources to bear in doing so. In the past distance-education providers were 'the only game in town' for adults wanting to pursue their education. This is no longer the case.

• While providing great opportunities for distance education, technology brings at least two threats with it. First, the costs of high technology are difficult to manage and can easily run out of control. Second, the lure of new technology tends to undermine the need for sound educational thinking.

• Although there has been a general trend towards the liberalization of credit transfer among post-secondary institutions in Canada, counter-trends have emerged. There is a system-wide pressure to maintain and increase enrolment levels, and institutions are becoming increasingly jealous of their turf. Distance-education institutions such as Athabasca University are heavily dependent on system-wide credit-transfer opportunities. The erection of barriers to credit transfer represents a real and immediate threat.

Issues to consider

The foregoing SWOT analysis seems to place distance education in a favourable position overall with reference to emerging trends in the educational environment. However, it is easy to become complacent, especially as conventional education must also respond. The following is a set of issues that we feel must be addressed in the near future if distance education is to take advantage of opportunities ahead and mitigate potential threats.

Industrialized education

It seems clear that post-secondary distance-education institutions must move beyond a Taylorist form of industrialized education. This system was once well suited to meeting the needs of an undifferentiated mass market of students who were unwilling or unable to access conventional educational opportunities. Through the establishment of a techno-structure similar to industrial models of line-production and management it was anticipated that courses could be developed, produced and maintained in an efficient manner. Furthermore, efficiency could be measured and thereby be subject to improvement. The line process of production had other advantages: economies of scale resulting in low per-unit costs of course materials; creation of large inventories to service mass markets; and the benefits of a division of labour which allows for the input of experts (e.g., subject matter, instructional design and editorial expertise) into a series of segmented tasks, thus, in theory, maximizing the value of each input.

Nevertheless, the industrialized model of distance education has never been totally successful. From the outset, for example, it has been obvious that the friction between the purposes of 'the academy' and the structure of the organization has never been resolved. Division of labour is the primary Taylorist means of increasing efficiency. But it necessarily fragments the work experience of employees. In addition, collective (and in universities, collegial) efforts to solve problems have been replaced by 'scientific' management techniques and faith in technological solutions.

In order to achieve efficiencies, bureaucratic solutions are offered that further formalize structures and functions. Thus Taylorist solutions can actually exacerbate the problems addressed. Other consequences of the Taylorist approach to the organization of distance-education institutions are becoming increasingly apparent. Among them are the following:

- There is an alienation of academic staff who have found the Taylorist organization antithetical to the ideals of the university as a community of scholars concerned with the organically linked pursuits of teaching, research and public service.
- There are limits to organizational learning, largely due to the difficulty and expense of building effective feedback loops throughout the system.
- Industrialized systems are slow to respond to change – and in particular to changing market demands – due to the complex set of formalized relations and processes that are a key to achieving their goals of efficient mass production.
- There is an inability to meet niche-market needs due to the inflexibility of systems geared to mass markets.
- There are high up-front costs and long project lead times – inevitable in a line-process production system.

As stated before, Taylorism as a management model for distance education, whatever its deficiencies, worked well in the past. But can this set of organizational principles alone respond effectively to the needs and demands of contemporary students?

Programme development

Traditionally, the educational provider has almost exclusively determined programme development in the university sector. Academics developing programmes of study have had to weigh three sets of factors: the need to maintain disciplinary integrity; the needs of the institution, which are usually resource driven; and the perceived needs of students. However, the contemporary student seems less interested in pursuing institutionally prescribed programmes and more intent on customizing their educational programme experience to meet a variety of needs.

The issue of programme development does not end with curricula. It extends to such matters as entry requirements, prerequisites for senior-level courses, residency requirements, pacing and provisions for transfer of credits. All the sub-issues can materially affect the attractiveness of programmes to contemporary students. The challenge, for both the distance and conventional systems of higher education, is to preserve the intellectual integrity of programme offerings while responding to the programmatic needs of contemporary students.

Accreditation

The recognition of prior learning is not an issue for the conventional student archetype except insofar as it relates to entry requirements. With contemporary students, prior learning is critical since students may bring with them a wealth of past learning that may be relevant to their programme of studies. This prior learning may be formal, such as course credits earned at a variety of accredited institutions, or it may be informal, such as on-the-job training or self-improvement courses. Ignoring prior learning obviously makes things more expensive, time-consuming and difficult for the contemporary students. It is also economically inefficient from a systems standpoint. While the issue of accrediting prior learning is certainly not the exclusive preserve of distance education, it is more pressing as distance education typically attracts older students who have had the opportunity to develop a store of prior-learning accomplishments. The accreditation of prior learning may prove to be one of the most thorny issues facing the higher-education sector.

Technology

It is a truism to say that technological change is affecting all of our lives, for good and ill. By definition, distance education is technologically mediated. Managing the financial and educational implications of technological change has become a critical issue for distance education. In the first instance, technology is a powerful cost driver. Rapid depreciation of hardware (computer equipment generally has less than three years of useful life) is not the only economic factor. The need for constant retraining of staff and the restructuring of work processes also has to be factored in. In addition, technology has the tendency to drive educational thinking and decision-making. There is constant pressure to make use of new, glamorous technologies because they are there and it is hoped that they will prove educationally effective. Politically, this tendency has been encouraged in the belief that technology will offer cheap solutions to the problem of increasing costs of education.

The challenge for distance-education institutions is to avoid a messianic faith in the promises of the 'technological fix'. By uncritically adopting high technology, distance-education institutions may well achieve the worst of both worlds: high costs along with inefficient and ineffective development and delivery platforms.

A final note

A generation ago candidate student populations for higher education could be neatly categorized into conventional and non-conventional students. However, student expectations and behaviour have undergone important changes and continue to do so. These changes affect both conventional and distance-education systems equally and are forcing both systems to rethink who their students are and how best to meet their educational needs.

We have tried to encapsulate these changes by referring to the emergence of a newly defined contemporary student: a concept that encompasses the traditional notions of both conventional and non-conventional students. The driving forces behind this convergence of learner types are largely economic. People are re-entering the higher-education system again and again throughout their working lives because they have to. And they are making use of both conventional and distance educational opportunities as best fits their needs.

While the needs and demands of the contemporary student affect all forms of educational provision, the responses of the conventional and distance-education systems will differ as each sector brings with it its own inherent strengths and weaknesses. As distance educators we have been primarily concerned with identifying the position of distance education: its strengths, weaknesses, opportunities and threats in the light of the new demands facing higher education in general.

References

Garrison, D. R. (1985) 'Three generations of technological innovation in distance education', *Distance Education* 6(2): 235–41.

Little, Don (1997) 'Financing universities: "Why are students paying more?"', *Education Quarterly Review* 4(2).

Nipper, Soren (1989) 'Three generations of distance learning and computer conferencing', in Robin Mason and Anthony Kaye (eds), *Mindweave: Communication, Computers and Distance Education*, Oxford: Pergamon Press, pp. 63–73.

Peters, Otto (1993) 'Distance education in a post-industrial society', in D. Keegan, *Otto Peters on Distance Education, the Industrialisation of Teaching and Learning*, London: Routledge, pp. 220–40.

Shermerhorn, J. R. Jr., Cattaneo, R. Julian and Templer, Andrew (1994) *Management: The Competitive Advantage*, Toronto: John Wiley.

Taylor, F. W. (1911) *Principles of Scientific Management*, New York: Harper & Row.

Wallace, Lori (1996) 'Changes in the demographics and motivations of distance education students', *Journal of Distance Education* 11(1): 1–31.

8 Canaries in the mine?

Women's experience and new learning technologies

Jennifer O'Rourke

Introduction

'Canaries in the mine' refers to a practice in which caged canaries kept in underground mines provided a first alert to potential problems. More vulnerable to oxygen deprivation than humans, a canary's death served as a warning of a dangerous gas accumulation, giving miners time to get out before the situation was fatal for them as well. In the same way, some sectors of a community or a society may be the first ones affected by a particular situation. Rather than isolating this group's experience as arising from their 'unique problems', it can be useful to examine how their response may be an indicator of the potential impact of the situation on many more people.

This chapter argues that, by examining the impact of new technologies on women distance learners, we may be able to develop some strategies for scrutinizing the effectiveness of new technologies for the whole range of learners we intend to serve. The issue becomes particularly critical as new technologies become more prevalent in both conventional and distance education and promises of their potential are increasingly persuasive. The elements of open distance learning that address important social factors could be submerged as conventional education adopts its techniques and technologies but not necessarily its social mission.

Defining new learning technologies

Briefly, in this chapter, 'new' learning technologies include the newer electronic technologies that can provide enhanced communication and interaction to support learning. These include:

- communications technologies such as videoconferencing, electronic mail, computer conferencing, and
- technologies that provide access to information, such as the Internet and the World Wide Web.

New learning technologies, like all technologies, are part of a system, as Franklin (1992) points out: 'technology involves organization, procedures, symbols, new words, equations and most of all, a mindset'. And although this chapter refers to some of the newer technologies, it will also consider the organizational dynamics and changes in mind-set that are part of the use of any technology, from books and libraries to the Internet.

Two dimensions: practical aspects and quality of learning

New technologies have implications for the practicalities and the quality of learning – two dimensions that interweave in open and distance education. We can begin by looking at them separately in order to identify specific issues, and then consider how they relate in day-to-day situations. As a practical approach to practical challenges, distance education is a means of serving those most affected by constraints to educational access. For many women, distance learning represents the only option that enables them to pursue education and accommodate their other commitments to work, family and community. And while distance education, especially in Canada and Australia, was initially designed to address issues of physical distance that preclude on-site learning, more recent developments have been prompted by the need to bridge social distances that excluded many adults from further education.

In addition to practical considerations, there is the question of quality and equality of learning. Women have sought to expand the scope of education so that it recognizes their reality and context and accommodates a range of approaches to learning. It is reasonable to expect that new technologies would support, rather than constrict, these achievements.

The practical aspects

For learners, access and cost are two critical factors in determining whether or not they can participate in an educational programme. In Canada, many institutions offer distance education programmes that enable learners to complete their studies without leaving their home community, by using course packages, in some cases supplemented by audioconferenced meetings; these programmes provide a reasonable level of accessibility in the face of physical distance and time constraints. In addition, some also make a concerted effort to address social distance (factors such as limited prior education or language skills; lack of a socially supportive context) by inviting increased community support, providing additional counselling and study-skills help, or developing customized programmes in partnership with agencies in direct contact with learners (Spronk 1995). For the most part, these initiatives depend largely on the human side of the system, rather than the technological side, and involve innovative strategies that require rethinking how people do things within an organization.

In countries where there is limited access to telephone service, much less to other technologies, many distance education programmes include occasional meetings at a study centre and support a more group-oriented approach to learning that is particularly workable for programmes designed for specific cohorts who share a common context, such as teachers or nurses. While there are certainly practical challenges in providing access and in ensuring that materials and tutorial support are available when needed, the key factors are the human and organizational systems, rather than a given technology.

If we look at the particular situation of a sample learner, we can get an idea of whether new technologies actually improve access for that learner. Suppose that Susan is a Canadian teacher who wants to complete a university degree. Because she works full time and has a family, she can take only one course at a time. Most of the courses in the programme are available as independent study packages, so she can work on them whenever she has a chance. She can call her instructor, and does so when she needs advice on a project. Some of her courses also have audioconference meetings, and she has to go to the local college to take part. In some cases there were good discussions among students and instructor: in other situations, the instructor simply lectured for an hour and there was little opportunity for interaction, so she felt it was not worth taking the time and trouble to participate.

Now suppose one of Susan's required courses has a compulsory computer-conferencing component. She will now need access to a computer equipped with a modem and communications software. If her family is one of the 16 per cent of Canadian households fortunate enough to have a computer with a modem, she may be fine, if she can negotiate with her spouse and children to use the computer when she needs to. Otherwise, she may be able to use a computer at school, if she can set aside the time. If she is already computer literate, she will probably have to learn new software for the con-ferencing system, and if not, will have to dedicate even more of her limited study time to learn about the computer itself (cf. Ross et al. 1995). But she also needs to be able to access the university's computer, either directly or through a local service that can connect her to the university. If there is no local service available, she will have to pay long-distance charges to connect to a service provider or the university. And, if she happens to live in a region where there are no private phone lines, she won't be able to take part in the course at all. If the university's computer system is in high demand in the evenings, she may find herself trying to connect at very odd hours, such as 4 a.m. If the conference is structured so that particular topics are addressed within a time frame, such as a week, the pressure will increase to find some way of getting connected and keep up with the course dynamics.

Now suppose the course requires access to the World Wide Web, as some Canadian distance education courses do. How does this affect Susan? She needs access to a computer that has sufficient memory to run software that can find and download material from the Web. She also needs a high-speed modem and a phone connection that has sufficient capacity to transmit Web-based material. Even if the school has a Web connection, there is no guarantee that the appropriate computers and software will be available, given education funding cutbacks.

Or perhaps the course has a required videoconferenced component. But there are many fewer videoconference sites than audioconference locations: satellite transmission is costly and broadband phone lines that can carry a videoconference do not yet reach beyond major urban centres. Even in Canada, where phone use is among the highest worldwide, it is estimated that it will be 2005 before 80–90 per cent of homes and businesses have this kind of service, and the priority will be to provide it to densely populated urban centres rather than rural areas. This means that Susan has to travel at least an hour, one way, often in winter conditions, to reach the video-conference location. The experience is comparable to audioconferencing with the addition of not very clear images on a monitor – sometimes a good discussion, sometimes a lecture with no interaction.

Not only does each of these technologies make access more difficult, they also shift costs to the learners. Many Canadian distance-education insti-tutions have had provisions for learners to have toll-free phone access to instructors, tutors and programme administrators. But as this is replaced by on-line communication, it is the learner who picks up the cost – of owning a computer, of connecting to a local computer communications service provider, and, in many cases, of long-distance charges. If a learner has to travel to a videoconference site, the learner also has significant trans-portation costs. These shifts in responsibility for obtaining and paying for access may not just be the outcome of a particular technology, but may repre-sent a fundamental shift in perspective away from the view that it is the insti-tution's mandate to provide the link to learners.

In many ways, Susan represents a more fortunate learner who has some options for access to technologies. If she were not a teacher, or lived in a rural area, or could not afford the additional costs, or if her first language were not English, new technologies could represent an insurmountable barrier. If this is the situation for a middle-class learner in Canada, what are the chances for a learner where resources and communications systems are much more limited?

Should distance educators be early adopters of technology?

It might be said that the problems outlined above are just the typical chal-lenges to be faced when a technology is first used. The rationale is: 'Sooner or later we'll all have access to this new technology and we will know how to use it. Look at how the use of VCRs grew exponentially so that 80 per cent of households had them a decade after they were introduced. We distance educators should be leaders in the use of these technologies.' This is certainly a well-rehearsed argument. But it begs the question: is it still the purpose of distance education to provide reasonable access to education for those who most need its flexibility? Why is there so much apparent pressure for distance educators to use technologies before they are readily available to learners?

Perhaps some institutions will use a new technology as a convenient means of excluding the more challenging learners. Like the fickle leprechaun in *Finian's Rainbow* who declares, 'When I'm not near the girl I love, I love the girl I'm near', some distance-education institutions may choose to redefine their mandate as serving those who already have technology access and know-how, rather than those who most need the educator to bridge the gap and reach out to them. In that case, it is likely that women learners will be among the first to be left out. Statistics Canada reports that computer ownership is twice as prevalent among two-parent families than single-parent households (the majority of which are headed by women), that computer use at home for on-line services was about 50 per cent greater for men than women, and that women's computer use at work tended to be more for routine clerical tasks than for management or professional communication (Statistics Canada Household and Facilities Survey 1996).

Videoconferencing technologies also present an access conundrum. By making it possible for one instructor to teach learners at several locations, videoconferencing may help the institution offer cost-effective programmes. But its higher costs and specialized equipment usually limit the number of sites, which may not help learners facing time and distance constraints if they must travel to participate in a programme at a particular time. Videoconferencing could provide the appearance of outreach without the reality, and by theoretically satisfying the institution's mission, limit its efforts to explore other ways of providing a genuinely accessible learning experience.

The fact that some new technologies may offer less access than 'old' distance-education technologies should trigger some questions about the purpose of distance education. Practical issues of physical access to learning opportunities are a reality for many adult learners, especially women: dismissing these issues as boring and passé compared to the exciting possibilities of new technologies is a way of limiting how much of the learner's reality is to be accommodated. Depending on one's goals and perspective, using new technologies without addressing access issues can be seen as 'segmenting the market', or as remarginalizing learners who were previously welcomed as those whom distance education was designed to serve. The use of these technologies in on-site education can obscure the issue by creating what appears to be a new clientele for distance learning, but many of these learners are already well served by conventional programmes. The potential drawback of convergence for genuine distance learners is that their needs can be overshadowed by the more commanding virtual and physical presence of on-site learners.

One of the rationales for newer technologies is their potential to enhance the learning experience by allowing for much greater interaction, an element considered important for learner persistence and success. It is worth exploring the extent to which these technologies actually support interaction and other features that contribute to the quality of learning.

Quality of learning

In addition to the practical aspects of accessibility and affordability, there is the question of what is learned and how it is learned. One of distance education's most significant contributions to the field of adult learning is its acknowledgement of the validity of the learner's context as a place to learn and as a source of learning. By making education accessible and enabling learners to incorporate their own reality in their learning, distance education practice has expanded the adult learning principle of valuing the learner's experience. However, this expansiveness is by no means universal, and there have always been opposing viewpoints which maintain that distance education should provide a close replica of the classroom by delivering the same goods to learners, and help them overcome the perceived disadvantage of distance from the source of knowledge.

Maintaining identity

But as Haughey has observed, distance is not necessarily a negative factor to be overcome, but is simply a reality to be recognized. Haughey notes that distance means 'standing apart', and 'in standing apart, we also stand *for* something, whether it is our community culture or our individual uniqueness' (Haughey 1995). For women, who have struggled to establish their own identity in the world of education, this 'standing apart' is particularly significant. As we consider strategies that can establish linkages and provide for communication among learners, we need to be careful that they are not also eroding the distinctiveness of learners' own context and reality. Just as wonderfully unique communities can lose their special charm once they are 'discovered' by tour operators and linked by four-lane highways to 'major centres', learners' particular experience and context can be overwhelmed by words and images delivered from afar. Print, audio and video each carry their own assumptions and authority, but newer technologies, such as Web-based materials, imply additional advantages of currency and inclusiveness, without necessarily offering opportunities for genuine scrutiny or critical reflection.

Supporting holistic learning

Over the past decades, feminist educators and learners have argued for more holistic approaches to learning that value social and cooperative learning, inclusion and validation of experience, and a recognition of the importance of process as well as outcomes. At first glance, it would seem that technologies that provide for more interaction among learners would support these approaches. How well do they fulfil this promise?

Issues of technology accessibility and affordability pose one challenge. If some cohorts of learners may be excluded entirely, and others have limited access, it creates inequities that erode the potential for building cooperative relationships. In non-formal learning situations, there are examples in which those with access to technology find ways of keeping others in the communications loop, but these arrangements depend on learners' time and goodwill, and should not be presumed in situations where it is the educator's mandate to ensure equitable access.

The more positive reports on computer conferencing describe small-enrolment graduate courses: intensive asynchronous seminars are conducted with significant levels of guidance, response and encouragement from instructors or tutors, who indicate that they invested considerably more time in these courses than in conventional classroom or distance courses (Burge 1994; Rossner and Egan 1995; Tagg and Dickinson 1995; Weisenberg and Hutton 1996). This latter observation indicates it might be worthwhile to explore the effect on learner satisfaction and success if the same level of support was provided in conventional distance education as in these technology-based courses. Women respond very positively to opportunities for social learning and support in distance education, and particularly value personal contact (von Prummer 1993, 1995). When this type of student support is curtailed due to financial cutbacks (Brindley 1995) at the same time as there are significant investments in new technology systems and technology-based courses, it raises questions about priorities. An assessment of the impact of a new technology should take into account the non-users who are affected by the diversion of attention, resources and funding away from activities that had supported them.

Trust and privacy

Situations in which learning includes integration of life experience often raise issues of trust and respect for privacy. As one women's studies instructor noted, participants in an audioconference or videoconference do not know who may be at other sites, making it more difficult to ensure the kind of safe environment that enables learners to speak about personal reflections and experience. People who are not part of the group may drop in unnoticed, perhaps to observe the technology in action, but potentially disrupting the group dynamic. (I was told about one case in which someone from outside the class sat in on a conferenced women's studies class unknown to participants at other sites, and made derogatory remarks about the discussion to people at his site.) Computer conferences can be vulnerable to unauthorized bystanders, if members of a household share one computer account and password. Some of these situations could be addressed with careful attention to protocols and to process, but they require a commitment on the part of the educational institution to ensure that its systems truly support trustful inter-action among learners and instructors. In a climate in which technologies are shifting accountability for access and costs to learners, this commitment seems less likely.

The packaging of knowledge

An even more challenging issue is the extent to which new technologies shape knowledge and give it authority. For those who believe in the cargo-cult approach to distance education, using any particular technology to 'deliver' knowledge may not be a problem, but for those who regard learning as a dynamic process which includes learners' reflections and reality, technologies that package information have many drawbacks. Gains made by distance educators and feminist educators in enabling more holistic experiential approaches to learning could be threatened if new technologies preclude that which cannot be easily transmitted in a crisp comment in an electronic conference, or presented on a web page. If learners' ability to make their own insightful connections is superseded by pre-made linkages on a website, what has been gained and what has been lost in terms of development of capability and confidence? And if women are less likely than men to find their reality reflected in traditional academic literature, is it more likely they will find it on the Web, where men are still the majority of authors and users?

Conclusions

This chapter has touched on some of the issues that new learning tech-nologies raise for women. These technologies will only be a benefit for women if they genuinely accommodate practical needs for flexible learning, allow for the inclusion of women's reality and support women's preferred approaches to learning to the same extent as current distance education strategies. Of course, it is to be hoped that the new technologies will represent an improvement on all counts, but I will leave it to technology's promoters to demonstrate that.

Exploring how women learners are affected by new technologies can help us develop strategies for comparing these technologies with current approaches to serving many other learners who need accessible, affordable and meaningful learning opportunities. Convergence could mean greatly expanded options for many more learners, or it could result in the strati-fication of programmes and segregation of learners based on funders' enthusiasm for the technology and learners' access to resources.

On behalf of learners, we have the right to scrutinize technologies and ask questions, such as:

- How does this technology help provide learning to those whom it is our mandate to serve?
- Are there trade-offs, in terms of access, cost, quality of learning, in using this technology?
- What are the benefits of this technology, and are these benefits important to our learners?
- Will using this technology redefine the teaching/learning interaction, and is this desirable?
- Does this technology broaden or narrow the possibilities for teaching/ learning approaches?
- Is the adoption of technology being used to change organizational assumptions or systems (for example, shifting more costs to the learner, reducing tutorial staff, etc.)?

More general societal questions also come to mind:

- Are new learning technologies being used to reverse gains that have been made in broadening access to education?
- Is technology being used as an excuse to redefine what it means to serve people's educational needs, particularly of those most vulnerable to constraints?
- Who stands to benefit from the increased use of technology in learning?
- How does using new technologies relate to the commercialization of education?
- What does increasing use of new communications technologies mean for countries that have limited resources and must serve large numbers of learners?

On the other hand, we could simply abandon the long-standing social mission of distance education to enhance access to quality learning, and seek out more durable canaries.

References

Brindley, J. (1995) 'Learners and learner services: the key to the future in open and distance learning', in J. Roberts and E. Keough (eds), *Why the Information Highway? Lessons from Open and Distance Learning*, Toronto: Trifolium.

Burge, E. (1994) 'Learning in computer conferenced contexts: the learner's perspective', *Journal of Distance Education* 9(1): 19–43.

Franklin, U. (1992) *The Real World of Technology*, 1990 CBC Massey Lectures, Toronto: Anansi.

Griffin, V. (1988) 'Holistic learning/teaching in adult education: would you play a one stringed guitar?', in T. Barer-Stein and J. Draper (eds), *The Craft of Teaching Adults*, Toronto: Culture Concepts.

Haughey, M. (1995) 'Distinctions in distance: is distance education an obsolete term?', in J. Roberts and E. Keough (eds), *Why the Information Highway? Lessons from Open and Distance Learning*, Toronto: Trifolium.

Menzies, H. (1996) *Whose Brave New World? The Information Highway and the New Economy*, Toronto: Between the Lines.

Ross, J. A., Crane, C. A. and Robertson, D. (1995) 'Equity of access to computer-mediated distance education', *Journal of Distance Education* 10(2): 17–32.

Rossner, V. and Egan, K. (1995) 'Using computers in teaching sophisticated conceptual material', in A. Tait (ed.), *Putting the Student First: Learner Centred Approaches in Open and Distance Learning*, collected papers of the 6th Cambridge International Conference on Open and Distance Learning, the Open University, Cambridge.

Spronk, B. (1995) 'Appropriating learning technologies: aboriginal learners, needs, and practices', in J. Roberts and E. Keough (eds), *Why the Information Highway? Lessons from Open and Distance Learning*, Toronto: Trifolium.

Tagg, A. and Dickinson, J. (1995) 'Tutor messaging and its effectiveness in encouraging student participation on computer conferences', *Journal of Distance Education* 10(2): 33–55.

von Prummer, C. (1993) 'Women friendly perspectives in distance education', keynote presentation to International WIN Conference, Umeä, Sweden.

von Prummer, C. (1995) 'Putting the student first? Reflections on telecommunications and electronic strings', in A. Tait (ed.), *Putting the Student First: Learner Centred Approaches in Open and Distance Learning*, collected papers of the 6th Cambridge International Conference on Open and Distance Learning, the Open University, Cambridge.

Weisenberg, F. and Hutton, S. (1996) 'Teaching a graduate program using computer-mediated conferencing software', *Journal of Distance Education* 11(1): 83–100.

9 A worthwhile education?

Pat Rickwood in collaboration with
Vicki Goodwin

Introduction

The intention in this chapter is to offer a perspective on the nature of the student experience within the higher education system in the UK over the three decades between the Robbins (1963) and the Dearing (1997) reports – a period of volatility and change, not least in the student experience and the way that the paths followed by full-time and part-time students have begun to converge.

Because any comparison of changing academic environments is necessarily largely qualitative, it is important to begin by setting out some facts. In terms of the extent of the student body, only 10 per cent of the 18–21 cohort (120,000) entered higher education in 1969, compared with 37 per cent (540,000) in 1997, and the number of the places to which they went rose from 43 institutions with the title 'university' in 1968 to 110 in 1997. In addition, the radicalizing innovations represented by the Open University (OU), the Council for National Academic Awards (CNAA) and the polytechnics did not appear until well after Robbins. In short the typical student experience of the early 1960s sprang from an environment that was relatively small, traditional and closed, in the sense that virtually all students were young and attended full-time. The number of part-time students was insignificant (so small indeed that official statistics do not record it), and insofar as they existed at all they were catered for within the London University External programme, by Birkbeck College, or through the minuscule extramural provision made by a few other universities. Thirty years later the Higher Educational Statistical Agency (HESA) returns show that over half of all first-degree students are now either part-time, mature or both. The OU itself adds upwards of 10,000 to the graduate population annually, and at least eleven other universities each admit more than 5,000 part-time undergraduates every year.

These facts help support the contention that the student experience in the Robbins era was of a different qualitative order from that found in the 1990s. What follows is a discussion of the social and institutional pressures over the intervening years that have contributed to this change in ethos and the process whereby full-time and part-time students increasingly came to share similar experiences. The change may in part be explained by the very growth of higher education – a process of semi-massification in student numbers and professional aggrandizement – but also to the different zeitgeists found during this period. Robbins signalled the dawning of a time of confidence, growth and rising resource. New greenfield universities were established, new disciplines entered the academic taxonomy, and grants, salaries and capital investment all rose in a way that is inconceivable nowadays. By the 1980s this mood of optimism had all but evaporated as the political agenda focused on a continued growth in student numbers but with no extra resources, funding the increase by so-called 'efficiency gains' and declining working conditions. A sort of pessimistic stoicism was perhaps the most characteristic mood to be found amongst academics as they awaited Sir Ron Dearing's proposals.

A brave new world?

This short scene-setting forms the context of the analysis that follows – one that takes as its starting point the assertion by Philip Healy (1994) that the funding crisis in higher education is threatening to destroy one of the pillars of our civil society. Even if we reject such a dramatic claim there can be no argument that a clash of cultures has taken place over recent years which in turn has triggered a fundamental teleological debate about university education. Ian McNay's four-part typology of institutional cultures (collegium; bureaucracy; corporation; enterprise) is well known (1995), whilst Stephen Yeo (1996) sees two contrasting paradigms competing for acceptance. What he calls the developmental humanist one accommodates concepts such as culture, aspirations, expectations, judgements, values, context and diversity. He terms this the 'primitive' view, in which there are beneficiaries rather than customers, and academic standards are grounded in reasoned argument rather than quantification. Opposed to this is what he calls the systems-fetishism paradigm, with a culture of measurement and accountability at its core, articulated through concepts such as competencies, skills, audit, ranking, uniformity, outcomes and results. The humanist paradigm is more diffuse and has rested traditionally on the moral authority of peers – the notion of the academic community pre-eminently – in contrast to the second, which represents the bureaucratic authority of the organization. We do not have to agree with Yeo's preference to find something of value in this distinction, although rather than being mutually exclusive, perhaps it is more sensible to see them struggling to cohabit? Might it be that current political, economic and social pressures are inexorably moving higher education away from valorizing the ideal of a clerisy towards a grudging and partial admiration of market values? This was the motif running through a recent analysis of higher education, broadcast on BBC Radio 4.

In the three-part series David Walker (1996) continually drew on such a contrast, often putting it in generational terms as between retiring and rising academics. Rachel Trickett, the novelist and academic, spoke about the need for academia to go back to its real purpose – the so-called 'narrative of return' – and rediscover its sense of moral commitment, its 'civilizing mission' and its dedication to 'the inner life'. During the discussion she put it thus: 'at the end of the day universities must discover what is good, not what is good for *them*' (whoever *they* might be) – even if this leads to what Alan Tuckett of the National Institute for Adult and Continuing Education half-jokingly referred to as 'an inchoate, seriously-useless education' (Tuckett 1996). One assumes the serious part of this statement makes the point that *no* education is useless, but what 'useless' *actually* means is that its utility is not immediately apparent – a point Mary Warnock had made several times over in her earlier pamphlet *Universities: Knowing Our Minds* (1989). Much of this debate was of course prefigured in Robbins, particularly in respect of the criteria which sought to promote 'the general powers of the mind' and notions of 'a common culture and citizenship'.

Certainly no one can doubt that from the mid-1970s the thrust of policy has been to superimpose an organizational culture upon the more humanistic one, and central to this new philosophy of metrics (to use Sir Ron Oxburgh's phrase, quoted by Walker (1996)) is the notion of 'critical review'. The process springs partly from the managerial task of doing more with less, but just as important are its ideological roots in the capitalist market process. Thus universities are seen as belonging to the weightless economy, providing marketable benefits such as knowledge, skills, guidance, credentials and employment opportunities to a range of customers who are principally their undergraduate and postgraduate students but also include corporate bodies in commerce, industry and the public sector, and their local population. This in turn has conjured up apocalyptic visions of the 'death of the university', as discussed in Ronald Barnett's most recent text (1997) and in Walker's (1996) analysis: 'No longer the disinterested pursuit of truth. The lust for money and for students has made them [the universities] ordinary. Fearful of government and subservient to business, they have bought too heavily into "what is", and given up on "what ought to be".'

There are at least two reasons why this commodification of higher education is such a difficult undertaking. The first is because the full cost is not paid directly by students, whether they are full-time or part-time, and therefore the market principle cannot really work. This in turn creates a fundamental contradiction: on the one hand, the social and economic improvement of society apparently requires an increasing access to higher education, whilst on the other hand a properly functioning market dictates that producers charge a price which at least covers their costs, and many potential customers of higher education are either unwilling or incapable of entering the market if they have to pay this true cost themselves. The first part of this contradiction suggests a mass system; the second suggests an elite one (Shattock 1996). The second reason questions the relevance of the market model from another direction, because the needs of a student are more complex than may be satisfied within the cash nexus. If you buy a car from Ford the company undertakes to replace it if it proves unsatisfactory. If they have sold you a bad car, then they will take it back and give you a good one. No university has yet devised a way of matching this sort of customer care, taking back a lower degree and giving something better in its place. The relationship cannot work like that because the 'price' the student pays includes a large intellectual and emotional payment over a considerable period of time, and is therefore not refundable.

The significance of the institution

The 1992 Higher Education Acts marked the creation of an enlarged and more unified university system in the United Kingdom. All polytechnics and several colleges of higher education received university status, and the Open University ceased to be a direct client of the government but was subsumed within the general (new) funding regime. The Council for National Academic Awards was wound up and its powers of validation more widely distributed. A plethora of bureaucracies such as the national funding councils, the Quality Assurance Agency, the HESA and the Teacher Training Agency were then created in order to resource, monitor and police this brave new world that was 'often futilely competitive and mindlessly managerial' (Pratt 1997) and preoccupied with funding, student numbers, research and teaching assessments. Although suffused by a competitive neurosis it has never been more than a simulacrum, steered and managed by this raft of agencies rather than springing spontaneously from market forces. Thorne and Cuthbert's contribution in *Working in Higher Education* (1996) makes interesting reading in this respect. In it they debate the whole notion of the 'appropriateness of market mechanisms and the utility of managerialism in [a] highly professionalised organization' (p. 170), and refer to Witzel's observation that two prerequisites for properly functioning markets are an adequate flow of resources and an adequate capacity for growth in order to stimulate and maintain competition – neither a characteristic of higher education in this country at the moment.

Institutions have sought a further competitive edge through devices such as Investors in People or British Standard kitemarks, in a sort of internal mimicry of this external control and audit. Gradually the old humanist discourse has been lost in a managerialist vocabulary of benchmarks, cost centres, performance indicators and stakeholders (Power 1996), perhaps because there has been a slow acceptance of the argument that the kind of restructuring experienced in other parts of the economy must necessarily wash over education as well. 'It's happening in the real world' we sometimes say, although it is interesting to ask why universities, with their vocation of disinterested research and employing some of the country's best intellectual talent, seem incapable of offering their own larger solutions to the problem. (Perhaps because they are still largely dependent on paymasters for whom such considerations are irrelevant?) It is also fair to say that these changes have been embraced by many of their staff with an appropriate enthusiasm, because such a brave new world is one ripe for colonization, offering the chance to develop careers and build reputations when such opportunities are drying up elsewhere. This element of personal advantage should not be ignored because it helps fuel the process from within the institution and encourages the growth of a vested interest that may be increasingly difficult to dislodge.

All this matters because the student experience is inseparable from its institutional setting. Although it does not determine every part of this experience, the setting necessarily provides both a context and a paradigm (see McDowell (ed.) 1991). Personal reflection tells you as much – most of us are held in thrall to some extent by the remembrance of our own student days. Indeed, this may be one of the sources of the alienation currently flowing through higher education. 'Most academics have a loyalty and a commitment to a higher education system that no longer exists' (Hounsell 1996), and one need only look to the writings of Mary Warnock or Christopher Ball (1985) to read similar sentiments.

Nowadays the notion of joining a clerisy when entering university must seem rather quaint. Contemporary discussion is much harder-edged. Three elements of this new discourse – quality, standards and accountability – are relevant to this study, because together they form the core of the institution's contribution to the learning experience (Alderman 1996). In fact there is nothing particularly new about this in the sense that peer review, external examining and entry standards for careers like medicine and the law have long been seen as ensuring a consistent quality, and a notional equality between qualifications and universities. With the increase in the number of institutions and the expansion of the student population from the 1960s onwards, other devices such as the CNAA came to be employed, awarding the imprimatur that ensured the necessary parity of esteem with universities for local authority sponsored polytechnics and colleges. This binary approach was based on the reasoning that you could be equal whilst still being different, and that one could establish some generally agreed standards of achievement. However, there is little comparability of *provision* between institutions, and variations in the unit of resource manifest themselves across the campus, from libraries and laboratories through to social and sporting facilities. Clearly such disparities can have a marked effect on the interaction between the institution, its staff and the student. Good facilities that attract and retain high-calibre staff should combine to provide a better learning experience for the student, creating a 'virtuous circle' that further enhances the institution's reputation and drawing power. Thus whilst we may argue that full-time and part-time experiences are moving closer, it could also be argued there is a tendency towards divergence amongst full-time campus-based students, depending on the standing of their institution.

Rights, responsibilities and outcomes: the contribution of the student

Before considering the contribution the student makes to fashioning the learning experience we need to unpack the semantics of that expression a little. 'Experience' may be used in two ways. One denotes the acquisition of some knowledge, skill or observation, which we will call the credentialist side of experience. Thus we refer to 'an experienced teacher', or comment on a probationer that she 'is inexperienced'. The second side has to do with undergoing, meeting with or being affected by some influence, as in 'that was a nasty experience'. This may be called the dispositional side of experience. Both are represented in the student contribution.

The vividness of the student experience is well documented in anecdote and research, as illustrated by these two rather negative references. In his autobiography *A Gorbals Boy at Oxford* (1988) Ralph Glasser described how as a working-class youth from Glasgow he won a place at Oxford in the 1930s and was taught by figures such as R. A. Crossman and A. D. Lindsay. The book is suffused by his resentment at what he saw as their arrogance and condescension. He recalled on one occasion being invited to a conversazione at Balliol in support of Basque refugees, only to discover when he arrived the reason why Lindsay had included him on the guest list. 'He led me round the room, a prize working class exhibit, as if to declare "who says we are out of touch with the workers"?' (p. 23). Today this situation can be found replicated in relation to ethnicity and gender also. A recent survey by the Institute for Employment Studies (1996) claimed that many ethnic minority students, particularly female ones, choose to avoid 'traditional' universities in favour of ex-polytechnics because of the image the former had as reservoirs of sexism, heavy drinking and cliqueishness. One of the researchers was quoted as saying:

> There is a class and cultural difference at old universities which affects minorities. Many have told us they felt under pressure to 'act white' as they put it. Asian girls who wore traditional dress felt uneasy. They also felt it was hard to explain that they did not want to go to the pub all night and that their culture meant they did not drink and went home early.

The survey also found that such students felt they were destined for poorer degrees than were white contemporaries of similar ability.

From the perspective of the university there is only one unfettered right within the institution/student relationship, that of choosing whether to admit a particular individual. From then on virtually all its actions are constrained by some obligation or responsibility towards that individual, up to the awarding of qualifications or the writing of references. The fashion for student charters is one expression of this responsibility; another example, admittedly still relatively rare, is the involvement of the law. A consequence of the Data Protection Act is that most institutions now make available the detail of their assessments, and this transparency gives students the opportunity to challenge failures or even classifications. The consumer culture has generally made students aware they have 'rights' and are 'owed' certain things, and indeed many institutions heighten these expectations by continually embellishing their advertising and prospectuses, even when it becomes harder each year to deliver on such undertakings.

Most entrants volunteer to go into higher education. Whatever parental or peer influences are at work, in the end they make a personal choice which presumably is based on promises, expectations, hopes or assumptions. So at this point it is worth considering two different models of student behaviour. One is the transactional model, which sees the student as a rational actor, making a sequence of decisions based on the weighing of costs and benefits. If universities operate within a competitive quasi-market it would seem logical for their students to seek assurances about the outcomes they may gain. They might well say, 'If I, or a third party, pay you a sum of money, and I undertake the requisite study under your direction, what will I obtain?' Invariably the institution would pledge a qualification appropriate to the study undertaken, and most would vouch for its benefit in securing employment. This is the transactional model in a nutshell, and any significant failure to deliver has the potential to involve legal recourse. 'Hard lessons in litigation: colleges that don't deliver what their prospectuses promise are likely to be sued by students with the help of a new breed of lawyers' (Hodges 1997). 'More and more students are taking legal action in order to pursue their grievances. Cases are beginning to flood into the courts, while universities and colleges brace themselves for an onslaught of litigation' (Green 1996).

The other model is more developmental – what Garland (1995) calls the achievement of epistemological autonomy. It portrays the student as self-consciously developing and growing intellectually, emotionally and experientially. Seeing each other in court is not what this model is about because it stresses reciprocation, and expects the student to be more active and responsible. It is more open-ended and variable and less prescriptive and specific. Garland argued it was about surrounding new students with enough support and guidance for them to grow in confidence and expertise, securing autonomy in their study to the extent that they might want to experiment, branch out or take risks. From the nature of this process the institution cannot necessarily be held responsible for its outcomes. It may help, facilitate, encourage and warn, but it cannot really make happen. It is tempting to see correlations between the humanistic ideal of the university and the developmental model of student behaviour on the one hand, and between the mechanistic approach and the transactional model on the other, but this is too simplistic; it would perhaps be more accurate to view the student experience as a hybrid of the two. To be a seeker after enlightenment does not prevent one from expecting certain standards of efficiency, consistency and objectivity – or indeed from desiring credentials and the opportunity to gain satisfying employment.

The student experience is also an elusive concept in that it is embedded within an institution without being totally *of* it (Hazelgrove (ed.) 1994). It contains many different elements, some of which have to be contributed by the individual. Personal qualities such as motivation, organization, effort, consistency, confidence and resilience can vary enormously, so that it is perfectly feasible for a multiplicity of experiences to be drawn from the same setting. However, facilitating the quality of the student experience should not be beyond the competence of an institution. At the least it should provide students with a supportive, secure environment, effectively managed, which they can then use to fashion something larger, which might be perhaps a mood, an emotion, a belief or a capacity as much as an achievement or a proof.

At this point it is worth asking whether there is anything nowadays which is clearly a *student* culture, as opposed to a more prevalent youth culture. Now that more students are having to live at home rather than away, or having to take paid work in order to survive, and bearing in mind the ubiquity of the pub and the disco, the existence of a distinctive student world may be a nostalgic misconception of 50-something academics. (Observations along these lines were made during a seven-programme series broadcast on BBC Radio 4 in February/March 1997. Entitled *The University*, it was a fly-on-the-wall documentary about life on the University of Warwick campus.) However, two ideas enjoying some currency are those of 'studentship' and 'graduateness'. Studentship seems a notion whose modishness is matched only by its opacity. Can there be some way of being a student that is different from the *experience* of being a student? Perhaps, in the sense of a predisposition which is required for the undertaking similar to a calling for the priesthood. Beyond that studentship possibly assumes characteristics such as self-confidence, an openness to criticism, a receptivity to new ideas and a rejection of collusion or fraud, alongside an appropriate sense of intellectual humility. Then it becomes difficult to see it composed of anything more than generalities, or attributes one might possess at some moments but not at others, as one's moods change. However, the concept is perhaps useful in signalling that unlike ordinary consumers, whose only responsibility is to pay the price of whatever they buy, students cannot simply purchase their higher education. They need to help produce it.

Education depends on the effort that students make as well as the leadership and support staff provide. Students are producers as well as consumers of their own learning. Knowledge is no longer delivered as largely fixed, but is transformed and created in the education process.

Education is no longer something that happens to you. It is something you do. . . . If we achieved this, we would be recovering and reclaiming traditions lost in higher education, traditions that have been undermined and devalued in the rush to the market-place.

(Fitzgerald 1996)

'Graduateness' is the other side of being a student, and is perhaps a more recognizable condition. After all, all graduates are such in the sense that they receive formal certification, but what is not so clear is whether all graduates are *graduates*. In this sense it is a statement about value, worth or expertise, rather than status. It is also a crucial question to ask of higher education providers – what *do* they produce from all the resources, time and effort involved? One approach is to define the product in terms of three interlocking kinds of attainments: of core skills, general cognitive skills and personal transferable skills. Another is to establish four sorts of outcomes: those of a trained mind, of being an educated person, of developing personally and of accepting the principle of lifelong learning (Pring 1996; for a more sceptical view, see Hyland 1997). At the time of writing the Higher Education Quality Council (1995, 1996) was attempting to work towards an agreed definition of the term (i.e., the Graduate Standards Programme), but in the meantime one might propose something of three parts: a public record of achievement, evidence of intellectual and social development, and a growth of self-confidence. If a person feels that their study has helped them in these directions then their experience of study must have been reasonably positive and beneficial.

The part-time and mature student perspective

So far we have looked at the student experience in a rather generic way, as it relates principally to a full-time, campus-based school leaver. HESA statistics actually show this to be a distortion because nearly half of those taking award-bearing courses nowadays are either part-time students, mature students or both. Clearly the part-time and/or mature experience is likely to be a very different one. First, even if one ignores any work commitments they might have, a mature student's education is typically only one part of a crowded and demanding life shared with partners, parents, children, neighbours, relatives and friends. Second, when they begin their studies they may lack personal or social confidence in a new setting or the study skills needed to buttress their position. This in turn might encourage them to retreat into a sort of ghetto, where they find comfort and mutual support amongst their peers. On the other hand they are able to mobilize a wealth of other experience to inform their student persona. One obvious result of this is that they tend to be more articulate, even vociferous, more enthusiastic about their studies, more driven to succeed. By the same token, because they come from many different places to arrive at the same starting point, they will be a more heterogeneous group than the typical cohort of school leavers, banded almost entirely by their A-level grades.

The breadth of the mature student experience has been considered in several recent pieces of research – particularly an NIACE-sponsored study by Veronica McGivney, Linden West's work on the motivations of adult students in higher education (both published in 1996), and a more colloquial account published by the University of Lancaster in their 'Innovation in Higher Education' series (Arksey, Marchant and Simmell 1994). McGivney synthesized a range of institutional or wider studies and although her principal concern was to investigate the issues of non-completion and retention, some of the material she brought together also reflected on the familiar problems of preparation, outside commitments, travel and, crucially, finance. She also made the point that some groups of mature students (for example, those on franchised courses or part-timers) were distinctly short-changed in terms of their study environments. The set of narratives edited by Arksey, Marchant and Simmell had the title *Juggling for a Degree*, which sums up the theme running through the different accounts, that most of the contributors had continually to balance competing commitments. 'Struggle, struggle, and more struggle', in the words of one of them. Even the financial strains of being a full-time student, worries about 'meeting the standard' or how to get back into the job market after graduation, all came second to finding the time. In fact the authors claim in their foreword that 'there is no common denominator in mature students' experiences' and that 'the "typical" mature student appears to exist only as figment of the imagination', although it is interesting to read the postscript to each narrative and discover that one common result was to want to continue to be a student. Most were intending to take, or were already studying on, masters' or doctoral programmes, or for professional qualifications.

Linden West's research used a methodology of biographical, longitudinal and reflexive analysis – a kind of 'secret history' or 'private lives' approach. The book contains a wealth of empirical material from which was constructed a 'narrative over time' centred on the personal and social dialectics involved.

> Many learners appear to experience fragmentary, even fragmenting processes in which the self becomes divided, to greater or lesser degrees, between private lives (as a parent or partner) and public spheres (as a student in higher education); and between experiential ways of knowing (personal, subjective, emotional) and academic knowledge (objective and abstract).
>
> (West 1996, p. ix)

Not surprisingly, if asked to make a choice between vocational or personal motives, most people will tend to give vocational justifications for their actions rather than anything more 'personal'. It is more respectable and acceptable to talk in such terms. These 'findings' are then used to reinforce the ideologically driven notion that higher education should serve primarily vocational and instrumental ends.

(ibid., p. 2)

West discusses what he calls this 'profound tautology' in the orientation of the students covered by his study, who were 'mirroring in their responses the rationalisations for educational participation most dominant and respectable in the wider culture, and in the process excluding, even repressing, the more personal parts of a story' (ibid.). He claims that this disjuncture creates 'a danger of being lost', and against this threat he argues that 'higher education is potentially a space in which to manage and transcend feelings of marginalisation, meaninglessness and inauthenticity in interaction with others; . . . to compose a new life, a different story and a more cohesive self' (ibid., p. 10). In short, he valorizes higher education because it offers mature students the opportunity for personal development and discovery – thus echoing, perhaps unintentionally, the views of commentators such as Warnock, Ball, Trickett and Walker.

Aspects of convergence

Up to this point the discussion has concentrated on the reasons why the students' experience has changed over the past thirty years and why by general consent it has deteriorated. As a significant proportion of the student population are now neither full-time in their studies nor particularly young, we must now focus more closely on this cohort, to consider some of the evidence for the convergence which is bringing it closer to the younger, full-time experience.

Finance is one such area. The apparent inequity of part-timers having to pay tuition fees whilst full-timers, however financially endowed, did not has now been corrected, albeit by demanding a portion of the cost of study from both. In addition, the burden of their maintenance is increasingly to be shifted on to the shoulders of full-timers, eroding their privileged position further.

Non-completion is another point of convergence, as the Society for Research into Higher Education (SRHE) has found. Traditionally this has been higher amongst part-timers but the current concern is about increasing full-time withdrawal rates, with some estimates putting the figure at 60,000 a year (SRHE/*Independent* 1998). Debt and financial worries are not the only reasons cited for this increase. Uninspired teaching, poor accommodation and the lack of pastoral support are also blamed, all issues with which part-timers, typically studying at the margins of an institution, have had a long acquaintance!

More flexible entry, exit and transfer and switches between modes of study (full-time; part-time; day/evening; part-time sharing with full-time, etc.)

emphasize the importance of credit accumulation and transfer, traditionally a concern of the mature student but now affecting younger ones as well as they struggle to handle their debts by finding employment. Indeed, some institutions no longer maintain a distinction between full-time and part-time students. At the University of Wolverhampton, for example, students are allowed to alter the pace of their study according to inclination or circumstance, so they may begin by studying four modules in one semester, drop to two the next, then move to three and back to four, thus moving from full-time to part-time and back. Thus the flexibility of study modes, engineered to meet changing circumstances, can be seen as another example of convergence. Pedagogic methodologies, too, are increasingly shared. Computer-mediated learning, forms of electronic communication (the Internet being the most obvious example) and various formats for distance learning are all contributing to a greater commonality of learning.

Finally there has been an alteration in expected outputs. An increasing number of part-time students in mid-life now are keen to enhance their employability in whatever way they can rather than simply fostering personal development (which has been the characteristic extra-mural mission), whilst debt, credit transfer and the flexibility of methods and modes may all encourage younger students to convert to part-time at some point in their study. The most recent evidence from UCAS indicates that there has been a significant drop in full-time applications from older people, down nearly 24 per cent between 1997/8 and 1998/9, and if many of these lost applicants turn to part-time routes instead this will also aid convergence by bringing numbers of students in each mode closer to equilibrium.

In these ways and others there has been a drawing together of experiences which were once very different. Convergence, however, is one thing; how and why it takes place is another. The worry is that rather than incorporating some of the richness and depth of the full-time experience into that of the part-time student, both will be driven by rising demand and falling resource to consolidate around a much lower point. Thirty years on from Dearing, will it be more meaningful to refer to a person who studies, rather than a student?

References

Alderman, G. (1996) 'The golden irretrievable', *The Times Higher Education Supplement*, 1 Nov., p. 12.

Arksey, H., Marchant, I. and Simmell, C. (1994) *Juggling for a Degree: Mature Students' Experience of University Life*, Innovation in Higher Education series, University of Lancaster.

Ball, C. (1985) *Fitness for Purpose: Essays in Higher Education*, Guildford: SRHE and NFER-Nelson.

Barnett, R. (1997) *Higher Education: A Critical Business*, Buckingham: Open University Press.

Dearing (1997) *Higher Education in the Learning Society: The Report of the National Committee of Inquiry into Higher Education* (The Dearing Report), London: HMSO.

Fitzgerald, M. (1996) 'Traditions lost in the market-place', *The Times Higher Education Supplement*, 22 Nov., p. 12.

Garland, M. R. (1995) 'Helping students achieve epistemological autonomy', paper presented to the ICDE conference, Birmingham, UK.

Glasser, R. (1988) *A Gorbals Boy at Oxford*, London: Chatto & Windus.

Green, J. (1996) 'Going to law to save your career', *Independent*, 22 Aug., Education Supplement, p. 23.

Hazelgrove, S. (ed.) (1994) *The Student Experience*, Buckingham: SRHE/Open University Press.

Healy, P. (1994) Opening address to Higher Education Foundation Annual Conference, Keble College, Oxford.

Higher Education Quality Council (1995) *Graduate Standards Programme: Executive Summary of Interim Report*.

Higher Education Quality Council (1996) *Graduate Standards Programme: Threshold and Other Academic Standards*.

Hodges, L. (1997) 'Hard lessons in litigation', *Independent*, 20 Mar., Education Supplement, p. 2.

Hounsell, D. (1996) Statement made during presentation of a research paper, 'Changing approaches to student assessment: a progress report on the ASSHE project', by D. Hounsell and M. McCulloch, at the SRHE conference.

Hyland, T. (1997) 'The skills that fail to travel', *The Times Higher Education Supplement*, 2 May, p. 12.

Institute for Employment Studies (1996) *Ethnic Minority Graduates: Differences by Degrees*. Report No. 309.

McDowell, L. (ed.) (1991) 'Putting students first: listening to students and responding to their needs', Standing Conference on Educational Development (SCED) Paper No. 64, Apr.

McGivney, V. (1996) *Staying or Leaving the Course: Non-completion and Retention of Mature Students in F&HE*. NIACE.

McNay, I. (1995) 'From the collegial academy to corporate enterprise: the changing cultures of universities', in T. Schuller (ed.), *The Changing University?* proceedings of the SRHE conference 1995, Buckingham: SRHE/Open University Press.

Power, M. (1996) 'I audit, therefore I am', *The Times Higher Education Supplement*, 18 Oct., p. 18.

Pratt, J. (1997) '1964 revisited: lessons from the history of Mr Poly', *The Times Higher Education Supplement*, 23 May, p. 14.

Pring, R. A. (1996) *Closing the Gap: Liberal Education and Vocational Preparation*, London: Hodder & Stoughton.

Robbins, Lord (1963) *Higher Education*, Cmnd. 2154, London: HMSO.

Shattock, M. (1996) 'Adding an annexe to the ivory towers', *The Times Higher Education Supplement*, 18 Oct., p. 20.

SRHE/*Independent* (1998) 'Non-completion: assessing the problem and seeking solutions', seminar, 3 Feb.

Thorne, M. and Cuthbert, R. (1996) 'Autonomy, bureaucracy and competition: the ABC of control in higher education', in R. Cuthbert (ed.), *Working in Higher Education*, Buckingham: SRHE/Open University Press.

Tuckett, A. (1996) Speech made at the 'Creating Two Nations' conference organized by Birmingham City Council Adult Education Service and the National Institute for Adult and Continuing Education, Birmingham, 28 Nov.

Walker, D. (1996) 'A degree of uncertainty', series of three programmes broadcast on BBC Radio 4, Aug.

Warnock, M. (1989) *Universities: Knowing Our Minds. What the Government Should Do About Higher Education*, Counterblasts No. 8, London: Chatto & Windus.

West, L. (1996) *Beyond Fragments: Adults, Motivation and Higher Education*, London: Taylor & Francis.

Yeo, S. (1996) 'Learning materialism', *Adult Learning* 7(5) (Jan.): 107–10.

10 Notes from the margins

Library experiences of postgraduate distance-learning students

Kate Stephens

Introduction

This chapter reports the findings of a twelve-month diary study of the use of libraries by postgraduate distance-learning students following courses delivered by conventional universities in the UK. A thematic consideration of the comments students made in the diaries is followed by a composite account of the experiences of a fictional student, 'Alice's Other Story', which draws on this evidence.

The subject of the chapter has implications for 'convergence' in two separately identifiable senses. The first is most closely related to the theme of this book, which is the convergence of open and distance learning with conventional education. In focusing on the library experiences of distance-learning students at dual-mode universities, the study invites comparison with the experiences of students at dedicated distance-learning institutions. It inevitably raises questions concerning institutional expectations, provision and responsibility, as well as concerning the importance and continued via-bility of reciprocal library access. The second sense is commonly referred to in the context of librarianship and information studies, that is the conver-gence of the traditional concerns of librarianship with new information tech-nology and services. It is in relation to this second sense of convergence that visions of the 'electronic library' have developed. The study here described and the larger British Library[1] research project of which it was a part provide an empirical background against which issues of comparison and viability raised by both these senses of convergence might be addressed. Both senses will be returned to in the concluding comments of the chapter.

While surveys have been conducted in Australia and North America (see Stephens 1996 for a summary of the literature) the larger research project of which this diary study is a part represents the first attempt to map distance-learning library use across the UK university sector.

The findings of the diary study confirm several of the conclusions of a prior large-scale questionnaire survey (Bolton, Stephens and Unwin 1998 and Stephens, Unwin and Bolton 1997). Dramatic evidence is presented for the battle with time, institutions and resources which many distance-learning students face. The study illustrates the sometimes clandestine nature of distance-learning students' library use, while confirming the value which students place on making personal visits to libraries in order to browse books on shelves. In addition, the study suggests that the burden of arrangement for library provision is not currently being fully met by providing institutions, with other universities, public libraries and specialist libraries fulfilling most student needs.

The sample

Library records were kept by forty-seven postgraduate distance-learning students for periods varying between three and twelve months from January to December 1995. The students' homes were widely spread across the UK. They were following courses, delivered by twelve dual-mode universities, in a range of subject areas. Between them, the diarists returned 830 records of library use, with thirty-five continuing for six months, twenty-two for nine months and nine for a full year. The diarists were volunteers invited through the earlier questionnaire survey, and included keen library users and some librarians. Their records offer a picture of what happens when enthusiastic library users try to meet what they perceive to be the requirements of their courses.

The sample included fifteen students of Education; twelve students of Management and fifteen specialists in Library and Information Science. Law was being studied by three, while two were students of medical-related subjects. The average age was 39, with ages spanning from 26 to 51. Women were in the majority, with thirty females and seventeen males. There were thirteen teachers, two educational managers, nine librarians, five in medical-related occupations, fifteen others held technical or managerial posts, and one was unemployed. The number of years participants had spent in higher education prior to the current course varied from none to ten, with three being the most common response. Professional experience averaged fifteen years, with a range from four to thirty.

Training in library use varied from having never received any at all, to very extensive experience in the case of one participant holding a senior position in an academic library. In all, six participants relied totally on previous experience in earlier courses, having received no training as part of the current course. A further thirteen had received an information pack about their institution's library, but nothing beyond this.

How were libraries contacted?

Table 10.1 indicates how many times each of a range of ways of contacting libraries was reported. It shows that by far the most common way of making use of the library was by means of personal visits, which account

Table 10.1 Frequency of reports of differing means of contacting libraries

Means of contact	Number of times library used	Percentage of diary entries
By visiting in person	585	70.5
By telephone	142	17.1
By post	72	8.7
Through another person	21	2.5
By on-line sessions	28	3.4
Total	848*	

*This figure is greater than the number of diary returns because in some cases the same return was given more than one code.

for the vast majority of the diary records. The next most common mode of contact was by telephone, with postal and on-line contacts representing only a very small proportion of the records received.

Use of the telephone was described for a variety of purposes, including enquiries about opening times, renewal of books on loan, requests for photocopies or books to be sent by post and requests for literature searches. Comments ranged from the delighted to the frustrated:

> [The librarian] is always so obliging and is able to answer queries. She always tries to get what you order and never appears to get tired of requests. (She gets a lot from me.)

> The lady who answered was very abrupt and told me she hadn't time to answer the phone and take details as she was busy – so ring next term when the students were back or better still call in next term and use the library myself. I was very angry.

Only 8.7 per cent of diary entries recorded use of postal services. Those who did use such services sometimes described great pleasure in receiving much-wanted books by post, although problems were also noted, such as books arriving after assignment deadlines had passed.

Access to library services via a networked computer from home or work accounted for a similarly small proportion of library contacts (3.4 per cent). Of the comments relating to on-line contact, the majority concerned the use of electronic mail. This confirms the finding of Ladner and Tillman (1992) that even for specialist librarians, the most frequent use of networked computers is for electronic mail.

> E-mail to librarian re library search she is conducting on my behalf.

I now have e-mail on laptop at home so can communicate with librarian whenever the urge takes me.

Sent list of 6 books/articles to house librarian via e-mail.

The following comments, all from the same person, concern difficulties in gaining on-line access for other purposes:

Access gained to . . . but couldn't get access to other libraries from there. Disappointing and time consuming and probably expensive. Will discuss with computer staff during summer school.

I originally thought that I would be able to access various journal data-bases and do searches of contemporary material. However, so far it appears that although I can get into various library catalogues for books, I cannot get any journal databases. This is a large disappointment because it appears I'm going to have to continue to wear out shoe leather and beg physical access to local universities and pretend to be a real student so I can use CD-ROM services.

This is where I get frustrated. I don't think I know enough about the technology to make full use of it and the longer I'm using the connection the more concerned I become about the cost.

Use of public libraries

While the diary group seemed to make proportionately less use of the public library service compared to the student questionnaire sample as a whole, nevertheless the public library seems frequently to be regarded as a good place to study and sometimes a surprisingly valuable source of material, as the following comment reveals:

No suitable finance or banking books – but OK for social sciences. . . . I'm surprised by the number of suitable books a small public library . . . holds. It's also a pleasant place to work and the staff are generally helpful.

Several comments suggested a high regard for the public library service, and indicate the manner in which its use can be a family affair which is integrated with other aspects of life:

The library at the end of our road stays open until 7.00 pm every Tuesday. So, most Tuesday evenings after tea the whole family pops down. While the children browse through the books I look over the fiction and non-fiction, perhaps read one of the local papers, occasionally order a book from another (county) library.

Use of the host university library

While the host university library seems to have been used a little less than public libraries, several entries were made regarding its use during residential periods or special visits. However, one student pointed out that the study school may not be the best time to select material:

> During the study school I really felt no pressing need to use the library – excellent though it is. It is not until I actually start working through the modules that I need library services.

Having decided to make a separate visit to the host university library, the comment below indicates the difficulties that can be experienced:

> I did not realise it was the end of term, the library is packed with students desperately trying to complete assignments. I couldn't get near a PC to carry out my search. (I should have thought about the timing of the visit, I had spoken to people at the university but no mention was made of difficulties accessing services at this time of the term.)

Another student, complaining of difficulties regarding loan periods for DL students, noted:

> I was told this system is geared to the full time students and could not be changed. (So much for equality.)

In the absence of any postal service, one diarist had this to say regarding her host university library:

> How can a DL student use a specialised library which is 108 miles away from her home (2 hours drive each way) and only borrow books in person – yet have to complete assignments where one of the criteria for marking is for evidence of further research beyond the set books?

Use of other universities' libraries

Over one-third of the records returned concerned visits to university libraries other than the host library. There can be problems gaining legitimate access to other institutions, with students sometimes relying on friends and relations for access.

One student described at length the problems she had in renewing an external reader's ticket and the response she received to a request to extend borrowing rights:

> I arrived today with the final book ready to discuss my case with the most senior person available if my card was still trapped. It was cleared as soon as the book went in. I asked about the date of expiry on my card and was told that it was up. The librarian offered to extend my card until August 1995, but once again warned me that the external readers' cards were 'under review'. I heard this phrase on the first day I received the card, which I believe was in June 1993. I questioned her further today about why this was continually under review and was told that the library's first priority was to their under- and postgraduate students. If too many demands were made from outside sources the students would suffer and the library would be failing to meet their needs. I asked for both an extension to the number of books I could borrow at one time and the time for which I could keep them. There was no leeway on either. The levels had been agreed by the sub librarians of each campus and were inflexible. I was also informed that many people were refused cards. Think yourself lucky . . . !

Sometimes access to short-loan collections is completely denied to the external reader, as is access to computerized databases. While problems with insufficient loan periods for normal-stock books were mentioned, some people clearly experience little difficulty in this area, relying on good relations with library staff:

> Had a letter from the librarian at the weekend to say that my books were overdue. . . . I almost always have my books overdue and take little notice of dates. The librarian also never seems to mind as long as he knows who you are and that you are reasonably responsible.

This diarist couldn't help being angry at poor communication, despite professional sympathies and feeling guilty about lack of entitlement to access:

> Returned very angry. [The library] was being completely revamped. When I arrived, I found the system was down and there was no access to bookstock. I asked at the counter and the assistant was very pleasant and said that there had been notices up for some time warning about this. Unfortunately as I don't go that frequently I had no way of knowing. So a long journey specifically to get items to use over the vacation was semi-wasted. Why couldn't I have been warned of this when I rang earlier in the week? Fortunately I could do some photocopying, but when my card ran out, they refused to give me change. I know this is a policy (we do the same) but it was quiet, just before Christmas –

what about a little goodwill? Too annoyed to complain (also that feeling of not really being entitled to access).

Use of specialist libraries

Almost a quarter of the records returned concerned use of specialist libraries, including professional and workplace libraries. Limited though such collections may be, students seem relieved to discover their potential, sometimes after frustrating experiences with university libraries:

> My organisation (a social work training agency) has a small in-house library. There are now few recent books but there is a reasonable collection of reports, journals and newspapers. We also have a daily press cuttings service. Through the librarian I have access to the British Library Lending Service which is my life line!

The same diarist commented:

> I have never used work library before my course – now it is a place of refuge.

The value of browsing

A clear message from the diaries is that students value the opportunity to visit libraries in order to browse the shelves and keep up to date with journals. The importance of this activity in getting a feel for relevant material when specified titles are not available, and for enlarging the reader's thinking outside given categories, is emphasized in several of the comments.

> I returned all the books I borrowed and spent about an hour browsing through the school science book shelves. Normally I would use the LIBERTAS computer index to search for books. In this case I was happy to just skim through books and choose the most appropriate.

> Found browsing of journals quite fruitful and photocopied a number of articles for consultation later.

> Check subject index and browse shelves and find a few interesting and useful background documents. Great believer in browsing.

> Eureka! It's amazing what you can find on the shelves if you really look.

Library use as a clandestine activity

In confirmation of one of the findings of Winter and Cameron (1983), who investigated distance-learning students' use of libraries in Australia, the diarists in this study also reported use of friends and relations to help gain access. At one time or other, fifteen of the sample gained access to libraries through other people's membership.

> My daughter is a student at . . . and so she said she would look for a book for me.

> I visited the library with my wife who is a postgraduate student at . . . and using my wife's card I borrowed four books.

It seems to be a distinctive feature of distance-learning students' library use that they operate around the margins of normal institutional services and practices. Library use does not for most such students occupy its own rightful space, but instead is achieved illegitimately and runs in parallel with whatever other life demands permit. It is slotted into the spaces which are left after the demands of daily and work life are met, and after institutions have fulfilled their functions regarding 'normal' students.

At its best this jigsaw puzzle of demands results in an integrated picture of apparently harmonized reading opportunities. Others see themselves as operating at the edges of acceptable behaviour:

> I had my twelve year old daughter with me who was going to do her homework while I carried out my own business. She felt uncomfortable as there were notices prohibiting school pupils from using the library as a study area. This was presumably due to lack of space but I was prepared to make a request for her to stay if we were challenged – we were not.

In the following extract borrowing books comes across in part as an act of theft, rather than a wholly legitimate affair:

> Now it is the school holidays. I had two little girls with me (the baby is in nursery full time so he is no problem). I sat them in a corner with some scrap paper, pens and scissors and told them to be as quiet as mice! In these circumstances, I have to find what looks promising as quickly as I can and then I can review it properly at home in my own time.

In the following comments library use seems as pleasurably clandestine:

> Children went back to school today so I sneaked a little time off work to do an hour on my current assignment. I could have done this at home or

in my office but there is something about library atmosphere which is settling and enjoyable.

I found myself with an unexpected afternoon off and it is the last day of school term so I indulged myself in simply sitting and writing. I have always found the library a helpful place to write since being an undergraduate and spending days in libraries. Today I did it with a sense of indulgence and really enjoyed myself.

Conclusions of the diary study

The age and experience profile of the diarists in this study seems to be fairly representative of distance-learning students in general. A range of geographical areas and disciplines are represented. Despite a weighting towards library professionals and, no doubt, library enthusiasts, there is a characteristic gap regarding training in modern library resources. The returns suggest that there remains a heavy weighting towards using libraries by making personal visits to them, despite forecasts of the imminent demise of the library as a physical place.

The most frequently used library resource is still libraries at universities other than the host. Problems of access include entrance barriers, restricted external-borrower status, limited loan periods, difficulty associated with short-loan collections, unfamiliarity with local systems, lack of information about systems and practices and absence of relevant stock. Better access is sometimes gained through personal connections. Concessions regarding the rules for use and borrowing can sometimes be gained through friendly contact with a sympathetic librarian.

Specialist, including professional and workplace, libraries form the second most commonly used category for this group. Despite sometimes limited collections, their use can be associated with a sense of relief after the battle for access to a university. The existence of such libraries is sometimes under threat from institutional reorganization.

Public libraries were third in order of frequency of use. There is a commonly expressed view that the middle classes have abandoned public borrowing in favour of buying books for personal collections. This study provides some evidence for the esteem and affection in which the public library service is held by the adult learner. It seems to remain an important source of academic material, and for some its use is integrated with family activities, such as children's reading and shopping. The role of the public library service needs better recognition and support.

The host university library was less frequently used than the other three groups. Problems in the use of the host university library include both distance and inconvenient opening times, when students visit either for organized residential courses or by their own arrangement. Breakdowns in communication regarding when facilities will be available sometimes occur, with libraries typically geared to the demands of the timetable of full-time, on-site undergraduates.

Postal services are valued where they exist, although the cost and the waste involved in ordering material which turns out not to be useful or relevant can be seen as problems. Getting information and making arrangements by telephone varies in success. Pleasure and relief at saving unnecessary and wasted journeys through use of the phone is opposed by the extreme frustration experienced when a telephone response is unhelpful.

Several mentions were made of the use of networked computers in order to obtain library services. Where this group used such facilities it was most frequently for electronic mail. One student described the disappointment she felt at being unable to access databases through an Internet connection with her host university library.

The need to browse books on shelves came across strongly from these diaries. In addition to a concern with time pressure, which mirrors the findings of our questionnaire survey, this study has revealed an air of illegitimacy in library use for distance-learning students. Such students see themselves as operating outside the normal expectations of academic life, and hanker after a legitimization of their study needs. It may be that this sense of illegitimacy can be partly alleviated through better communication and training.

Students want the opportunity to browse for extended periods before deciding what to take home and read in depth. Access as external borrowers to nearby university libraries can be expensive, as well as being limited in terms of the services which are offered. Use of networked CD-ROMs, for example, may be excluded. But even if these difficulties can be overcome, the stock of a local institution may not reflect the reading demands of a particular course. Despite this, extensive use is being made by this group of local university libraries, in excess of the use made of the host university library.

It seems that students would benefit from a library service which integrated some measure of local university access with some measure of special arrangements by the host institution, ensuring that access is available to the specialist material that a course may require. With the increasing participation of the conventional university sector in distance education, and the overall increase of postgraduates studying in this mode, there is a pressing need for more formal arrangements. While ideas about electronic collections and remote access to databases have captured the imagination of many, the daily realities and needs of distance-learning students suggest the inadequacy of this vision. In the short term at least, remote access to computerized catalogues and databases, where this is available to the student, seems only likely to increase the appetite for access to material only currently available by visiting libraries in person.

A distance-learning student's day (or 'Alice's Other Story')

The Follet Report (HEFCE 1993) on the future of university libraries offered a vision of the convergence of library and information services in the form of a sketch of a day in the life of an imagined university undergraduate. Briefly, in the report 'Alice' is pictured working from her study bedroom and communicating with her tutors and the library via a networked computer, with access to a campus textbook server and electronic journals, which she pays by credit card to download. In the Follet vision of converged learning, the on-campus student is served by an electronic learning environment in which the roles of librarian and teacher merge in the compilation of learning texts. This vision re-casts the learning relationship for the traditional on-campus student in a shape more easily associated with the distance learner, yet no view is presented of the current realities for distance-learning students in the more conventional sense.

Below is an account of another fictional Alice, but one which is grounded in these realities as they have emerged in the research which this chapter reports. This second Alice is, perhaps, the mother of the first. At any rate, she is old enough to have children of her own entering higher education for the first time, at the point when she herself is rediscovering what being a student might mean. The story attempts to give a composite account of her experiences.

Half-way through the course Alice discovered the need for a library. The course provided self-study materials along with a good deal of supplementary reading, but still there were points to clarify, and one or two things she would like to follow up out of personal interest. Already ideas were beginning to form for the dissertation, for which some wider reading would be necessary.

She hadn't much of a notion of what was available at the host university library. There had been vague talk at the introductory residential of registering with the library, but time had not been allocated for this and after waiting for her personal tutorial on the Sunday she could see that the building was already closed. Perhaps it wasn't open at weekends at all!

She had a vague idea that the public library should be fulfilling some kind of a need here, and although she used her local library regularly for her own leisure reading, and for such things as holiday guides and consulting *Which?* reports, as well as to encourage the children to read, she was sure that the stock would have little to offer for the specialist nature of the course. She went nevertheless to see what was available. The librarian on the enquiries desk was interested in her situation, having once enrolled for a distance-learning course herself. They shared a couple of experiences about the stresses and strains of doing such a course, found a useful basic text on the shelf, ordered a couple more references from the County Library via the local computerized regional catalogue, and processed three interlibrary loan requests.

It was difficult choosing the titles to order with a so far limited knowledge of the field, and not being able to browse. She was pleasantly surprised how cheap it was (only 50p an item) but held back before ordering another five titles for the next assignment. On the way back home, thinking about how long the librarian said it might take, she regretted this. She hoped that the librarian would do as she had promised, and try to hurry things up in view of her situation. But she didn't really know how much influence the librarian would have, and wondered whether everyone could expect such special treatment.

At home, she decided to take a bit more initiative and give the local university a ring. She was passed around several people before finding someone to answer her enquiry. When she was finally able to explain her situation fully, she felt that the words 'distance learning' and 'another university' had not gone down well. The response was unsympathetic: 'We have enough on looking after our own students without catering for the semi-detached variety.' It felt like a major setback, as if she was being treated as a non-person. She decided not to give up and planned a visit to her old university, 25 miles away, but a lot nearer than the one running her present course.

It was nice to be in a familiar place. She crept around rather guiltily, not absolutely sure if she had any right to be there. Last time she came here it had been rather a quiet place, and she remembered straining her eyes on the microfiche and having to consult the card catalogue for references earlier than a certain date. Now, students were queuing to use computer terminals which she supposed accessed the on-line catalogue, which she hadn't a clue how to use. It would be hard to spend a long time learning and making mistakes, with that queue growing longer behind. She didn't know if you needed some kind of password to get in. There was a small crowd of students jostling for attention at the enquiries desk. It was like a bazaar. Not at all the quiet and seemingly under-used place of her undergraduate days.

She decided this time to chicken out on the catalogue and go straight to the shelves. She could have done with some direction in finding the right class numbers, but didn't like to ask for help in case she was asked to justify her presence. Browsing the shelves turned out to be more useful than she had expected. She didn't find any of the titles on her list, but did find a later reference by one of the same authors, and spent a useful hour scanning some other related titles. She also found the current-journals section and got side-tracked reading a completely unrelated piece about something her daughter was studying. She considered photocopying the article, but was put off by the queues and decided to leave it for another day, whenever that might be. She had to go anyway, but made a mental note that the library closed for the day at lunchtime on a Saturday. She went home excited by the experience and determined to give her next visit priority, perhaps even over reading the course materials.

It turned out to be another three months before she felt she could afford the time for a second visit. This time she had a few hours owing at work. She decided to leave early in the afternoon and make an evening of it, when perhaps the place would be less crowded. The traffic on the motorway was worse than usual and she arrived, later than she had expected, at about 4 o'clock. She was dismayed to see that the library closed at 5! Surely last time she had noted this as a day for late-evening opening. Reading the notice with some care, she now saw the words 'In term time' and the dates showing that this was still (for some!) the vacation.

Suppressing a feeling of frustration, she planned at least to make the best of the hour she had. But something had changed. The porter on the entrance desk had been replaced with an entry barrier with a sign reading 'Insert Card Here'. A notice beside the barrier directed students to another building to register for the new swipe-card system. Students were fumbling in bags for their cards, and carefully passing through, as if the barrier had only recently been installed. A library assistant was standing nearby instructing students new to the system. Alice's plans to make furtive use of the library were completely scotched. No option but to announce her presence and find out what the proper rules were for using the library.

The library assistant directed her to a door marked 'Private' adjacent to the barrier. She introduced herself more cautiously this time than she had when telephoning the other place. She said she was a graduate of this university and that she understood that as a former student she could make use of it in order to pursue some research of her own. The response wasn't quite so warm as at the public library, but she felt that the librarian was basically sympathetic, and rather apologetic that the rules were a bit tighter than they had once been. She gestured through the glass partition towards the queues at various points in the library and explained that an external reader's ticket could be offered at a reduced rate due to her former student status, but this would only allow her to borrow a small number of books and for short periods. The short-loan collection and interlibrary loans would be unavailable.

It seemed like a lot of money, but Alice decided that this year's holiday fund would have to stand it. She couldn't help thinking, though, having financed herself through the course, she was paying for library services twice over. Once the forms were filled in and the cheque written, the library was about to close. This time she took a wad of information leaflets, including a guide to opening times and one about CD-ROMs available for student use. The librarian told her that a good time to come for a bit of peace and quiet was after the exams had started and before the summer courses began. There would be a window of a couple of weeks then when the place would be less hectic. It would still be officially term-time, so the late-evening opening would still operate.

When she managed the next visit, it was more like the library she remembered. There were no queues and she found somewhere to leave her things while she went off to browse. At first she just sat, gathering some thoughts about the direction she would like to take in her dissertation.

First stop this time would be a database search. She had no experience of using computerized databases, but the subject librarian was happy enough to spend half an hour starting her off. Having joined officially, she now felt it was legitimate to ask for help. It took her a further hour and a half to download and print something that looked like a respectable database search. What if she had missed something? She wasn't confident that she had defined her terms well enough. She sensed that she would still have to find other ways of trailing the key material.

A search of the library's own catalogue showed her the limitations of the library she had just paid to join. Hardly anything of relevance turned up in the Online Public Access Catalogue. Her first reaction was to feel she had been cheated. Remembering her experience on the first visit, she went back to the shelves and found one or two relevant titles and a collection of papers by a relevant author which had not turned up in the search. From a quick flick through a periodical she had not heard of before, she found two papers that she could see were immediately relevant to her study. At least the journey was not wasted, but there was one key reference from the reading list which was referred to in some of the material she had found and which she knew she must read in order to see how present approaches to the field had come about. She knew now that the next stop would have to be her own university. They, surely, would have a collection more comprehensively covering her field of study. If they didn't keep this particular reference, she knew she would be able to ask them to get it through interlibrary loan.

From home, she made one or two telephone calls and finally spoke to the subject librarian at her own university. The librarian was prepared to admit that, yes, distance-learning students have a problem, and, yes, as a special concession to her she would personally photocopy a couple of references and send them, along with a key monograph, by post, as long as she was able to pay the return postage. She was sympathetic to the problems and expressed some concern about students sticking too closely to a narrow range of material and course providers not thinking things through. Surely universities who had been around in distance learning longer would have sorted this one out?

The librarian also said that, with the expansion of courses like hers, the university was considering ways of improving services, but this would depend on additional staffing. Existing staff were pressed enough as it was. She looked forward to the day when distance-learning students could search databases from home and make e-mail requests for material to be sent by post. She said that the university had an experimental project looking at just this.

Alice wondered whether this would increase the demand to come and look at books, rather than reduce it. She was beginning to think of her guilty and unannounced presence in her old university library more as the exercise of a basic freedom to browse. Thinking of her own success in extending the boundaries of a reading list and a computer search by defining relevance for herself, she remembered that this was one of the things you were supposed to learn at a university. She wondered, half seriously, if the day would arrive when a readers' version of a mass trespass would be needed to secure the rights of citizens to access a national resource of materials for learning in libraries.

Convergence and flexibility for distance-learning library provision

At the beginning of this chapter two senses of convergence were identified in relation to the study described. Regarding the first, convergence of distance learning with conventional educational provision, it appears that the emergence of distance learning in traditional universities throws up a number of questions regarding the appropriate direction of this process in the UK. The most pressing question concerns whose responsibility it is to provide a library service for distance-learning students. While professional guidelines in North America indicate that this should be the responsibility of the institution running the course, this may be unnecessarily inflexible in a context where a library at some other university is frequently fairly close. The development of co-operative arrangements between institutions is perhaps a better principle in this context than the convergence of one set of practices with another.

The second sense of convergence concerned the integration of traditional library provision with new information-technology-based services. This study raises the question of how those needs which are usually met by walking into a library are to be met by electronic means. Visions of the 'electronic library' seemed to have little reality for the students in this study. Electronic resources sometimes restrict access more than they extend it. Technology in the form of electronic barriers can be used to restrict access to physical collections, before basic questions have been addressed regarding provision of access by other means. While development in this field is swift, it is risky to assume that questions have been answered, when they have barely been asked. Flexible integration of electronic with physical access to collections, in order to meet the reading needs of students, seems to be a better principle than a technologically driven convergence.

Note

1 The research project was conducted at the University of Sheffield from 1994 to 1996 and was directed by Lorna Unwin and Neil Bolton. The project is fully reported in Unwin, Stephens and Bolton (1998).

References

Bolton, N., Stephens, K. and Unwin, L. (1998) 'The use of libraries by postgraduate distance learning students: whose responsibility?', *Open Learning* 13(1): 3–8.

HEFCE (1993) *Joint Funding Council Libraries Review Group Report*, Gloucester: HEFCE.

Ladner, S. J. and Tillman, H. N. (1992) 'How specialist librarians really use the internet', *Canadian Libraries Journal* 49(3): 211–15.

Stephens, K. (1996) 'The role of the library in distance learning: a review of UK, North American and Australian literature', *The New Review of Academic Librarianship* 2: 205–34.

Stephens, K., Unwin, L. and Bolton, N. (1997) 'The use of libraries by postgraduate distance learning students: a mismatch of expectations?', *Open Learning* 12(3): 25–33.

Unwin, L., Stephens, K. and Bolton, N. (1998) *The Role of the Library in Distance Learning: A Study of Postgraduate Students, Course Providers and Librarians in the UK*, London: Bowker-Saur.

Winter, A. and Cameron, M. (1983) *External Students and Their Libraries: An Investigation into Student Needs for Reference Material, the Sources They Use and the Effects of the External System in Which They Study*, Geelong: Deakin University.

11 The convergence of distance and conventional education

Some implications for policy

Alan Tait

This chapter begins with the acknowledgement that conventional educational institutions in the UK have begun substantially to use open and distance learning (ODL); that is to say the array of educational approaches and technologies which permit learning to take place to a substantial degree away from the teacher's physical presence have been adopted in many post-secondary environments. It is in this sense that convergence is for the most part taking place. In more detail:

- the scaling up of learning opportunities to achieve mass higher education looks to ODL methods at least in part to deliver these policy objectives;
- the broader context of lifelong learning looks to ODL and the new technologies to provide the necessary flexibility to permit, or indeed expect, learning to support work more intensively;
- ODL methods are also thought to be capable of delivering financial economies, both absolutely and of scale, in the context of the generalized downturn in governmental spending and the related increased pressure on profitability in private enterprise;
- the increased range of technologies, in particular those supported and delivered by computer-mediated communications, are fast accelerating the convergence process;
- the increasing international commodification of education sees ODL as particularly suited to reinforcing the concept of education as a range of saleable products and services.

The secret garden of open and distance learning has become public, and many institutions in the UK are moving from single conventional-mode activity to dual-mode activity, that is to say offering a range of modes of study from the full-/part-time and conventional/distance spectrum. The process was made explicit in the UK in 1990 at a National Extension College conference with the title 'Open Learning: Moving into the Mainstream' (National Extension College 1990). At least since then the Open University's hold on the market of part-time adult undergraduate students has been challenged by the substantial interest on the part of higher education in the adult-learner cohort as a whole, and in geographical areas where the OU has hitherto had a monopoly of supply, by the new entrepreneurial franchising arrangements between further- and higher-education institutions which has meant that the reach of those institutions has been extended (Mills and Tait 1997; Rumble 1992). Further, the Open Polytechnic (now Open Learning Agency), established in 1990 to develop distance-learning collaborative approaches amongst conventional British universities, has made substantial impact particularly in vocational and professional development fields. Most recently, the UK government has announced the establishment of a 'university for industry', intended according to the 1998 green paper in an explicit parallel to the OU to use new technologies to 'change attitudes to learning and acquiring skills in the new century' (Department for Education and Employment 1998, p. 20). Over and above national development, we have seen major policy statements and programmes of action from the EU (Tait 1996), Unesco (1997) and the World Bank, all recognizing and seeking further to promote the potential of open- and distance-learning methods to expand educational opportunity on a widespread basis, with economic objectives central in importance.

The implications of these moves are manifold. First, we can see in recent policy the construction of a larger than ever proportion of the population as lifelong learners, driven by analyses which relate education and training directly to economic growth. Arising from this is the need for conventional institutions to retool and retrain with ODL methodologies, in order to achieve volume and efficiency measures, and the concomitant threat to the market of distance-teaching institutions. This process of institutional change also challenges the identity of distance educators, who have hitherto, through necessity and to some extent choice, defined themselves as a separate professional sub-group.

All these are significant issues. One, however, has not hitherto been discussed, and that is the future for that significant part of the distance-education tradition which has defined itself as operating in the interstices of social policy and on the margins of societies, providing educational opportunity which the state and private institutions choose not to prioritize. In other words, if distance education through convergence has at last become a major avenue for what can be broadly termed governmental policy, as well as for employers private and public – its methods, language and to some extent personnel made respectable and adopted into larger structures – what sort of loss accompanies at the same time what is rightly seen as a victory?

'The other': redefining the excluded

In considering how exclusion from educational opportunity and social equity is affected by convergence, the notion of 'the other' can be illuminating. The use of this term is from Said (1995), with references to its application in adult-education contexts both in India (Steele and Taylor 1995) and domestically in the UK (Stuart and Thomson 1995). By the term 'the other' is intended those who are seen as different from 'us', not integrated within 'our' culture nor included in 'our' society, and who therefore need development or deserve exclusion or punishment. The term in the adult-education context derives from analysis of the disputes under the British Raj in the development of adult education in India, the conflict between attempts either to anglicize Indians through British educational norms and practices or alternatively to recognize their legitimate alternative ideas and value systems. Needless to say the former, which constructed Indian culture as 'other', was dominant. However, as has been pointed out, construction of 'the other' has worked systematically on a domestic basis also. It has been argued that in the context of nineteenth-century political development, 'Within the new European nation states cultural and political elites established their own ways of being in and knowing the world as the norm . . . and constructed the different peoples of their own countries as inferior and ignorant' (Stuart and Thomson 1995, p. 4).

The importance of this analysis for assessing policies of educational access is clear, and particularly at this juncture for the convergence of ODL approaches with so-called conventional education. For while ODL in the mainstream opens access to many (and this chapter does not seek to belittle that commitment and achievement), it at the same time constructs new 'others', new categories of the excluded whose non-incorporation into the purposes of contemporary economic life is legitimized through their failure or unwillingness to adopt the necessities of lifelong learning. Those who are not participants in converged lifelong-learning systems are becoming as 'strange' as the 'Orientals' whose identity Said revealed was constructed through the process of Western imperialism. They are the newly categorized or re-categorized 'inferior and ignorant', to use Stuart and Thomson's phrase. They thus become responsible for their own exclusion from employment and accommodation, and are punished for acts of rebellion.

Who will work in the margins?

The issue identified here relates to the question as to whether the balance of power in the world of social policy has shifted even further into the hands of established structures through the incorporation of the powerful mechanisms of open and distance learning. Issues of social justice, while on one hand ameliorated by the wider opportunities which convergence brings, are at the same time paradoxically themselves marginalized, as distance education gives up its sometimes dissident role within societies and becomes the servant of the very social and economic structures which it originally came into being to compensate for or challenge. There is a danger that along with the expansion of opportunity which convergence has undoubtedly brought, the long debate of issues of access – meaning that nexus of issues around participation, life opportunity and social justice, mediated primarily through the social geography of class, gender and ethnicity – has been silenced. The tradition of oppositional discussion of education and society that has taken place in different ways in the UK in the work of Charles Dickens, Thomas Hardy, D. H. Lawrence, Raymond Williams, Stuart Hall and the Centre for Contemporary Studies, Birmingham, and finally the practice of the OU UK itself (Sargeant 1996) risks being insidiously stifled by the incorporation of lifelong-learning policy. The very convergence and mainstreaming process itself, it is to be feared, has sanitized and de-radicalized ODL, so that it becomes a new product from the emergent colleges-cum-companies that reinforces the educational and social structures it once challenged.

ODL and the broader canvas of convergence

It has been observed before that ODL has a habit of living an isolated life, accepting its own rhetoric as an adequate account of its social function (Tait 1994). It is important therefore to emphasize that the convergence of ODL and conventional education represents only one part of a wider range of shifts, other larger convergences and alterations of pattern, and these should be identified so that a fuller understanding of the changes taking place can be arrived at. These convergences can be further examined under two main headings:

- social institutions and businesses
- the compulsory nature of lifelong learning.

ODL, social institutions and businesses

Colleges, universities and indeed schools are not alone in finding their identities defined away from social institutions of a different type towards business organizations for whom profitability, or at least survival, in a competitive environment becomes the prime purpose (Shumar 1997). Over the last twenty years in the UK this trend has additionally moved, at least to some extent, into health care, community care and social work, and the public media (viz. the BBC). This trend is not of course an objective natural force but the result of purposeful activity by those who espouse such a view, and in the UK and elsewhere over the last twenty years, of explicit public policy. Such developments have created both a reality and an ideology that there is no alternative to liberal globalizing economies and societies essentially organized to serve them. Organizations that take moral, cultural and political objectives as their primary purpose find their vision of reality and their modus vivendi more difficult to sustain than ever in competition with 'the real world' of the bottom line, i.e. profitability.

Significant actors on the social stage outside the market, driven by values other than profit and competition, include the churches and other religious traditions, NGOs and pressure groups in a range of social, political and environmental fields. These important counter-currents do not, I suggest, alter but throw into relief the predominant trends, while at the same time revealing the still-contested nature of social development which ensures its discussion remains worthwhile. However, non-commoditized relations, which are not subject to the imperatives of profitability and the associated instrumental rationalities of managerialism, have retreated to these organizations, and to the very limited environments of family and friendships, themselves often damaged and diminished by the social currents in which they attempt to sustain themselves.

It is within this broad picture of society, a challenging and difficult one rather than a vision of worldwide economic prosperity and well-being, that this writer sees ODL playing an increasingly important role, accelerating the change of educational institutions into businesses and serving more closely than ever before through the imperatives of the market current economic needs, rather than access, opportunity and social justice, which have been relegated to second-order objectives.

The compulsory nature of lifelong learning

As businesses increasingly become the predominant social world on which life centres itself, so personal identity is increasingly moulded to serve the superordinate life task for the employed, which is paid work. Both the volume and pace of work for individuals increase to meet ever tighter demands for profitability, squeezing out other activities and absorbing greater and greater proportions of available personal energy. Lifelong education, which began its days as a series of policies predicated on remedying past educational exclusion, has turned predominantly into the construction of a series of policies and practices which support individuals in keeping themselves employable and organizations in maintaining and increasing competitiveness and profitability. Learning throughout life is constructed more and more as a necessity and less and less as an option, for those who want to stand a chance of being employed. What used to be termed post-compulsory education – i.e., that which took place as a voluntary activity after the age when the state insisted on attendance – is now taking on both formal necessity (as, for example, for members of certain professions who must undertake some elements of continuing education in order to remain registered) as well as more widely, and more importantly, an informal necessity for those who want to remain attractive in the labour market.

It would now be seen as an act of rebellion or resistance (depending on one's point of view) to refuse training on the grounds that one had other things to do with one's life. ODL serves to reinforce this trend of the non-voluntary nature of post-secondary education and training, offering flexible solutions which shift the burden of study for employment into the individual's private time. At the same time ODL in the mainstream assists in the internalization of the legitimacy of such demands with terms such as 'independent learning', 'flexible learning' and indeed 'open learning' – terms which seek to persuade people, through language that now owes more to marketing than educational theory, that they should seek to transform themselves into the sorts of infinitely accommodating and flexible individuals wanted in contemporary organizations. ODL serves as an increasingly important agent in the disciplining of the population into these new regimes – a disciplining process which demands that more and more study is dedicated to servicing and managing employment, and that more and more of private life is similarly dedicated to it through the exploiting of hitherto 'private' time, i.e., the extension of learning into the home through convergence.

Who will be marginalized by convergence?

As this chapter has sought to demonstrate, the convergence of ODL and conventional education is only one part of a broader pattern of economic and social policy development which convergence serves to reinforce and accelerate. The new marginalized are therefore broadly those who cannot be accommodated by the wider economic and social changes. A number of dimensions are immediately apparent.

First, the vocationalization of education for the post-secondary sectors significantly diminishes the life opportunities of those who are without work. With the present figure of some 18 million unemployed in the European Union, and higher rates in other newly marketized economies in the post-communist countries, this is no insignificant issue. Vocationalization also serves to exclude the increasing cohorts of the retired, with 20 per cent of the EU population expected to be over 60 by the year 2000 (Eurostat 1992).

Second, the increasingly important development of market approaches to education serves to exclude those without the means to pay at the point of delivery. This impacts again on the unemployed, but also on the low-paid, and generally those living in poverty (now as high as 11 million people according to recent research in the UK, having increased by 50 per cent in the last decade) (*Independent* 1997). Within the framework of the articulation of exclusion, these disadvantages are likely to continue to express themselves with further acuteness on women and ethnic minorities.

Third, the increasing emphasis through converging systems of the home as a place of study serves to exclude the homeless and the overcrowded, both of which categories have increased. The implications for the education of school-age children have been noted by researchers for Shelter, the leading NGO working in the field of homelessness in the UK, but are equally pressing for adult learners (Power, Whitty and Youdell 1995).

Fourth, the increased necessity for home-based computers for the delivery of both content and process through computer-mediated communication will represent a concrete example of very firm barriers to those who do not possess hardware or have access in the workplace. The model of provision at present is almost entirely one of individual acquisition rather than social or community provision.

Lastly, the cultural capital needed to study 'independently', 'flexibly' and 'at a distance' is not likely to be evenly distributed throughout the population, but skewed in its distribution. Not to be overlooked in this context is the seriousness of literacy problems in developed countries, and as more and more educational opportunity through convergence demands both functional literacy and associated cultural capital, those without are going to see educational opportunity made even more remote and the fences which create marginalization more solidly built (Kozol 1985). Those who already fall into the category of 'the other' will find their exclusion reinforced.

Refocusing ODL's tradition of access

This chapter concludes with some proposals for refocusing the tradition of access to education which ODL brings to the convergence process, and which it has been argued is being overlooked.

First, we need at a broad level to be aware of the social-policy dimension which the excitement of seeing ODL methods accepted may lead us to forget. The most important research carried out in this field has been in Australia, where recent work by Campion (1997), Evans and Nation (1997) and Jakupec (1997) amongst others has provided a series of sharp and critical examinations of the series of major governmental interventions into the higher distance education scene. Work in this area has been begun in Canada (Haughey and Roberts 1997; Roberts and Keogh 1995), and I have contributed a study of ODL policy in the European Union (Tait 1996). However, more needs to be done as consideration of convergence at only the micro-level will permit the larger social implications of such developments to go unnoticed.

Second, in order to maintain and build the traditions of access and educational opportunity we need to raise within discussions of new policies of convergence at international, national and institutional levels the issue of how exclusion is reasserting itself. Amongst the questions which need to be debated are:

- What are the implications of new market-related fees policies? How can financial exclusion be diminished? How can the new hierarchies which a market system brings be identified and opposed, e.g. the funnelling of less well-off students to the lower-quality provision, or their exclusion altogether, and their allocation to the less attractive life opportunities?
- What are the effects of convergence on the already educationally disadvantaged? What educational support is there so that independent and flexible learning strategies do not provide a rationale for continuing to exclude cohorts starting, at least formally speaking, from further back?

- How is the heterogeneity of learner populations with more varied cultural backgrounds than ever before to be accounted for in the creation of new converging learning systems, with assumptions of the possession of cultural capital that are not in fact universally shared? How will the risk be diminished that the already disadvantaged and minorities will find their continued exclusion legitimized?
- How will the availability of technologies be addressed as convergence brings its use into more and more delivery of educational opportunity? Will there be social availability of hardware through institutional or civic facilities (e.g. local cybercentres), rather than systems dependent on domestic ownership which will marginalize the less well-off?

Through the construction of a series of questions such as these, those committed to the access element in the ODL tradition can find appropriate ways of impacting on the convergence discussion and on educational and social development as a whole.

Conclusion

This chapter is not intended as a polemic against convergence, or indeed against ODL. The major contribution to educational access which flexibility of learning strategies allows is acknowledged, as well as the excellence of both structured curriculum and learner support which well-designed ODL systems provide. The potential of the new technologies in reinforcing and indeed expanding opportunity in large-scale flexible education systems has been acknowledged in other places.

However, the chapter does represent an attempt to problematize convergence, to point out that educational disadvantage and marginalization will be re-articulated by the economic and social currents which the convergence of conventional and ODL systems themselves accelerate. Some important elements of the ODL tradition which are being brought to the marriage are concerned with access and social equity. These need to be reasserted in the light of the recent increase in unemployment, homelessness, poverty and illiteracy, in order to ensure that the exclusion of the 'other' is not normalized. This requires a unifying consideration of both policy and practice as convergence takes hold, and the maintenance of a dissident, oppositional and critical approach to power and social opportunity which is so significantly mediated and reinforced by education.

References

Campion, M. (1997) 'Open learning, closing minds', in T. Evans and D. Nation (eds), *Opening Education: Policies and Practices from Open and Distance Learning*, London: Routledge, pp. 147–61.

Department for Education and Employment (1998) *The Learning Age: a Renaissance for a New Britain*, Command 3790, London: HMSO.

Eurostat (1992) *Europe in Figures*, 3rd edn, Luxembourg: Office for Official Publications of the European Communities.

Evans, T. and Nation, D. (1997) 'Opening education: global lines, local connections', in T. Evans and D. Nation (eds), *Opening Education: Policies and Practices from Open and Distance Learning*, London: Routledge, pp. 1–6.

Haughey, M. and Roberts, J. (1997) 'Canadian policy and practice in open and distance schooling', in T. Evans and D. Nation (eds), *Opening Education: Policies and Practices from Open and Distance Education*, London: Routledge, pp. 63–76.

Independent (1997) 'Hunger and cold: facts of life for 11 million Britons', 22 July, p. 2.

Jakupec, V. (1997) 'Reforming distance education through economic rationalism: a critical analysis of reforms to Australian higher education', in T. Evans and D. Nation (eds), *Opening Education: Policies and Practices from Open and Distance Learning*, London: Routledge, pp. 77–89.

Kozol, J. (1985) *Illiterate America*, New York: New American Library.

Mills, R. and Tait, A. (1997) 'The ecology of the Open University UK', in *The New Learning Environment: a Global Perspective*, conference papers of the 18th International Council for Distance Education world conference, University Park, Pa.

National Extension College (1990) 'Open learning: moving into the mainstream', papers prepared for the National Extension College/CRAC conference, National Extension College, Cambridge.

Power, S., Whitty, G. and Youdell, D. (1995) *No Place to Learn, Homelessness and Education*, London: Shelter.

Roberts, J. M. and Keogh, E. M. (eds) (1995) *Why the Information Highway? Lessons for Open and Distance Learning*, Toronto: Trifolium Books.

Rumble, G. (1992) 'The competitive vulnerability of distance teaching universities', *Open Learning* 7(2) (June): 31–46.

Said, E. (1995) *Orientalism: Western Conceptions of the Orient*, repr. with a new afterword, London: Penguin Books.

Sargeant, N. (1996) 'The Open University', in R. Fieldhouse and Associates, *A History of Modern British Adult Education*, Leicester: National Institute for Adult and Continuing Education, pp. 290–307.

Shumar, W. (1997) *College for Sale: a Critique of the Commodification of Higher Education*, London: Falmer Press.

Steele, T. and Taylor, R. (1995) *Learning Independence: a Political Outline of Indian Adult Education*, Leicester: National Institute for Adult and Continuing Education.

Stuart, M. and Thomson, A. (1995) *Engaging with Difference: the 'Other' in Adult Education*, Leicester: National Institute for Adult and Continuing Education.

Tait, A. (1994) 'The end of innocence: critical approaches to open and distance learning', *Open Learning* 9(3) (Nov.): 27–36.

Tait, A. (1996) 'Open and distance learning policy in the European Union 1985–1995', *Higher Education Policy* 9(3): 221–38.

Unesco (1997) *Open and Distance Learning: Prospects and Policy Considerations*, Paris: Unesco.

12 From marginal to mainstream

Critical issues in the adoption of information technologies for tertiary teaching and learning

Diane Thompson

To speak of technology is to speak of complexity, for 'technology' is a multi-faceted entity, far more than its individual components. As Franklin (1990, pp. 14–15) wrote:

> It [technology] includes activities as well as a body of knowledge, structures as well as the act of structuring. Our language itself is poorly suited to describe the complexity of technological interactions. The inter-connectedness of many of those processes, the fact that they are so complexly interrelated, defies our normal push-me-pull-you, cause-and-consequence metaphors. How does one speak about something that is both fish and water, means as well as end?

Hence it is with due recognition of, and regard for, the complexities entailed, that this discussion attempts to address some of the critical issues when new technologies at the margins are brought towards the centre. As technologies advance so rapidly and offer potential in so many areas, we struggle to use them effectively and responsibly and to make well-grounded decisions about their viability. Effective use of 'cutting-edge' technologies requires new synergies in working relations and much rethinking as they are integrated into the fabric of tertiary life, impacting on teaching, research and administration. As Stoll (1995, p. 200) wrote, to say something 'is poised on the cutting-edge of technology . . . sounds painful, doesn't it?' To take something beyond the cutting-edge involves a complex and often confused and confusing set of interrelated matrices. It sounds painful because it can be painful; but, as this discussion suggests, one's attitude and where one is situated greatly influence how such experiences are interpreted.

The perspective of convergence

To move from the peripheral to the core, from marginal to mainstream, is to converge, for such movement is premised on the bringing together of disparate elements. In the specific context of this discussion where adopting information technologies for tertiary teaching and learning is the focus, three issues of convergence are underpinning elements. The first is the recognition that technologies themselves are converging under such banners as 'multi-media' and 'digital', and this of itself appears to mandate a movement towards the mainstream. The second is that when tertiary teaching is the environment, what were once seen as discrete and single modes of education with clear demarcation and division are increasingly coming together as mixed and multi-mode models. Further, the link between distance education and technology is umbilical and, as on- and off-campus tertiary education merges, so all tertiary education is engaged with adopting information technologies for teaching and learning.

The convergence of technologies seems, in one sense at least, to make the situation clearcut. There is an implication of total inclusiveness – of all and everything. Apparently discrete uses of technology (such as desktop video-conferencing) now are digitally driven through the Internet. Commonly accepted technologies, such as the telephone, are being augmented by Internet Relay Chats (IRCs) and Internet phone systems. There seems nothing – including print publishing – that is not computer-generated. A computer sits on nearly every academic's desk, many academics do not travel without their 'laptop' and there is an increasing expectation that all students have access to computers, ideally with CD-ROM and modems. Yet, when one looks more deeply into computer-based teaching and learning applications the reality is not what one would expect and it is fascinating to consider the reasons for what is commonly termed the gap (or chasm) between the rhetoric and the reality.

Although correspondence has remained the foundation of most distance education, morphological differences between distance and mainstream education are falling away as technology allows a closer simulation of the usual educational exchange between teacher and student. Whereas the distinctive nature of distance education was stressed in the 1970s, by the end of the 1980s some prominent scholars seemed to modify their views. For instance, Sewart, writing in 1981, contended (p. 11) that 'the process of learning at a distance is generically different from the conventional mode', yet in 1987 he claimed (p. 157), 'all teaching and learning is based upon the same fundamental principles. . . . There are no unique principles inherent in distance education which are not also inherent in mainstream education.'

While this, of itself, suggests convergence it should be appreciated that one of the hallmarks of distance education was information technology. In 1990 Wagner (p. 53) claimed that the relationship between the fields of distance education and educational technology is a strong one, with every indication of becoming even stronger. For Wagner (pp. 65–6) 'distance education provides educational technologists with an exceedingly rich research and application environment, while educational technology provides distance educators with methods and means of improving performance'. Three years earlier Garrison (1987, p. 45) had written, 'Distance education is inexorably linked to the technology of delivery. . . . Without the use of technology, distance education would not exist.' This is not a novel or radical view: as early as 1973 Moore (p. 664) claimed that media skills 'must' be employed in distance teaching. Now it is customary for media skills to be employed in face-to-face teaching as well, as educators strive to accommodate mission statements that stress such words as 'open' and 'flexible' and as more curricula need to model approaches that ensure relevance to a society where, in western developed economies, computers are a fundamental constituent of work practice and, to an increasing extent, of home life.

Recognizing that 'one of the most important developments in educational theory and practice in recent times' concerns technology – most notably communications technology – Green (1993, p. 9) asserted that this development would 'inevitably require, as many have observed, decisive shifts in how we think about and conduct curriculum and schooling, at every level'. A decade earlier, Schrag (1982) had contemplated such 'decisive shifts' at the university. Fearing the technologies that result in a 'fully formalized cybernetic world' would displace language and thought (p. 112), he urged for the university a recovery of the maieutic artistry of the Athenian Socrates. He wrote (p. 112):

> This would make it possible for us to reestablish learning as an adventure in the pursuit of knowledge. It would enable us again to approach communication as a creative process of dialogue and dialectics and thus restore both language and thought to their deserved eminence in the life of the university.

Yet technologies, rather than displacing language and thought, have the potential to help create the university culture Schrag envisages. Technology has not only supported, but has facilitated and influenced teaching and learning for tertiary off-campus students. Further, approaches to teaching so-called 'distance' students have influenced approaches to on-campus teaching. It is possible, for instance, that audio and video teleconferencing may help 'restore' oral language to more university students, while particularly providing access for those most obviously deprived of such communication: the off-campus learners. Computer teleconferencing, as well as interactive programs, fosters a level of contact that cannot necessarily be assumed as part of the on-campus experience.

It is, for me, an inescapable conclusion that technology does have the potential to allow creative approaches to what is at the heart of all education: communication. Whether that potential is realized is far less clearcut and hence the whole issue of convergence in this context is open to question. For although there appears to be consensus that educators are inevitably concerned with matters of technology, the question of whether technology (in whatever form) is celebrated or condemned, scrutinized or passively accepted, sought out as desirable or imposed and endured, is far more ambivalent and contested. Evans, for example (1991, p. 179), engendered a sense of foreboding with the word 'loom' when he wrote, 'In fact, they [matters of technology] often loom large over the entire teaching and learning processes.' There is now greater recognition of the complexities and implications that attend educational technology and, justifiably and correctly, increasing concern to scrutinize and problematize. Theorists such as Bigum and Green (1993), Campion (1991) and Harris (1987, 1991) offer insightful and thought-provoking critiques of the present, and scenarios of the future, as they raise pertinent questions about how choices and applications of technology impact on the design, delivery and reception of education, suggesting that some decisions to employ such technologies have been made with scant appreciation and understanding of their consequences. Even when they are selected in the context of a particular educational paradigm, as Harris (1991, p. 223) contended, it is 'now impossible to hold to educational technology as a universal discipline, offering principles of design that are so obviously superior as to need no justification or argument'.

Hence to the crux of this discussion: as information technologies and modes of tertiary education converge, what are the critical issues in moving from the experimental and narrow band of use (the marginal) to what is regarded as part of the core (mainstream) with wide use?

Dollars or attitude?

Whenever there is a perceived and shared need for something to happen and that something does not, in fact, occur, lack of resources almost inevitably gets blamed. Generally this is reduced to money: 'We can't afford it.' Occasionally the human as well as fiscal costs are mentioned.

Is money the critical issue in this debate? I am inclined to think not. There is money in the tertiary sector and money is being spent on information technologies. As just one example, in 1996 it was claimed that over a million dollars for each US college and university ($3–4 billion in all) was spent on academic computing alone (Geoghegan 1996). Then there is the much less readily quantified expenditure on the necessary supporting components, from administrative and institutional overheads to apportioning opportunity costs. However, while resources may be available, access to these resources is a different matter.

There is a further twist to the resource issue. As put bluntly in a recent Australian report to the relevant government body (University of New South Wales 1997, p. ix): 'The universities which get IT right will attract resources; those that get it wrong will not.' The issue is not bringing technologies to higher education – print has assumed mainstream status for generations of students and computer-based technologies are becoming increasingly pervasive – it is which technologies will make the transition from the experimental, the 'marginal', to be widely used by a broad band of the tertiary sector. Elsewhere (see, for example, Holt and Thompson 1995), I have referred to the 'imperative' of the use of IT in the tertiary sector. It seems axiomatic that information technologies will be highly significant in the delivery of teaching and learning; the real debate is over the issue of 'which sort', with 'when', 'where' and 'why' being key underpinnings. To get it 'right' such questions have to be correctly answered.

The critical issue in leveraging the university community to adopt a particular technology – or suite of technologies – is persuading and convincing the multiple decision makers that such a move is prudent and, indeed, essential. Beyond that there is a need to mobilize the academics, and at this stage in the process to a far lesser extent the students, to implement the 'vision'.

The different worlds of the enthusiast and the adopter

As a way of conceptualizing this issue I decided to use the term 'enthusiasts' for those who are actively involved in the emergent stages and 'adopters' (following Rogers 1995) for those who take on what is regarded as 'innovative' and bring it, with greater and lesser success, into the mainstream of teaching/learning for an individual curriculum at the micro-level and as a part of a cultural change within the university at a macro-level. I appreciate that this binary distinction simplifies the gradations of adoption from early to late participants and from small groups to large cohorts, but I still consider it a useful way of foregrounding issues.

The so-called 'true believers' in IT tend to be the enthusiasts. Their world is, indeed, a rarefied one in that they tend to work in an environment with access to top-end equipment and with solid support at the innovative and experimental stage. When your own computer runs at 200 MHz and is connected to a highly robust and permanently accessible network it is difficult to envisage the situation for others when they struggle to download networked data and only have dial-up access to the Internet. The gulf between these worlds is well exemplified when demonstrators, who are intimately involved with the process and work in a context where much is intuitive and taken-for-granted knowledge based on considerable experience, attempt to 'show' a product to neophytes. Moreover, where too much is taken for granted, there is sometimes justified complaint of receiving bits of information while the picture as a whole remains elusive. Often, and sadly, the more developed and sophisticated the product the less effective the presentation will be, as what is demonstrated seems so remote from the real-world experience of the tertiary educator. It is understandable that in such demonstrations it is the product that dominates. Yet of critical importance in the evolution of that product has been the process, and the separation of the two inhibits acceptance because much of the rationale has been clouded. The likely success stories here are those where academics – also of the 'enthusiast' variety – have been closely involved with all stages of the development and where they can identify more closely with the teaching sector and are more sensitive to such concerns.

If a technological 'solution' is going to be mainstreamed it is essential that it is presented in such a way that it seems useful. One of the strong inhibitors to a wider take-up of many apparently superb innovations is the 'add-on' factor. The enthusiasts (both technical and academic staff) often have the early period of development as a core function of their work. For the average teaching member of staff, the would-be adopter, the new development is cumulative and can be perceived as oppressive. 'Value-adding' is important and there are justifiable concerns regarding equity and access, but the reality is very often that the innovation is set alongside what is in place and so the demand on the academic staff is increased – at least in the vital early stages where decisions are being made to persevere or not. Not only is such redundancy in delivery extremely costly in monetary terms but the human effort is often insurmountable. While there may be acceptance, for instance, that computer conferencing is a 'good thing' in and of itself, in the final analysis it is not taken up widely because staff are not so convinced of its usefulness for them as teachers that they will let other things go, for they have made a judgement that the time cost is too high. As well, it is often difficult to convince such people that investment of their time in learning to use new technologies effectively will provide long-term gains, most especially in the current tertiary climate of competing priorities and demanding deadlines.

Moreover, for the enthusiast, the development process may be an end in itself: even if the final product does not function as intended, a considerable amount is gained from the experience itself. This is in direct contrast to the adopter, who generally wants a working system almost solely for what it can provide. Further, the enthusiast is challenged by the unknown; the potential adopter seeks proof – evidence that 'it' will work and clearly articulated statements of resultant teaching and learning outcomes. However, in the early stages before mainstreaming there is unlikely to be a robust body of evaluation or research to provide such assurance and, despite a huge literature in the field of educational technology, there is still inadequate understanding of how learning processes are mediated by technologies.

Further, while the enthusiast is likely to be tolerant of failure, to enjoy the whole risk-taking process, the adopter wants any technology to be failure-proof and non-disruptive. Academics quite rightly hesitate to expose students to cutting-edge technologies and for this reason much of the early development is separated from the teaching/learning experience. When it is delivered for the first time there is a strong likelihood of problems – of things not going quite as desired. Where the development is backed up by formative evaluation and the experience strongly supported, there is a reasonable likelihood that the knowledge gained will be reworked into a better product. This is especially the case if all concerned (including the students) are fully informed about the status of the new approach and feel a sense of involvement in the process. If the experience is seriously flawed, however, it is unlikely that further involvement will be welcomed.

Infrastructure

For IT to be mainstreamed the infrastructure must be there to support it. By 'infrastructure' I am referring to more than the conventional variant of an information technology service provider, important though that this. My definition includes management and professional development.

In the conventional service context, in the early stages infrastructure is less important mainly because, if and when there are failures, not only is the enthusiast likely to be more understanding and forgiving, but the effect of such failure is likely to be minimal. For instance, a server failure that is a minor irritant to the developer can be highly problematic for the students who are doing a computer-generated and -assessed examination. Moreover, it only takes one such experience for the academic community to become very wary. The enthusiast is likely to be very aware of the infrastructure; the adopter's awareness is likely to be tied to problems such as when the network is 'down'. The crisis in IT support is well documented (see, for example, McClure, Smith and Sitko 1997) and while 'help desks' fail to give timely assistance and responses are unhelpful in the current climate where so much is expected of the working week, it is tempting to give in and resort to well-known and less time-demanding and often less frustrating avenues of teaching. Again the gulf is wide as the enthusiast is likely to be able to solve the sort of technical problems that the adopter seeks help for, and finds it difficult to appreciate that what are often small areas of misunderstanding are not trivial, as perceived by the enthusiast, but significant hurdles to the adopter.

If the management infrastructure is fragile, then it is highly unlikely that the necessary steps will be taken at the right times to mainstream technologies. Dolence and Norris (1995) have their own response to Franklin's 'push–pull' metaphor as they advocate a fusion of learning vision 'pull' with the 'push' of technology application. If transformation towards the mainstream is to be accelerated then, as they argue, strategic thinking must precede strategic planning, with academic programmes and resource allocations closely aligned with institutional strategies. Where, as so often is the case, the focus is on specific technology products, the very success of these can place enormous pressure on support agencies (most especially technical) and, when they cannot cope with what is sometimes unexpected as well as burgeoning demand, their failure reverses the trend towards the mainstream, sometimes irrevocably.

Seeding grants for the development of cutting-edge technologies are welcomed by management because they bring external funding and often prestige to the institution. Sometimes they raise expectations of use beyond the funded trial period and, where management is weak, the enthusiasts are left in isolated positions. This is generally because they do not have the support necessary to involve others. Where management decides not to use university resources once the project period ends there is sometimes a failure to communicate this to the enthusiast and, quite often, innovations are left to wither over time, with attendant frustration. For good reasons some technological developments will remain marginal, and the enthusiast has a role in keeping such innovations alive; but, where the expectation is for possible mainstreaming, it is clear that the enthusiast, alone, is not in a position to achieve this.

Even where strong management decisions are made to mainstream, they tend to be ineffectual unless and until they are supported by effective professional development. Where the sense is one of technologies imposed on the university community with minimal sensitivity to the academic sector they are to serve and the reality of that world, the response is likely to be resistance. As constituent elements of professional development, opportunities must be provided not only for training in the technologies but for debating and discussing the pedagogical implications of their use. Showing what can be done by a given technology – with all its complexity as well as its promise – is inadequate. For the technological innovation to be mainstreamed the process must be owned, at least in part, by those who are to implement it – the adopters. The intricacy and elegance of the technology are likely to be compulsive motivations for the enthusiast but are likely to be irrelevant to the adopter who is seeking straightforward and nonthreatening technologies that do not demand a steep learning curve over a considerable period. As argued above, sharing the development process is valuable, but for those adopters who have not had this opportunity, they must be able to be active contributors to how the technology is applied in their own curriculum.

The student factor

Most institutions can point to at least some occasions where technologies have been developed well ahead of possible general adoption for students. Early CD-ROMs are a useful illustration. The rationale has generally been that such expensive prototypes have value at the margins for specific uses and users, and that much will be learned from the exercise. As a second illustration, the present comparative rarity of desktop videoconferencing in any university (let alone workplace or home) makes its movement into mainstream distance education in the next few years highly improbable.

It is not many years ago that it was politically incorrect to assume that all students would have computer access; consequently, any aspect of a course that was delivered in so-called 'non-traditional ways' had also to be delivered traditionally (usually face-to-face for on-campus students or in print for off-campus students). Not surprisingly, students responded to this duplication by resisting investments in computers until they could be convinced that they were necessary and would contribute in a unique way to their learning. There was a huge tension here. On the one hand, IT enthusiasts argued that the gains from using a particular technology were substantive and pointed to the uniquely defining characteristics: for instance, of facilitating peer as well as mentor interaction by computer conferencing with its written record of the exchanges. On the other hand, until such learning outcomes could be integrated into the fabric of the curriculum they were destined to remain peripheral. Yet they could only be integrated when it was assumed that all students had access to such base equipment. Increasingly this is the case. While internal surveys at the university where I work have shown access above 90 per cent for the whole of this decade, the most recent data released from the Australian Bureau of Statistics show that 41 per cent of all households have computers, with the popularity of CD-ROM drives and modems growing quickly (*Australian*, 1 July 1997). Such access is a necessary underpinning of mainstreaming.

Student response can be influential as new technologies move from small pilot groups to larger cohorts. The product and the infrastructure must be strong for student acceptance to occur. An excellent website that cannot be readily downloaded by modem from a lower-end machine will not be used. A fine conferencing system where the academic concerned rarely checks the folders and more rarely contributes is likely to die unless the students themselves – as does happen – are convinced of its usefulness. Further, students need assurance that the technology is adding value to the study and is not there for its own sake or for reasons that do not clearly relate to the curriculum. In this regard specialist instructional design that integrates technology and pedagogy is likely to achieve the desired learning outcomes and is an important element. Professional development should have a role in sensitizing academics to instructional design issues but is not a replacement for professional assistance.

Conclusion

Information technologies are having a major impact on tertiary institutions. Perhaps this is most clearly seen in the administrative sector, where already there is compelling evidence of huge investments in IT and changing work practices for staff. However, we are not yet at the stage where the rhetoric of the virtual university is our shared reality in terms of teaching and learning.

The Chair of the Higher Education Council of Australia, Professor Gordon Stanley, was quoted recently (28 May 1997) in the higher education supplement of the *Australian* as saying: 'Universities must move away from experimenting with information technology and begin to use it to make their programs more efficient and effective if they are to function competitively.' The exhortation to function competitively is not new to academics, nor is it without its difficulties for those involved in this cultural change. The interest in this comment here is the causal connection between success (as judged in competitive terms) and the use of IT, interpreted as integrated into the curriculum and delivery of higher education. While this directive through government adds its own force to the issue of mainstreaming, it is of concern that according to this edict 'experimentation' is to be shunned. Fundamentally, the basis of implementation is experimentation, and innovation is a tenet of the academy. Further, it is doubtful that many of the 'new media and information technologies' referred to in the chapter are readily integrated to the extent envisaged as necessary.

I have noted a tendency in the literature for experimental work to be reported as if it were integrated and systemic, when, in fact, on follow-up investigation it has been revealed to have touched a very small percentage of the university's staff and student population. Further, at a Research in Distance Education conference (see Thompson 1994) there was compelling evidence from representatives from a wide sector of Australian tertiary institutions of the difficulty of reporting 'failure' and even problems in this context, with much emphasis being on situating one's institution in a perceived most-favourable light. Hence problems tend to be buried and government agencies and university management often do not have the necessary information from sanitized reports on which to base decisions.

Hence, I conclude that, as far as cutting-edge technologies are concerned, the transition from enthusiast to adopter is often difficult to accomplish. Much is still with the enthusiast, who often has a narrow focus and needs strong institutional support if such experimental work is to be strategically aligned and implemented. As Geoghegan (1996) advised, we should nurture the innovators as they are the source of much creativity and they can provide models for mainstream adoption. University managers should see their role in this complex period of convergence as providing informed support and being responsive to the many and often competing demands. They should nurture both enthusiasts and adopters and assist at all levels as their institutions mainstream information technologies.

References

Bigum, C. and Green, B. (1993) 'Changing classrooms, computing and curriculum: critical perspectives and cautionary notes', *Australian Educational Computing* 8(1): 6–16.

Campion, M. G. (1991) 'Critical essay on educational technology in distance education', in T. Evans and B. King (eds), *Beyond the Text: Contemporary Writing on Distance Education*, Geelong: Deakin University Press, pp. 183–203.

Dolence, M. G. and Norris, D. M. (1995) *Transforming Higher Education: A Vision for Learning in the 21st Century*, Ann Arbor: Society for College and University Planning.

Evans, T. (1991) 'Technology in distance education: introduction', in T. Evans and B. King (eds), *Beyond the Text: Contemporary Writing on Distance Education*, Geelong: Deakin University Press, pp. 179–82.

Franklin, U. (1990) 'The real world of technology', CBC Massey Lectures Series, Concord: Anansi.

Garrison, D. R. (1987) 'The role of technology in continuing education', in R. G. Brockett (ed.), *New Directions For Continuing Education*, No. 36, San Francisco: Jossey-Bass, pp. 41–53.

Geoghegan, W. H. (1996) 'Instructional technology and the mainstream: the risks of success', Maytum Distinguished Lecture, SUNY College, Fredonia.

Green, B. (1993) 'Curriculum, technology, textual practice: images and issues', in B. Green (ed.), *Curriculum, Technology and Textual Practice*, Geelong: Deakin University Press, pp. 9–31.

Harris, D. (1987) *Openness and Closure in Distance Education*, Barcombe: The Falmer Press.

Harris, D. (1991) 'Towards a critical educational technology in distance education', in T. Evans and B. King (eds), *Beyond the Text: Contemporary Writing on Distance Education*, Geelong: Deakin University Press, pp. 204–25.

Holt, D. M. and Thompson, D. J. (1995) 'Responding to the technological imperative: the experience of an open and distance education institution', *Distance Education* 16(1): 43–64.

McClure, P. A., Smith, J. W. and Sitko, T. D. (1997) 'The crisis in information technology support: has our current model reached its limit?', CAUSE Professional Paper Series, No. 16, Boulder, Colo.

Moore, M. G. (1973) 'Toward a theory of independent learning and teaching', *Journal of Higher Education* 44(12): 661–79.

Rogers, E. M. (1995) *Diffusion of Innovations*, 4th edn, New York: Free Press.

Schrag, C. O. (1982) 'The idea of the university and the communication of knowledge in a technological age', in M. J. Hyde (ed.), *Communication Philosophy and the Technological Age*, Tuscaloosa, Ala.: The University of Alabama Press, pp. 98–113.

Sewart, D. (1981) 'Distance teaching: a contradiction in terms?', *Teaching at a Distance* 19: 8–18.

Sewart, D. (1987) 'Staff development needs in distance education and campus-based education: are they so different?', in P. Smith and M. Kelly (eds), *Distance Education and the Mainstream: Convergence in Education*, New York: Croom Helm, pp. 156–74.

Stoll, C. (1995) *Silicon Snake Oil: Second Thoughts on the Information Highway*, New York: Doubleday.

Thompson, D. J. (1994) ' "And will we write a letter?" Research to inform the selection of educational technologies', in T. Evans and P. Murphy (eds), *Research in Distance Education 3*, Geelong: Institute of Distance Education, Deakin University, pp. 103–14.

University of New South Wales (1997) *Managing the Introduction of Technology in the Delivery and Administration of Higher Education*, Canberra: Department of Education, Employment and Youth Affairs.

Wagner, E. D. (1990) 'Looking at distance education through an educational technologist's eyes', *American Journal of Distance Education* 4(1): 53–68.

13 Building tools for flexibility

Designing interactive multimedia at the Open University of Hong Kong

Ross Vermeer

Introduction

Over the past nine years, the Open University of Hong Kong (OUHK) has quickly established a reputation as a leading Asian distance-education institution. After a series of accreditation procedures and a nervous period wondering if sufficient time remained in the Hong Kong legislative council's schedule to consider an Open University ordinance before the territory's July 1997 handover to the People's Republic of China, the former Open Learning Institute (OLI) did indeed, in May 1997, become the OUHK. Even in this time of celebration, however, the OUHK faces the same challenges as other tertiary institutions around the world: scarce funding, technological changes and increased competition. The issue of 'convergence' is inextricably tied to these challenges.

These several challenges cannot all be addressed here – an impossible task. Instead, this chapter will focus on one challenge facing the OUHK: dealing with new technologies.The discussion begins with a brief introduction to some of the challenges facing distance-teaching universities in general with respect to new technologies, particularly ones associated with a possible convergence between 'traditional' and distance teaching institutions; it outlines details of non-print media development at the OUHK; and it finally focuses on a particular project, a CD-ROM dealing with the history of Hong Kong. An attempt will then be made to highlight some of the tensions inherent in the development of multimedia-based learning materials that are often ignored or downplayed in the rush to 'keep up' with trends in both the uses of technology and in teaching.

Technology and convergence

The claim that fundamental forces of change are at work in the educational community in general, and distance education in particular, is now a commonplace. Equally true is that many of the forces are focused on uses of technology. Among the important changes listed by the International Council for Distance Education (ICDE) task force on the educational paradigm shift was 'the shift to technologically mediated processes of

communication and learning' (ICDE 1996, p. 4). Also of interest was the discussion of both 'drivers of educational change' and the perceived 'barriers
and blockages to the educational paradigm shift'. The drivers are:

- the explosion of information;
- information technology;
- the changing nature of work; and
- the changing student population.

(ibid., pp. 8, 9)

Concerning the opposite forces, the report noted a general resistance to
change, along with the following specific barriers:

- resistance to new learning theory and practice;
- rigidity of organizational structures;
- the tyranny of time;
- traditional faculty roles and rewards;
- assumptions about learning content;
- constraints of regulatory and accrediting practices; and
- traditional funding formulas.

(ibid., p. 10)

Although these 'drivers' refer to distance-teaching universities in general,
they can reasonably be applied to many 'traditional' universities as well.
Given this common challenge, it is worthwhile considering how both types
of universities will address it, and to ask whether such attempts will in fact
fuel convergence.

Distance-teaching institutions would appear to have a head start in harnessing the drivers, overcoming the barriers and applying new technologies,
largely because of their lack of historical commitment to traditional classroom technologies. They do not customarily have physical classrooms, but
have groups of learners linked to tutors and teachers through learning
materials and a variety of forms of interaction, whether it be by television,
mail, the telephone, the computer or other means. The institutions have
developed sophisticated procedures and practices for providing courses
and support remotely to their students. Their course materials, even if
print-based, usually exist in digital form. Conventional institutions have
had to scramble to catch up in many of these areas (Murphy, Tsang and
Vermeer 1996). This apparent advantage would apply equally to both the
institutions and to distance-education students themselves. Distance-
education students are accustomed to receiving and discussing their courses
remotely, and so their ties to face-to-face education are not usually as strong
as their mainstream counterparts.

But the picture is not entirely rosy. Distance-teaching institutions face
challenges both from newer institutions, and, ironically, from older ones.

For example, several first-rank American universities (including Michigan, Chicago, Duke and Dartmouth) are offering very profitable degrees (MBAs) in Europe and Asia using Internet-based education, therefore simply bypassing the 'traditional' channels of distance education altogether. It would be bitter indeed if conventional universities responded more constructively to new technologies than the supposed experts in distance learning because, as Tony Bates (1996) points out, traditional universities' agrarian/medieval structure is actually more nimble and adaptable than that of the modern/industrial distance-education university.

New technologies are thus placing pressures on institutions to make decisions about how distance education is to function in the future, and if those pressures are not faced successfully a new generation of distance-teaching institutions will emerge. Decisions to be taken are thus fundamental to the survival of existing institutions:

> distance educators cannot afford to wait until this evolving situation is fully understood and some standardized plan for innovation can be constructed. . . . Backward-looking metaphors focus on what we can automate – how we can use new channels to send conventional forms of content more efficiently – but miss the true innovation: redefining how we communicate and educate by effectively using new types of messages and experiences.
>
> (Dede 1996, pp. 5–6)

All universities, distance or not, need to become more flexible and responsive to change, whether technological, political, economic or demographic. A more flexibly organized university is a university better equipped to deal with change, period. The new distance-education university would feature: 'a high degree of decentralization, but overall leadership and direction in terms of broad but clear goals . . . customized products and services, alliances with key partners that provide complementary services . . . and highly networked and flexible communications systems linking them with their clients' (Bates 1996, p. 15). A new vision of the distance-education university might also include more space for producing new knowledge, as well as for new ways to pass conventional knowledge on to students. But that university would be quite unlike either the traditional university of the western tradition, or the twentieth-century distance-education 'mega-university'. Envisaging the 'new university' is, however, a fairly pointless exercise unless concrete steps are taken to address the challenges of rapid technological change. Distance-education universities must not assume they are already adequately doing so, simply because of their historical expertise with educational technology.

The experience of distance-education students in this new university also calls out for attention. Distance-education students should, we might reasonably assume, be more comfortable constructing their own educational programmes, their educational goals, and perhaps, given their experience with distance-learning techniques, their understanding of course materials as well. Yet are students really prepared for study in a dencentralized, post-modern university where technology pervades exchanges between themselves and teachers, and even amongst themselves? Will such a university provide the best possible learning environment for them – or even a decent learning environment at all?

These challenges come to the forefront, therefore, in the design of electronic learning tools and environments, for it is at this level that dealing with these abstract administrative and pedagogical issues becomes a reality. The rest of this chapter takes a background look at the OUHK's institutional response, then focuses in on this specific project-design level.

The Open University response

Although the OUHK was originally envisaged as part of a consortium to be supported by the other local conventional universities, that vision was never realized (Hong Kong 1989). This failure closed off many possible paths for co-operation, and hence convergence, with conventional tertiary institutions in Hong Kong.

In the nine years of its existence, then, the OUHK has relied primarily on print-based course materials. Many of these courses were in fact bought in or adapted from materials produced by the UK Open University (OUUK), and new courses developed at OUHK have followed the basic OUUK style and philosophy of course development and presentation. The OUHK has also managed, with occasional government help, to become self-supporting. It therefore cannot afford to spend vast resources on technology developments. It has relied upon well-established technologies, such as broadcast television, to supplement its primarily print-based course materials. Audio tapes are also used, along with a few computer applications. In addition, there is limited use of an electronic bulletin-board service.

The Open University of Hong Kong is, however, a highly appropriate place in which to conduct investigations into the uses of multimedia teaching methods. Although it cannot currently be described as a leader or innovator in educational methods, the OUHK serves a technologically sophisticated clientele in a highly competitive market environment, so institutional focus is beginning to shift from 'getting on our feet' to becoming a respected centre for educational research and the application of up-to-date teaching methods. Inevitably, therefore, the OUHK, on both a formal and a more piecemeal basis, has committed itself to both an increasing use of multimedia teaching tools and to beginning to teach courses on-line. Given recent criticisms of the failure of highly bureaucratic distance-teaching institutions to respond rapidly to changes, this opportunistic approach to using new technologies may not be a bad thing.

The development model the OUHK has adopted combines existing design capacity with outside expertise in the technical aspects of programming and production. Overall, this makes effective use of limited resources, and does not commit the university to a particular technology. Current developments include two management information systems to enhance OUHK's administration. One is the development of interactive voice response systems for students for selection of tutorial groups, course registration, loan applications, transcription applications and the checking of mailing dates for course materials. The other enhancement is the development of a document imaging system to store, view, print and scan documents.

The OUHK also intends gradually to change its computer network towards up-to-date networking technologies, using standards such as data link, physical layer protocols and network wiring standards. Optical fibres will be used to implement the wiring backbone, and the network will be upgraded to support applications such as client-server, imaging, multimedia and videoconferencing. An 'electronic library' with a CD-ROM network is now partially operative, allowing staff and students to access CD-ROM databases for learning, and for research and development. The OUHK has also arranged to provide Internet services to all students, both at the OUHK campus and through special reduced-rate packages negotiated with a commercial Internet service provider. Course teams are being encouraged, and in some cases required, to provide web pages for many OUHK courses.

The OUHK is thus making a number of strategic decisions with respect to the new technologies. These decisions are based on both local and global factors, including:

- local conditions;
- the present and future operation of the Internet;
- the needs of Hong Kong learners;
- the availability of the technologies;
- resource constraints, both on the institute and its students; and
- the desired teaching and learning approaches.

To further assist in this decision making, the university funds a number of research and development projects. It has committed staff and funds to two interactive multimedia programs delivered on CD-ROMs: a Hong Kong history program and a program for teaching Mandarin Chinese to Cantonese speakers. Each project is a small-scale example of the application of new technologies.

The history of Hong Kong

Choosing to produce the program

An internal OUHK survey carried out in 1994 showed that only thirteen of our courses had a computing component, and – much more telling – that all of these computing software packages were externally produced. We decided that making a leap into the fray of multimedia development would be worthwhile, since we had a likely candidate, our newly developed history of Hong Kong course, *AW213 A History of Hong Kong 1842–1984*. An interactive multimedia program seemed the best way to integrate *AW213* course materials and visual and audio resources easily obtained from Hong Kong's government archives and museums.

The program was developed under the auspices of a research project headed by Ross Vermeer, a course designer, and Linda Chung, an educational technologist, both members of the OUHK's Educational Technology and Publishing Unit. The project has also enjoyed the collaboration of the original course writer, Dr David Faure of the University of Oxford, who added his expertise by writing additional explanatory text and guiding the selection of visual materials.

We chose a history course as a starting point for several reasons: this was a project of manageable dimensions; it could be served by a fairly straightforward interface design; much raw visual material was already sourced via our development of the history course; and the course provided text that could be adapted.

Designing the program

We decided to produce an IM program that made up only part of a course, but that could also stand alone as an independent supplement. Such a program would be designed to be accessible to both students taking the course and anyone else who wanted to learn about Hong Kong history.

The OUHK has no staff with the necessary programming and interface design experience, so we had to look outside for an external producer. After an open-tendering process involving bids from both educational institutions and commercial producers, the project was awarded to a team of specialists in multimedia development from the Centre for Applied Learning Systems (CALS) at the Adelaide Institute of Technical and Further Education in Adelaide, South Australia. This international cooperative effort gave the project a unique perspective, but also caused some difficulties, to be discussed below.

Work proceeded on a simple, flexible development model based on a commercial model designed by Roy Strauss and published in *New Media* magazine. This model comprises four basic stages: research, design, production and testing. The OUHK researchers acquired resources from local government sources; managed the project as a whole; and contributed to the general program design. Staff from CALS provided additional project management, graphic and interface design, and coding.

We pursued the following general project objectives:

1 To develop an interactive multimedia program delivered via CD-ROM disks to supplement the course content for *AW213*.
2 To evaluate the interactive multimedia program produced.
3 To develop ETPU staff expertise for future non-print media projects.
4 To prepare a program that helps OUHK students deal with modern technologies essential in an information-driven society such as Hong Kong.
5 To develop institutional experience in delivering sophisticated non-print instructional material.

Project results

The finished program features text articles, photographs and video footage. These elements are arranged and accessed through what has turned out to be a quite visually elegant interface. The program's visual design is perhaps its highlight; it is of a high standard, comparable we believe to commercial products costing many times the budget for this project.

In its final design, the program comprises four main sections:

1 A timeline showing key events in Hong Kong history and a pictorial history of the development of Hong Kong's famous harbour and skyline. The print-based course materials begin by helping students learn to put historical events into order and into context so that they have a chronological framework for understanding historical trends and themes. This section of the CD-ROM should enhance those activities. The timeline is designed as a dragon; the events or years are marked as scales on the dragon's back and belly.
2 A large section on historical themes, comprising articles, photographs and video clips covering Hong Kong's economic, social, industrial and political development, as well as the Territory's experiences in World War II and the period of rapid change and unrest that followed. This part of the program contains most of its resources. This wide range of topics is covered in depth, with hundreds of photos and about twenty video clips accompanying well over 100 text articles. The design of this section is perhaps closest to what one sees in many data-heavy CD-ROM programs, as well as on many Web pages: the organization is hierarchical, and links are mainly up and down that hierarchy. Text is broken up into small chunks on consecutive screens, allowing for a fairly large pitch size for the text, enhancing readability.
3 A map-driven section on certain towns and districts in the Territory. This section depicts the changes in Central, Kowloon, Shatin and other locations around Hong Kong over the years. Users gain access to the various places by clicking on a map-menu, then read articles

about the place they clicked on, or view an 'interactive slide show' of photos of that location in the historical era they choose.

4   A comprehensive look at the 'Life of the People' of Hong Kong. This section focuses on the way the majority of people in the territory have lived their lives, rather than on the minutiae of colonial administrations that so many of Hong Kong's historians have addressed. Text, photos and video clips are closely aligned in this section, which depicts the lives of the poor, the wealthy and the great majority of Hong Kong's people, the working and middle classes. Particular attention is paid to details of ordinary Hong Kong life: housing, leisure activities and day-to-day tasks such as running small businesses, finding housing and going to the movies.

Altogether, the program contains several hundred text articles, several hundred photographs and other graphical images, and over thirty minutes of video footage. A word-search facility is also provided; this engine gives users immediate access to any part of the program that appears as a search result.

So has this project met our list of objectives? So far we think it has, and we hope it will continue to do so. The primary objectives – developing a useful learning tool for our students, using a new technology and gaining experience in such projects – have been achieved. The researchers have gained the experience they were looking for, given the amount of time they had to devote to the project. The university now has a project under its belt, and perhaps can better look forward to continuing to develop its commitment to multimedia development.

The work of David Faure, as subject matter expert, particularly benefited this project. Since Dr Faure also developed the original course *AW213*, his work on this project has built a seamless connection between printed material and CD-ROM content. It has therefore proved very easy to integrate this CD-ROM into the *AW213* course work. This fulfilled another of our goals; we have no way of knowing now, of course, but we believe that choosing a commercial producer might have jeopardized this aspect of the program's content, particularly if the producer were determined to make the program more 'marketable'. Working with another academic institution precluded this possible conflict of intentions.

On the whole, then, the project has gone as planned, save for the timing. We are particularly pleased that the project has been completed well within its designated resource limits. We have proved that collaborative multimedia work across international boundaries can be done, and done well, given a reasonable budget (about US$90,000 was enough for this pro-ject) and a sufficient time frame (over two years overall; and about fifteen months after contracting CALS).

Putting the program into use

This project will continue to evolve and bear fruit as we track the actual use of the new CD-ROM in *AW213* course presentations. The first presentation is currently under way; the program was made available to April 1997 semester *AW213* students. The *AW213* course team has focused on integrating the use of the CD-ROM into the extant printed course materials. We are doing our best to avoid asking students simply to wander about the program trying to absorb useful knowledge from its hypertext environment (Laurillard 1994): activities and assessment included in the printed course materials have been developed to guide students' use of the program, and to focus their 'reading' of this electronic text while maintaining their freedom to browse and follow links that interest them.

There is great possibility for further development of the program itself. Although copies, once pressed, are permanent, the program itself is easily updated and expanded. If the OUHK decides to make a commitment to in-house multimedia development, this program can easily be kept up to date. It also provides a wealth of well-organized materials that would be appropriate for translation to a website (assuming the necessary copyright issues could be resolved).

The CD-ROM on Hong Kong history provides a useful tool for all of the Special Administrative Region's tertiary history students, and will be of general interest to most Hong Kong people. We hope, therefore, that developing such teaching tools will help raise the OUHK's profile in the local tertiary community, and serve as the catalyst for future collaboration, and convergence, if you will, on similar projects.

Inherent tensions

Although initial indications are that this OUHK CD-ROM development project was a success, and that principles and skills acquired through it will be useful for the creation of future multimedia learning environments in OUHK courses, the project also raised questions about the efficacy and appropriateness of multimedia teaching methods in general. There were points in the design and development processes that challenged the development team's assumptions and expectations about designing teaching materials. This section is an attempt to address one of the most important of these issues: the need to balance the flexibility of hypertext with the coherence of historical narrative.

In particular, our concerns were with neither teaching nor learning *per se*, but rather with the context in which they take place. It is not enough simply to show that learning can be mediated through electronic means. Research is needed to help show how such learning can be actively fostered and enhanced, and to explore the ways the learning environment affects its quality. In other words, the design and use of electronically created and mediated learning environments compels investigation into what it really means to 'read' and understand electronic texts – to redefine what 'literacy' really means – an issue coming under increasing scrutiny (Kaplan 1995). Enthusiasts such as Myron Tuman (1992) assure us that students set free in a hypertext environment will take on the characteristics of the 'playful' readers, who, given a number of starting points and paths through texts, images and other information, will exult in this freedom and exert their own imaginations and meaning-making powers in constructing knowledge. The flexibility of hyperlinked information compels a new, and exciting, way of reading and understanding.

Yet is all of this 'flexibility' really the best way to structure an electronically delivered, multimedia-based learning environment? In other words, is providing a learner with hypertext – the ability to link to related information – enough? Is there not something lost in providing such flexibility? Specifically, in the case of subjects such as history, is there not a greater narrative order lost, a framework – whether it be chronological, thematic or otherwise – that simply cannot be recreated by students working in a hypertext environment? Is it intellectually responsible to present the history of a single geographical and political entity such as Hong Kong in a randomly accessed selection of brief, 'atomized' articles? How can the natural chronological and narrative flow of such a history be adequately maintained in a hypertext-dominated technology? Still other concerns surround the issue of language competency: OUHK students are overwhelmingly *not* native English speakers, yet, as part of an international studies degree programme presented in English, the program is exclusively in English as well. Is extra guidance therefore necessary, or can students who are often quite uncomfortable using English in the first place be trusted to enjoy a 'playful romp' through historical hypertext?

Balancing hypertextual flexibility with a desire to retain a coherent narrative recounting of key historical themes and events was therefore a daunting design task. As we planned this program, we found ourselves taking constant difficult decisions in trying to balance the narrative unity of a theme or episode in Hong Kong's history against the need to keep blocks of text short, and flexibly accessible to the program's users. Although no such compromise can ever be wholly satisfactory, we believe we struck a reasonable balance. We allowed the topic of a particular article to determine its length: this meant making some of the thematic articles significantly longer than we had originally planned (i.e., in the range of 1,000–1,500 words); we decided some sacrifices in design elegance had to be made in order to maintain narrative integrity.

Similar problems were apparent in placing photographs and video clips. Rather than simply place them in a 'gallery' in chronological order, or arrange them in pretty but ultimately forgettable collages, we worked hard to 'embed' all visual images within environments that would lend them meaning. An analogy with a printed book is instructive here: collections of photographic plates set together in one series of pages in the middle of a book are useful, but they are not as useful as having a photo available on the page of text to which it is related. We wanted to avoid too much unnecessary 'paging' back and forth from images to text, so we again tried to strike a balance, with individual photos and video clips coming up only on 'pages' where they are firmly embedded in a greater narrative structure. We hope this will ensure that students have a context for making sense out of what they see, so that their journey through our multimedia learning environment will have a sense of direction and purpose, instead of being a random wander through a rich country where the forest cannot be seen for trees. The timeline and map section will also, we hope, provide additional frameworks to help signpost and structure student learning – in these cases, chronological and geographical frameworks, respectively.

Finally, we also gave up any and all attempts to present one continuous path to 'reading the whole history'. At the project outset, we had hoped to design a program that could 'tell the whole story' of Hong Kong's history. Indeed, this would not have been impossible, but it would have required the inclusion of thousands upon thousands more words of text than we wanted to ask our students to read on screen. Taken on its own, therefore, the program will not give a novice a fully adequate picture of Hong Kong's history. We maintain that a taught course is necessary to provide this organizing experience, and that, in that vein, many of its future users will be students taking Hong Kong history courses at other tertiary and upper-secondary institutions in the Hong Kong Special Administrative Region and perhaps beyond. What the program will do, we hope, is to bring that history alive for students who are already immersed in the printed course materials or a conventional classroom experience, and to provide an attractive 'appetite whetting' to anyone who picks up the CD and uses it outside the context of the course itself.

In the end, one cannot help but wonder whether, having worked through the entire contents of the program, a learner would be able to construct an accurate narrative account of Hong Kong's history – or even whether this is a useful and worthwhile goal. Yet we would like to think our efforts in creating this program were worthwhile. It remains to be seen, therefore, to what degree, and in what specific way, using this program enhances our students' learning. This question, like the ones above, provides fertile grounds for continuing research into the efficacy of electronic learning environments.

What we have discovered so far is that the challenges of developing flexible and effective learning tools extend well beyond the logistics of programming and funding, and in fact call into question many long-held assumptions about how teaching and learning should take place.

Implications for convergence

What light, then, does this experience shed on the convergence of distance and 'mainstream' or traditional face-to-face instruction? I will highlight three areas in which I think our experience can help to illuminate how that convergence is taking place; why, on the whole, such convergence is to be sought; and yet what dangers such convergence may pose.

1   The production of interactive multimedia programs, World Wide Web pages, electronic texts distributed by various means – all hold in common their essentially digital natures. As digital resources they can, with varying degrees of difficulty, be transported, transcribed and some-times transformed into an infinite variety of shapes or vessels. They are portable, reproducible and malleable in ways traditionally printed texts or face-to-face lectures can never be. Our program, although delivered via CD-ROM, has already been excerpted for an OUHK web page, and has been used by students in school settings. We expect in the future that it will be revised, adapted and excerpted for other uses we did not really anticipate when we initially conceived the program. Such possibilities for a variety of uses highlight the power and flexibility of electronically mediated teaching materials: they can be used or adapted by a variety of institutions for a variety of learners, and they can be altered to meet specific learners' needs. The possibility for both distance education and traditional institutions to draw upon and adapt the best available electronic teaching tools makes convergence both more likely, and more palatable.

2   We learned that researching and sorting through thousands of photo-graphs, dozens of hours of video material and reams of printed docu-ments took a lot of time and effort. One undeniable reason, then, why convergence should take place is the chance to avoid the replication of such efforts. Sharing electronically mediated teaching materials makes good financial sense, and it promotes institutional co-operation. It gives students the chance to access some of the best teaching efforts avail-able from a range of institutions, not just their own. And it also helps staff in both distance-education and traditional institutions learn about 'how things are done on the other side'. Such cross-pollination of ideas and approaches should only benefit learners in the long run.

3   Again, however, I will close with a note of caution. Our troubles in designing and structuring the Hong Kong history program exposed one of the pitfalls of electronically mediated teaching in general, and interactive multimedia programs in particular: if great care is not taken, the narratives that surround and hold together the transmission of information and ideas to learners can be obscured, or even lost. Even if a course draws together the very best available electronic teach-ing resources, those excellent individual parts may add up to a very

inadequate whole if they are not held together by some other narrative – a teacher, or a well-designed printed study guide, or the like. In the current educational climate, this is surely a greater danger for distance teaching institutions, but as boundaries between distance and traditional teaching blur, this problem will face almost all institutions looking to make use of electronically mediated forms of teaching.

Conclusion

The OUHK's first complete CD-ROM project has served as a useful intro-duction to multimedia development. It has also, however, been time-consuming and often frustrating, and has sparked off questions within the university that will likely continue to be debated as multimedia and on-line technologies come into greater and greater use.

The future of effective multimedia development includes CD-ROM delivery, but the field is expanding rapidly into networked services, especially those transmitted via the Internet. CD-ROM-delivered programs can still better handle complex and visually detailed material, but that too is changing as transmission technologies improve. The OUHK is pleased with its first foray into multimedia development, but should also be ready to continue its commitment to continuous and systematic research into new teaching technologies.

In a sense, the OLI/OUHK was 'set aside' years ago to develop alone as a distance-education provider, clearly separate from the rest of Hong Kong's tertiary sector. It would be somewhat surprising, however, if technological developments and the resultant changes in educational practice at all kinds of tertiary institutions allowed this gap to remain intact for much longer, in spite of – or perhaps just despite – the pitfalls such convergence may engender.

References

Bates, A. W. (1996) 'The impact of technological change on open and distance learn-ing', keynote address delivered at the 'Open Learning: Your Future Depends on It' conference in Brisbane, Australia, 4–6 Dec.

Dede, C. (1996) 'The evolution of distance education: emerging technologies and distributed learning', *American Journal of Distance Education* 10(2): 4–36.

Hong Kong (1989) *The Report of the Planning Committee for the Open Learning Institute of Hong Kong.*

ICDE (1996) 'The educational paradigm shift: implications for ICDE and the distance learning community', task force report, ICDE Standing Committee of Presidents' Annual Meeting, Lillehammer, Norway.

Kaplan, N. (1995) 'E-literacies', *Computer-Mediated Communication Magazine* 2(3): 11.

Laurillard, D. (1994) 'Adapting multimedia technologies for academic learning', in M. Thorpe and D. Grugeon (eds), *Open Learning in the Mainstream*, Harlow: Longman, pp. 261–76.

Murphy, D., Tsang, E. and Vermeer, R. (1996) 'Interactive multimedia development at the Open Learning Institute of Hong Kong', paper delivered at the ET2000 international conference in Singapore, 15–17 Aug.

Strauss, R. (1994) 'Budgeting and scheduling a CD-ROM project', *New Media* 4(2): 99–101.

Tuman, M. (1992) *Word Perfect: Literacy in the Computer Age*, Pittsburgh: The University of Pittsburgh Press.

14 A case study of convergence between conventional and distance education

Using constructivism and postmodernism as a framework to unconverge the mind

Gill Young and Di Marks-Maran

Introduction to the BSc (Hons) in Health Promotion: setting the scene

The BSc in Health Promotion at the Wolfson Institute has been run as a taught programme for several years. Although the course was well evaluated by the students undertaking the modules within the programme, many of them began expressing concern that it was becoming increasingly difficult for them to organize their work and domestic lives to come to the university to attend the taught sessions, despite the fact that we have provided these at varying times of the day. More and more of our existing students were asking whether they could undertake the modules via distance learning. Additionally, at recruitment events an increasing number of potential students began requesting that this programme be available via distance learning. For these reasons, as well as to increase the potential of our market, in 1995 we took the decision to further develop this programme so that it could be delivered at a distance, either through paper-based packages or over the Internet. We decided in the first instance to focus on delivering the year-three modules via distance learning.

The Centre for Teaching and Learning at the Wolfson Institute took the lead in providing the necessary staff development for teachers to produce distance-learning materials, to explore and develop the kinds of learning support techniques that would be required for students learning at a distance and to provide the administrative systems to enable students to enrol, receive materials, have queries and problems dealt with and manage the submission of assessments. The Wolfson Institute has been exploring distance education and other educational initiatives such as problem-based and practice-based learning. As part of this work, theoretical frameworks of teaching and learning were being examined and explored so that the decisions we made about our approach to new learning initiatives could have a sound and defensible rationale.

This chapter will explore the theoretical underpinning of our approach to distance education from a constructivist and postmodernist perspective and how this particular programme is based on these two approaches. It also includes a case study in enhancing quality in distance education and a look to the future of educational design and delivery in distance education and conventional higher education.

Using constructivism and postmodernism as frameworks to unconverge the mind

In recent years in the field of health care there has been a rise in the importance of evidence-based health-care practice. Evidence-based practice is an attempt to ensure that clinical decisions made by doctors, nurses, midwives and other health-care professionals are made by critically evaluating all available evidence. The aim of this evidence-based approach in health care is to ensure that clinical decisions are based not on ritual or routine (Sackett and Rosenberg 1995) but on sound and reasoned argument and thinking for the ultimate good of patient care. However, there is increasing concern that the criteria for what is to count as 'worthwhile' evidence is based on a modernist understanding of one reality, with scientific, empirical, quantitative evidence being regarded by some clinicians as the only legitimate evidence. Postmodernist thinkers in health care are now suggesting that legitimate evidence for making health-care decisions should come from multiple sources, first because there is often insufficient quantitative, empirical data available to support many clinical decisions and second because scientific, quantitative data, even when and where they do exist, do not provide all the answers to clinical questions. New definitions of what is to count as legitimate evidence are arising, to include the values, beliefs and preferences of clients (Page 1996) and qualitative data using such methodologies as phenomenology (Benner 1994); in the absence of data, theory is sometimes used to make clinical decisions (Parse 1992). But what is particularly significant is that health care is demanding that decisions have a rationale and that health-care decision makers can justify and defend their actions with reference to available evidence, regardless of how that evidence is defined.

So what has this to do with the convergence between conventional and distance education? It seems appropriate that decisions about teaching and learning in higher education should also be evidence-based. But this raises some obvious questions: What is to count as evidence-based practice in teaching? Where can we find evidence for making decisions about how best to enable our students to learn? How do we know that the evidence we uncover is sound evidence and applicable to the decisions we have to make about our teaching? How can we turn evidence into practice? These are

- Qualitative and quantitative research studies into how students learn.
- Values, beliefs, assumptions and ideologies of individual teachers and institutional mission statements.
- Learning theories and models.

Figure 14.1 Sources of evidence-based teaching

questions that are arising within conventional education and within open and distance learning.

Like health care, evidence-based teaching in this postmodernist age will rely on a number of sources (see Figure 14.1). In this chapter an overview of some of the issues related to sources of evidence, particularly learning theories, will be presented.

Theories about how students learn have existed for thousands of years either implicitly or explicitly and can be reviewed by examining teaching and learning practices over time. Fowler, Mayes and Bowles (1994) suggest that early informal education often took the form of discussion or dialogue between mentors (teachers) and their protégés (students). Protégés learned by directly questioning the mentor and noting the mentor's responses to questions asked by other protégés. Over the centuries, this original mentor/protégé dialogue approach has shifted to a deficit model of teaching and learning. Dialogue has become less important; transmitting information from the one who knows (the teacher) to one who does not know (the student) has become the model for teaching and learning in higher education. Renshaw (1995) suggests that this transmission model is based on a number of assumptions about teaching and learning (see Figure 14.2). Within this

- Learning is correct performance of a task.
- Teaching is giving accurate information.
- Learning is cumulative.
- Teaching is sequential.
- Learning is receptive.
- Teaching is direct.
- Learning comes from outside in.
- Teaching is structuring the environment.
- Learning is practising and performing.
- Teaching is rewarding performance.

Figure 14.2 Assumptions underpinning the transmission model of teaching and learning
Source: Renshaw 1995

theoretical position the excellent teacher provides a sequential, cumulative, highly controlled, rewarded and successful set of learning experiences. Incomplete or inaccurate performance by the student is immediately corrected by feedback so that ultimately only correct responses are practised (ibid.).

If we were to place a theoretical label on this approach it might be called didacticism or instructionalism (Fowler, Mayes and Bowles 1994), although Renshaw (1995) suggests the term 'transmission model'. In many respects, that which is termed 'conventional' education has largely been guided by a transmission model. It is evident in academic timetables, and recent evidence suggests that despite changes in theoretical understanding about learning, the lecture remains the most commonly used form of teaching practice in higher education (National Committee of Inquiry into Higher Education 1997).

At the opposite end of the spectrum – although within postmodernism such opposites are not necessarily in conflict with each other – lies constructivism. Draper (1994) suggests that constructivism is a label for an epistemological position which holds that there is never enough knowledge or information for a person to be sure of the belief she/he holds. The reason for this, according to Draper, is that although experience can prove our beliefs to be wrong/false, it can never prove them true. In this respect, constructivism fits (philosophically) into sceptical arguments as described by others (e.g., Kripke 1982). Draper suggests that as a consequence of this, an individual's beliefs are not just a reflection of external reality but result from two factors interacting with each other: those constraints from external events which may refute our beliefs, and our prior mental content (which Draper refers to as the 'history of the mind' (1994, p. 3)). As a theory of interplay between these two factors, constructivism does not really have an opposite, as was intimated by Renshaw (1995). Instead, constructivism appears to be in opposition to both rival theoretical positions, each of which claims that one factor overrides the other. Objectivism or realism claims, according to Draper (1994), that external inputs determine a person's belief, while extreme relativism proposes that only prior mental contents matter. In line with postmodernist thought, constructivism reconciles these two conflicting extremes by suggesting that beliefs arise from the interplay between the two.

Constructivism, then, proposes that individual beliefs are formed in part by the student's prior mental contents and in part by external inputs. In taking this point of view constructivists suggest that both objectivism and extreme relativism are each partly right but are also both equally wrong in opting for a single-factor theory. Single-factor theory suggests one truth. Constructivism holds that we can never be sure that we have arrived at the truth; that beliefs are not all equally valid and that they have to fit external inputs. Constructivism suggests that learning depends upon both current external inputs and prior mental contents. Where transmission works, the learner's beliefs converge closely with external inputs (e.g., concepts, information, tasks or explanations). Where transmission does not work, it is often because the contribution of prior mental contents dominates (Draper 1994). In practical terms, what counts as a good explanation for me will depend upon what I do or do not already know: prior knowledge acts as a hook upon which to hang the new explanation. Additionally, constructivism also suggests that teaching can never be seen as the major cause of learning. Teaching is merely an external input. Without recognizing, and harnessing, the student's prior mental contents, the external input of teaching will not result in learning.

Draper (1994) suggests that constructivism in learning is where students build their own understanding through interactive processes. Renshaw (1995) argues that like the transmission model, the constructivist model has its own set of assumptions about teaching and learning which will influence how decisions are made to enable learning to happen. These can be found in Figure 14.3. In many respects, open and distance learning practices have subscribed to the assumptions identified in Figure 14.3. The best learning materials set challenging tasks for learners, enable learners to interact with knowledge, provide opportunities to develop personal understanding, and so forth. But this is not to say that some conventional education practices have not also worked in this way.

Renshaw (1995) offers two alternative models for learning and teaching, both of which go beyond the continuum of transmission versus constructivism. His impetus for doing this came from his critique of work by Biggs (1994). Both Biggs and Renshaw suggest that what is to count as excellent teaching involves active engagement by both teachers and learners. Renshaw's two new models are the sociocultural model and the metacognitive model.

- Learning is personal understanding.
- Teaching is setting challenging tasks.
- Learning is interpretative and selective.
- Teaching is observing and interviewing.
- Learning is active.
- Teaching is supporting learners' activity.
- Learning is constructive.
- Teaching is creating dissonance.
- Learning is reviewing and integrating.
- Teaching is helping learners to reconsider.

Figure 14.3 Assumptions underpinning the constructivist model of teaching and learning
Source: Renshaw 1995

- Learning is social.
- Teaching is a joint activity.
- Learning is assisted performance.
- Teaching is guiding the conversation.
- Learning is interactive and co-constructive.
- Learning is self-regulation among the group.
- Teaching is helping joint constructions to form.
- Learning is evaluating shared values.
- Teaching is enacting community values.

Figure 14.4 Assumptions underpinning the sociocultural model
Source: Renshaw 1995

The sociocultural model, according to Renshaw, views the learner as someone who is in the process of entering the practices, values, norms, mores and ways of thinking and articulating of a wider community. Therefore, social participation is central to the learning and teaching process. With the company of others and guided by the teacher, the group learns the culture of that community: how to speak its language, adopt its practices and values, and take on its forms and structures. Teaching is therefore largely a social process, helping students to create connections between the personal and local domain and the domain of the abstract and more general. The assumptions about learning and teaching which underpin Renshaw's sociocultural model are found in Figure 14.4.

The other new model suggested by Renshaw, the metacognitive model, suggests that it is necessary for learners to use and develop methods which allow them to step back from a learning activity, to monitor their learning and consider how they can improve their understanding. Metacognition – reflecting on learning activities in order to reach a goal – has been highlighted as important in light of other evidence that shows that students very rarely seem able to apply and use relevant knowledge in new situations. Barrows (1979) found this in his study of medical students and demonstrated that medical students achieved very high exam scores in their relevant subjects in medical school (e.g., anatomy, physiology, microbiology, and so forth) but when faced with a real patient in a real clinical situation were unable to call upon their knowledge. This led Barrows to adopt a problem-based learning curriculum for medical students. This problem-based curriculum, now widely used around the world in medical, nursing, midwifery, occupational therapy and other health curricula, puts into practice much of the metacognitive model suggested by Renshaw, combined with a social constructivist approach. The assumptions underpinning the metacognitive model are outlined in Figure 14.5.

- Learning is mindful engagement.
- Teaching is explicating expertise.
- Learning is strategic management of learning tasks.
- Teaching is modelling strategies.
- Learning is reflecting and self-monitoring.
- Teaching is supporting and assisting reflection.
- Learning is adapting, applying and transferring knowledge.
- Teaching is application across concepts.
- Learning is self-evaluating.
- Teaching is providing criteria for evaluation.

Figure 14.5 Assumptions underpinning the metacognitive model
Source: Renshaw 1995

Both of the models proposed by Renshaw reflect a commitment to deep rather than shallow learning, to self-regulation and direction rather than control and regulation by others; both argue that, over time, learning should be self-sustaining. The convergence of conventional with distance education will rely more upon the extent to which teachers in higher education – whether they are supporting students learning at a distance or whether they are working with students on campus – adopt a metacognitive and sociocultural model of working.

With regard to developing and delivering our BSc in Health Promotion by both paper-based and Internet delivery modes we looked to both the sociocultural and the metacognitive models (see Figures 14.4 and 14.5). In some respects the metacognitive model was our first consideration. It led us to design our learning packages (paper-based and Internet) so as to:

- allow students to engage with the material;
- enable students to tap into the expertise of the teacher, even though studying at a distance;
- incorporate reflection and self-monitoring into the material and the process;
- incorporate teacher support in the reflection and self-monitoring process;
- provide specific learning activities which adapt, apply and transfer prior learning to new situations;
- provide students with criteria for engaging in self-evaluation.

With regard to support for students learning at a distance, it seemed to us that the sociocultural model could provide a valuable additional source of theoretical evidence. Replicating the social learning environment through distance learning is a challenge, and we are exploring how we can maximize social learning even though students are geographically distant from the teachers and from each other. Building in study periods where people on the same programme meet to engage in group learning activities is the ideal, but for many, this is impossible. Using e-mail tutorials, e-mail communication between students, computer noticeboards and discussion groups, fax tutorials and telephone tutorials goes some way to provide this social component of learning. When technology improves and becomes more readily available we will examine computer conferencing and video-conferencing more extensively. We are also exploring the possibility of setting up study centres in geographical areas where we have a large number of students undertaking distance-learning programmes. Once these learning-support systems are in place, even more interactive and group learning activities can be built into the learning packages. The challenge of distance learning is creatively establishing learning-support structures to enable students to engage with each other, through the activities in the package, and with the teacher, to allow learning to be interactive and co-constructive.

It is not always easy for teachers to seek and find evidence upon which to base decisions about what to teach, when, where and how. Theoretical frameworks and models about teaching and learning provide one of the sources of evidence to make sound and defensible decisions about design, delivery and support for learners in distance-learning programmes.

Using evidence to enhance quality: a case study

This case study provides a concrete example of how some of our thinking about theoretical frameworks and the need to look to gradually bringing together conventional and distance learning is working in practice. Our decision to write quality criteria for learning support was influenced strongly by the sociocultural model.

A core theme in developing this honours degree was providing both a flexible and a quality learning experience for the individual learner. To aid this task quality criteria were designed at both the macro- and the micro-level, and in the Wolfson Institute's 1997 restructuring the needs of both conventional and distance learning students were taken into consideration.

Starting at the macro-level, as part of the institute's 1997 restructuring a Centre for Teaching and Learning was established. This centre has four units: an educational development unit with responsibility and resources to design distance-learning materials either in paper-based or electronic forms, and to provide leadership in innovation in teaching and learning in the institute; a research unit to undertake educational research into the effectiveness of the institute's innovations in teaching and learning; a distance-education administration unit to co-ordinate all the administration activities required by distance-learning students, acting as an interface with the conventional administration functions; and the praxis laboratories, which support the development of practice skills in nursing and midwifery programmes.

Without the creation of this centre and especially the education-development and distance-education administration units this and other programmes could not be developed or run successfully. Experience from our own university and others informed us that for distance learning as for 'conventional' education, quality materials, quality teaching and quality administration systems are necessary, but they are not identical. At present neither our university nor any other we have investigated has an administrative system which can meet the needs of both conventional and distance-learning students. For example, assessment units usually require students to deliver, collect and sign for assignments in person, an arrangement unsuited to distance learners. However, it is not a matter of setting up totally different systems, but of putting in place a one-stop shop which will interface with the 'mainstream' university administration systems on the student's behalf – for example, receiving students' assignments by post, fax or e-mail and passing them on to the assessment unit. As the distinction between conventional and distance-learning students diminishes, the need for separate administrative systems may disappear.

Staff in the Centre for Teaching and Learning have developed evidence-based (wherever possible) quality criteria, using an input–process–outcomes model to enable the centre's four units to be evaluated. This model was chosen because it correlated with the university's and the institute's outcomes approach to learning, and it was congruent with the findings of the Higher Education Quality Council, the National Health Service Executive and the Northern and Yorkshire Regional Health Authority's 1996 project, 'Improving the effectiveness and quality assurance systems in non-medical care education and training'. Figure 14.6 gives an example of the criteria designed by and for the distance-education administrative unit, which will form the basis for annual audit by the Centre for Quality Enhancement at Thames Valley University.

As part of the Wolfson Institute's 1995 strategic plan a quality-enhancement project ran for approximately eighteen months. One aspect of the project was related to identifying criteria for describing, measuring and monitoring the quality of teaching and learning at the micro-level of student/lecturer interaction. A task group consisting of nurse managers from a number of NHS Trust hospitals, lecturers and students was established. A review of the literature showed that there was limited work at this micro-level of the teaching/learning experience.

The same input–process–outcomes approach was used by this group, who started their work by writing a list of generic outcomes that they believed students should develop as a consequence of quality learner support in health-care education. What emerged was a list of nine lifelong learning skills needed by practitioners to work effectively in the social context of

Materials in stock in sufficient quantity to meet needs.	Unit staff establish materials requirements, based on student numbers and module schedules, and arrange production/acquisition and storage accordingly.	Academic staff provide timely information of student materials requirements for each module, together with schedules specifying when materials are needed and their source.
Tracking system for student communications data and assignments is efficient and effective.	All communications with students handled by, or through, the unit are logged. Tracking system is updated regularly with details of materials, assignments, etc., sent to/received from students, and handling thereof within the institute.	Administrative and academic staff have clear procedural guidelines (and training where required) for the handling of student communications, data and assignments.

Figure 14.6 Extract from distance-education administrative unit's draft quality criteria

today's health-care environment. For example, 'use judgement and discretion to take risks sensitively and maturely, recognising the consequences of own actions, and acknowledging that there is seldom one right way' and 'access and analyse evidence upon which to base practice'. These skills had to be as applicable to students studying at the university as to those studying with the university from a distance, thus fulfilling a key concept of the university's mission. However, these are not measurable statements, so the next stage was to break them down into testable criteria.

To move the work forward the task group needed frameworks within which to organize their thinking, and in a moment of brilliance came up with two ideas. The first was a 'where students are learning' framework; the second was the mirror image of this, viewing *teaching* wherever it was taking place. The first idea emerged from a realization that in health-care education most of our planning is based on a binary model of teaching and learning occurring either in 'classrooms' or in practice settings, and that this model was no longer useful when students were learning in a wide variety of locations. The idea was influenced by our belief that knowledge is an individual and social construct and therefore the context of learning should be taken into account. Particularly in health-care education where teaching activity is orientated to assisting students to use theory in the practice setting, and to understand how practice influences theory, uniting 'knowing that' with 'knowing how' to form a single construct of knowing is essential.

The 'where students are learning' framework identified six main locations in which our students may be learning: in classrooms; at a distance; in practice; in a learning resources centre (LRC); in a praxis laboratory, i.e., science, physiology and clinical skills labs; and during social and leisure activities. Although we realized that we would not be able to establish criteria for learning during social and leisure activities it was deemed important to retain this aspect in the framework in order formally to acknowledge it as a site where learning occurs. This correlates with work on lifelong learning that posits a convergence between education, leisure and entertainment (Edwards 1997). The task group then wrote specific outcome criteria for the five other locations based on the list of nine generic outcomes written previously. Then process criteria (i.e., delivery of learning support and input criteria, design of materials and preparation of students and staff for learning) were drafted, based on educational research and literature. Many criteria were found to be generic to learning in all of the locations, but some were very specific. This exercise enabled us to clarify our thinking about how location affects teaching and learning. Other projects and research being undertaken currently at the Wolfson Institute are further developing this work, for example a practice-based education project being undertaken in conjunction with St Mary's NHS Trust Hospital, London.

Another task group then took these criteria for learner support and turned them into questions that could be used to evaluate the quality of, and set a standard for, modules and programmes. They designed a set of questions for students and then, using the mirror-image idea of learning and teaching, wrote questions for lecturers and practice-based educators/assessors mirroring the students' questions. These formed the basis of a new evaluation strategy to support and monitor the individual learning experience for students learning at and with the Wolfson Institute.

Implications for the future

If there is to be a convergence of conventional and distance education then programmes to prepare adult educators will need to change in order to develop teachers who can work '"professionally" with adults, whoever and wherever they may be, and within a variety of learning situations, both inside and outside formal educational institutions' (Usher, Bryant and Johnston 1997, p. 27). The adult educator of the future will need to provide programmes which are available in a variety of delivery modes to allow students to choose the mode best suited to their requirements. These decisions will frequently be made as much on social and lifestyle grounds as on educational ones. Allowing students to direct what mode of delivery is used for a module or a whole programme is congruent with the valuing of 'consumption' within postmodernity.

To work effectively in the future, curriculum designers will need to understand that in the postmodern world, with its blurring of the boundaries between education, training and leisure (Edwards 1997), it will not be enough to provide modules and programmes in a variety of modes. There will need to be something extra, something which seduces students, persuades them to register for one university's programme rather than another's. This 'extra' may be the degree to which the student controls not just the time and place of delivery but the content of the module/programme. To some extent this is an inherent feature of open and distance learning, since the student can use the support material however they wish; but the overall content is still dictated by the institution.

Will there come a time when a module may be defined and validated only on its learning outcomes, assessment criteria and the quality of its learner support, with every other aspect being framed later as the teacher and students work in partnership to identify the content, supporting resource material and communications medium(s)? This would allow a module to be running with several groups of students concurrently, in a variety of delivery modes and with differing content. However, all would be aiming to achieve the same learning outcomes and would receive the same standard of learner support, although the medium (i.e., face-to-face, telephone, e-mail, Internet) would vary. Even achievement of these learning outcomes could be measured by a variety of assessment methods, provided the assessment criteria remained the same. At the Wolfson Institute the basic requirements for this change are in place: all programmes and modules have learning outcomes; generic assessment criteria for academic levels 1, 2, 3 and M are used by all programmes; and we have quality criteria for learner support. However, it will require a fundamental change at institutional level and a radical role-change for many teachers to fit into a new educational world defined not by the teacher's view of learning needs but by student wants, with few fixed reference points. The firm support of the module specification and module study guide would be replaced by the shaky ground of a module for ever changing and evolving.

In sum, staff and students in the post-secondary education sector have a good deal of adapting to do. We are not discounting the power of and need for the modernist discourse of progress, but are positing that the established grand narratives of further and higher education should be viewed with scepticism (Lyotard 1984). We have made a case for educational development based on constructionist theoretical frameworks to enhance student learning and have based the development of a specific degree programme, quality enhancement framework and evaluation strategy on this. Few aspects of education are more steeped in the modernist concept of progress than the present focusing on quality and evaluation we see in further and higher education. But at the same time we doubt that continuing to design and deliver modules and programmes using these models, or using this approach to quality and evaluation, will continue to meet the educational requirements of post-secondary education in the future. This world is one of ephemeral created images (Harvey 1991) and is therefore unstable and subject to change. The skill for educationalists in the future will be in designing programmes to meet student wants, and in predicting at least the short-term educational trends. The success of the programme discussed here will depend on how well we have predicted and met the demands of students at the end of the twentieth century.

References

Barrows, H. S. (1979) 'The rationale and structure of problem based learning', *The Learner* 7: 39–41.

Benner, P. (1994) *Interpretative Phenomenology*, London: Sage.

Biggs, J. (1994) 'What are effective schools? Lessons from east and west', *Australian Educational Researcher* 2(1): 19–40.

Draper, S. (1994) 'Constructivism, other theories of the teaching and learning process and their relationships', discussion paper presented for the NATO Advanced Studies Institute, Glasgow, Aug.

Edwards, R. (1997) *Changing Places?*, London: Routledge.

Fowler, C., Mayes, T. and Bowles, B. (1994) 'Education for changing times', discussion paper presented for British Telecom, Martlesham Heath.

Harvey, D. (1991) *The Condition of Postmodernity*, Oxford: Blackwell.

Kripke, S. A. (1982) *Wittgenstein on Rules and Private Language*, Oxford: Blackwell.

Lyotard, J.-F. (1984) *The Postmodern Condition: A Report on Knowledge*, Manchester: Manchester University Press.

National Committee of Inquiry into Higher Education (1997) *Higher Education in the Learning Society* (The Dearing Report), London: HMSO.

Page, L. (1996) 'The backlash against evidence based care', *Birth* 24(4): 191–2.

Parse, R. R. (1992) 'Human becoming: Parse's theory of nursing', *Nursing Science Quarterly* 7(1): 35–42.

Renshaw, P. (1995) 'Excellence in teaching and learning: external environmental scan', Brisbane, Queensland: Department of Education.

Sackett, D. L. and Rosenberg, W. M. C. (1995) 'On the need for evidence based medicine', *Auditorium* (Journal of the Anglia and Oxford Region) 2: 3–7.

Usher, R., Bryant, I. and Johnston, R. (1997) *Adult Education and the Postmodern Challenge*, London: Routledge.

Index